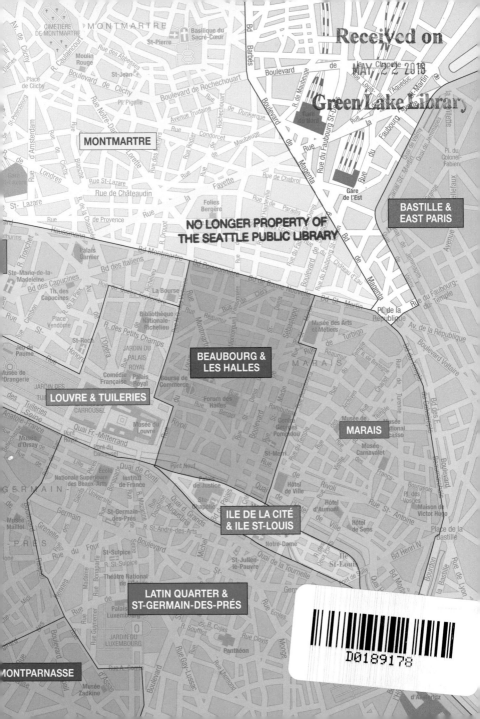

MONTMARTRE

BASTILLE &
EAST PARIS

BEAUBOURG &
LES HALLES

LOUVRE & TUILERIES

MARAIS

ILE DE LA CITÉ
& ILE ST-LOUIS

LATIN QUARTER &
ST-GERMAIN-DES-PRÉS

MONTPARNASSE

INSIGHT ⊙ GUIDES

PARIS
CITY GUIDE

www.insightguides.com/France

◉ Walking Eye App

Your Insight Guide now includes a free app and eBook, dedicated to your chosen destination, all included for the same great price as before. They are available to download from the free Walking Eye container app in the App Store and Google Play. Simply download the Walking Eye container app to access the eBook and app dedicated to your purchased book. The app features an up-to-date A to Z of travel tips, information on events, activities and destination highlights, as well as hotel, restaurant and bar listings. See below for more information and how to download.

MULTIPLE DESTINATIONS AVAILABLE

Now that you've bought this book you can download the accompanying destination app and eBook for free. Inside the Walking Eye container app, you'll also find a whole range of other Insight Guides destination apps and eBooks, all available for purchase.

DEDICATED SEARCH OPTIONS

Use the different sections to browse the places of interest by category or region, or simply use the 'Around me' function to find places of interest nearby. You can then save your selected restaurants, bars and activities to your Favourites or share them with friends using email, Twitter and Facebook.

FREQUENTLY UPDATED LISTINGS

Restaurants, bars and hotels change all the time. To ensure you get the most out of your guide, the app features all of our favourites, as well as the latest openings, and is updated regularly. Simply update your app when you receive a notification to access the most current listings available.

Shopping in Oman still revolves around the traditional souks that can be found in every town in the country – most famously at Mutrah in Muscat, Salalah and Nizwa, which serve as showcases of traditional Omani craftsmanship and produce ranging from antique khanjars and Bedu jewellery to halwa, rose-water and frankincense. Muscat also boasts a number of modern malls, although these are rare elsewhere in the country.

TRAVEL TIPS & DESTINATION OVERVIEWS

The app also includes a complete A to Z of handy travel tips on everything from visa regulations to local etiquette. Plus, you'll find destination overviews on shopping, sport, the arts, local events, health, activities and more.

HOW TO DOWNLOAD THE WALKING EYE

Available on purchase of this guide only.
1. Visit our website: www.insightguides.com/walkingeye
2. Download the Walking Eye container app to your smartphone (this will give you access to both the destination app and the eBook)
3. Select the scanning module in the Walking Eye container app
4. Scan the QR code on this page – you will be asked to enter a verification word from the book as proof of purchase
5. Download your free destination app* and eBook for travel information on the go

* Other destination apps and eBooks are available for purchase separately or are free with the purchase of the Insight Guide book

Contents

Travel Tips

THE BEST OF PARIS: TOP ATTRACTIONS

At a glance, everything you can't afford to miss in Paris, from the emblematic Eiffel Tower and Arc de Triomphe to the world-class museums and the cutting-edge architecture of what is a thoroughly modern city.

△ **Château de Versailles.** A palace truly fit for a king, it is an awe-inspiring confection of gilt, art, mirrors, lavish fabrics, stunning architecture and landscaped gardens. See page 264.

△ **The Arc de Triomphe.** The famous arch honours Napoleon's armies, and is the focus of national celebrations in France. The view from the top is breathtaking. See page 148.

▽ **The Louvre.** The glass-and-steel pyramid is an inspired addition to the venerable architecture of the best museum in the world. See page 130.

△ **The Jardin du Luxembourg.** As well as an art museum, this park boasts an apiary, an orangery, a bandstand, a boating pond, chess tables, tennis courts and a lovely civilised atmosphere. See page 200.

▷ **The Musée d'Orsay.** Once a railway station, it is now one of the world's finest museums of Impressionist art. See page 228.

◁ **St-Germain-des-Prés.** This quarter still evokes memories of its 1950s heyday of intellectual prowess and easy-going chic – though these days fashion has largely replaced philosophy. See page 198.

▽ **The Moulin Rouge.** A Parisian landmark that keeps the spirit of Montmartre's cabaret heyday alive. See page 151.

▽ **Notre-Dame cathedral.** With its soaring arches and wonderful rose windows, this Gothic masterpiece is one of the best-known churches in Europe. See page 84.

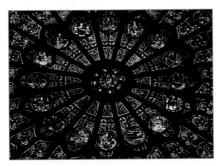

▽ **The Centre Pompidou.** This international icon of inside-out high-tech is as much of an attraction as its contents, which include the Musée National d'Art Moderne. See page 108.

▷ **The Eiffel Tower.** Built for the centenary of the Revolution, the city authorities originally planned to take it down after a few years. The tower is the city's number one visitor attraction, and a global icon. See page 226.

THE BEST OF PARIS: EDITOR'S CHOICE

Unique attractions, festivals and events, top cafés and shops, family outings and money-saving tips personally selected by our editor.

The breathtaking view over Paris from the Eiffel Tower.

ONLY IN PARIS

Eiffel Tower. Savour the city's skyline from the top one hour before sunset, and the tower's shimmering costume of light after dark. See page 226.

Sacré-Cœur. Look down on the city, as night falls, from the steps in front of the basilica. See page 155.

Grande Arche de la Défense. The Arc de Triomphe's modern sister is in the business district. See page 244.

The Mona Lisa. See that enigmatic smile at the Louvre. See page 117.

Musée d'Orsay. Admire France's Impressionist artworks here. See page 228.

Musée Rodin. The beautiful garden is full of Rodin's sculptures. See page 222.

Musée National Picasso. Picasso's legacy to the French state – an amazing collection of 20th-century art. See page 94.

Palais Royal. Stroll through these elegant 19th-century shopping arcades. See page 129.

Place des Vosges. This delightful square is the centrepiece of the Marais. See page 90.

Bastille. Explore the areas's offbeat boutiques and hip cafés. See page 170.

Montmartre. Away from the seedy Place Pigalle, there are quiet backstreets, arty shops and bars to discover. See page 158.

Père Lachaise cemetery. Wander among the famous graves. See page 175.

Les Catacombes. Subterranean passages, packed with skulls and bones. See page 205.

St-Germain-des-Prés. Enjoy a coffee and a croissant in a literary café and browse through the boutiques. See page 197.

Paris Mosque. Sip a mint tea in the delightful Moroccan tearoom. See page 191.

Pont des Arts. Pack a picnic and bottle of wine for an evening near this cast-iron footbridge. See page 199.

Palais de Tokyo. Take in some late-night contemporary art. See page 215.

Paris-Plage. Enjoy open-air swimming followed by drinks on the terrace at the floating pool on the Seine in July and August. See page 206.

Cinémathèque Française. A tribute to French movie-making. See page 179.

MK2 Quai de Loire and Quai de Seine. Two cinemas on opposite banks of the Canal St-Martin, linked by a nifty little ferry. See page 207.

Modern Métro. A 21st-century take on public transport: the "driverless" trains on Métro line 14. See page 178.

The opulent foyer of the Opéra Garnier.

BEST SHOPPING

Printemps. The department store that tops them all: six floors of fashion. See page 139.
The Marais. Funky boutiques and designer stores on and off Rue des Francs-Bourgeois. See page 92.
Colette. Pioneering concept store that picks the best of what's stylish and innovative. See page 123.
Galerie Vivienne. The best preserved of the capital's 19th-century shopping galleries, elegant precursors of the department store. See page 129.
Diptyque. Gorgeous candles and perfumes.
Le Bon Marché. The oldest, and still the most chic department store in Paris.
Rue de Rivoli. From souvenir shops to high-street fashions, they're all here. See page 123.
Marché aux Puces de St-Ouen. Wander among the bric-a-brac stalls of this huge flea market. See page 59.

Printemps is a long-established fashion mecca.

BEST MUSEUMS AND MONUMENTS

Centre Pompidou. Masterpieces of modern and contemporary art in an icon of high-tech architecture. See page 108.
Les Invalides. Testament to the imperial ambitions of Louis XIV and Napoleon. See page 221.
Musée Carnavalet. A fascinating insight into the history of Paris. See page 93.
Musée Guimet. Buddhist sculptures from Angkor and other treasures from the Orient. See page 216.
Musée du Quai Branly. Tribal art housed in one of the city's most dynamic buildings. See page 217.

Musée du Louvre. The Mona Lisa, Venus de Milo, the new Department of Islamic Art and much, much more – all in palatial surroundings. See page 130.
Musée de l'Orangerie. A refurbished Monet showcase. See page 122.
Musée d'Orsay. A treasure trove of Impressionist masterpieces. See page 228.
Musée Zadkine. An intimate glimpse of the artistic past of Montparnasse. See page 203.
Palais Garnier. Opulence at the opera in the grand staircase and magnificent foyer. See page 137.

PARIS FOR FAMILIES

Aquarium Tropical. Catch up with the crocs and tropical fish at the Palais de la Porte Dorée. See page 241.

Bois de Boulogne. The Parisian's favourite Sunday afternoon playground, with woods, gardens, lakes and cycling tracks, an amusement park for children and even a folk museum. See page 235.

Canal St-Martin. With its nine locks, the tranquil canal makes for an attractive boat trip, starting from Bastille. See page 172.

Disneyland Paris. The most popular tourist attraction in Europe. See page 246.

Grande Galerie de l'Evolution. Revamped natural history museum with a truly impressive collection of stuffed animals. See page 193.

Jardin du Luxembourg. Puppet shows, tennis courts, model boats, playgrounds, chess tables and honey bees in the quintessential Parisian park. See page 200.

Jardin des Tuileries. The well-manicured garden adjacent to the Louvre is the perfect pleasure park: avenues of trees, statues, pony rides, toy boats, cafés and children's trampolines, as well as a giant Ferris wheel at Christmas and Easter. See page 120.

Musée Grévin. A fun waxworks museum, full of cheerfully incompatible figures from Marie-Antoinette to Pope Francis. See page 136.

Notre-Dame. Kids love climbing steps: ascend the towers of Notre-Dame for a bird's-eye view of the gargoyles. See page 84.

Parc des Buttes-Chaumont. Ice-skating, a boating lake, a fake mountain and waterfall, puppet shows and donkey rides. See page 239.

Parc de la Villette. Science museum, music and dance conservatory, a giant IMAX screen and children's museum, all set in futuristic gardens. See page 237.

Enjoy some family fun at the Mad Hatter's Tea Cups ride in Disneyland Paris.

GOURMET PARIS

Berthillon. Ice-cream on the Ile St-Louis. See page 83.

Chez René. Timeless bistro atmosphere and the perfect coq au vin.

Drouant. A revamped classic that puts a new spin on the hors d'oeuvre concept.

Fauchon and Hédiard. Famous delicatessens brimming with visually stunning and mouthwatering delicacies. See page 140.

Guy Savoy. Light and sophisticated dishes: a gastronomic treat.

La Coupole. For an oyster feast and classic brasserie experience.

Ladurée. This elegant salon de thé is a Paris institution, famous for its melt-in-the-mouth macaroons.

Le Comptoir. Yves Camdeborde's no-choice set menu is the talk of the town – but you'll need to book for it months ahead.

L'Ourcine. Run by one of a new generation of young chefs revisiting bistro cuisine.

Marché d'Aligre. Sells some of the best and cheapest produce in Paris. See page 174.

Marché Biologique. Organic produce at the Sunday morning market on Boulevard Raspail. See page 196.

Tempting macaroons at Ladurée.

BEST EVENTS & FESTIVALS

Feb–Mar. Salon de l'Agriculture. A festival of regional food.
Apr–May. Foire du Trône. A huge funfair comes to town.
June–July. Paris Jazz Festival Open-air jazz in the Parc de Vincennes.
21 June. Fête de la Musique. Free street concerts and dancing.
Late-June. Gay Pride.
July. Bastille Day. Street party on the night of 13 July at Place de la Bastille. On 14 July, a military parade and fireworks.
July–Aug. Paris Plage. The seaside comes to the Seine.
Sept. Festival d'Automne. Modern theatre and dance.
Oct. La Nuit Blanche. Museums, monuments, cinemas open all night.
Dec-Jan. Ice-skating at the Hôtel de Ville and at the Champs Elysées Christmas Market.

Foodies and hipsters flock to Chez Prune.

The beach comes to the French capital during Paris-Plage.

BEST CAFÉS

Bistrot Beaubourg. Designer café by the Centre Pompidou with a chic clientele and a great terrace.
Café Charbon. A coal merchant's shop turned café that's a neighbourhood fixture.
Café de Flore. The Left Bank literary café still retains something of the charm of its intellectual heyday.
Café de la Ville. Trendy hangout on the Grands Boulevards.
Café du Marché. Classic neighbourhood café with a good menu of market-inspired food.
Café Marly. The Louvre's classiest café, with a superb terrace overlooking the Pyramid.
Chez Prune. A cornerstone of the trendy Canal St-Martin area.
Le Procope. The oldest café in Paris, established in 1686.
Le Sancerre. One of the best cafés in Montmartre, drawing an eclectic, young, arty crowd.
To read more about café life in Paris see page 97.

MONEY-SAVING TIPS

Paris Museum Pass. Sold at museums, tourist offices, FNAC, Paris airports and online (www.parismuseumpass.com). Chose from 2, 4 or 6 consecutive days with unlimited access to 60 museums and monuments around Paris. Gives you priority and discount entrance at the Louvre.
Metro Tickets. A single Métro ticket costs €1.80 while a carnet of 10 tickets costs €14.10 from Métro stations and newsagents. The Paris Visite card is valid for 1, 2, 3 or 5 consecutive days, allowing unrestricted travel on the Métro, bus, tramway, RER networks and Montmartre Funicular. Buy from Métro stations and online (www.ratp.fr/en/ratp/r_61634/paris-visite/).
Le Kiosque Théâtre. 15 place de la Madeleine; place Raoul Dautry, Montparnasse and 3 place des Ternes; www.kiosquetheatre.com. Sells half-price theatre tickets from 12.30pm for performances that day.
The sales. The sales (les soldes) are held in July and early January but many shops offer mid-season reductions.
Free museums. Entry to the permanent collections of the municipal Paris museums is free, including the Musée Carnavalet, Musée d'Art Moderne, Musée Cognacq-Jay, Musée Zadkine, Musée de la Vie Romantique, Petit Palais, Maison de Victor Hugo and Maison de Balzac. Most Réunion des Musées Nationaux (RMN) museums are free on the first Sunday of the month.
See http://en.parisinfo.com/discovering-paris/themed-guides/inexpensive-paris for free or inexpensive activities.

The Pont des Arts aptly attracts musicians, street performers and romantics alike.

Dim lighting is de rigueur in any Parisian café.

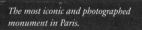

The most iconic and photographed monument in Paris.

A CITY FOR ALL SEASONS

France's chic capital has as much substance as style and offers plenty to entertain visitors whatever the month. Scratch the surface and uncover a liveable city where old meets new and the finer things in life make up for an often-painful past.

"I love Paris in the springtime," wrote American composer and lyricist Cole Porter, who then went on to say that he also loved it in the fall, the summer and the winter. Paris is a seductive destination at any time of year, whether strolling along the banks of the Seine in muggy August, when most of the city has shut up shop, or ice-skating on the Champs-Élysées in the chilly depths of December.

Wherever you head in Paris you are surrounded by its (often turbulent) history, usually in places you least expect to find it: the reconstructed Roman amphitheatre off Rue Monge in the Latin Quarter; the 14th-century city walls, underground, in the Carrousel du Louvre; the church of St-Roch on Rue St-Honoré, whose facade is dotted with the scars of 18th-century Revolutionary shoot-outs.

Artwork in Montmartre.

Paris has long been known as the place to go for a good time: from the 19th-century Montmartre cabarets famously painted by Henri de Toulouse-Lautrec to the current vogue for stylish cocktail bars.. Then there is the galaxy of Michelin-starred restaurants, not to mention a few of the world's best sporting events like the French Open and the final leg of the Tour de France. Look hard enough and you'll find something to suit all tastes and budgets.

Métro sign.

This might be one of the world's greatest cities but Paris manages to retain the feel of a large town; it is very easy to get around on foot. Each district has its own unique character – from the smart shops and cafés in St-Germain to the ethnic markets and restaurants of Belleville – and it is often said that the French capital is merely a collection of villages.

In recent years, thanks to former President Sarkozy's reforms including the *Grand Paris* project, which aims to improve transport links with the suburbs and build 1.5 million new homes by 2030, Paris has been reluctantly dragged into the 21st century. The successful *cohabitation* between ancient and modern is exactly what makes Paris attractive to so many visitors.

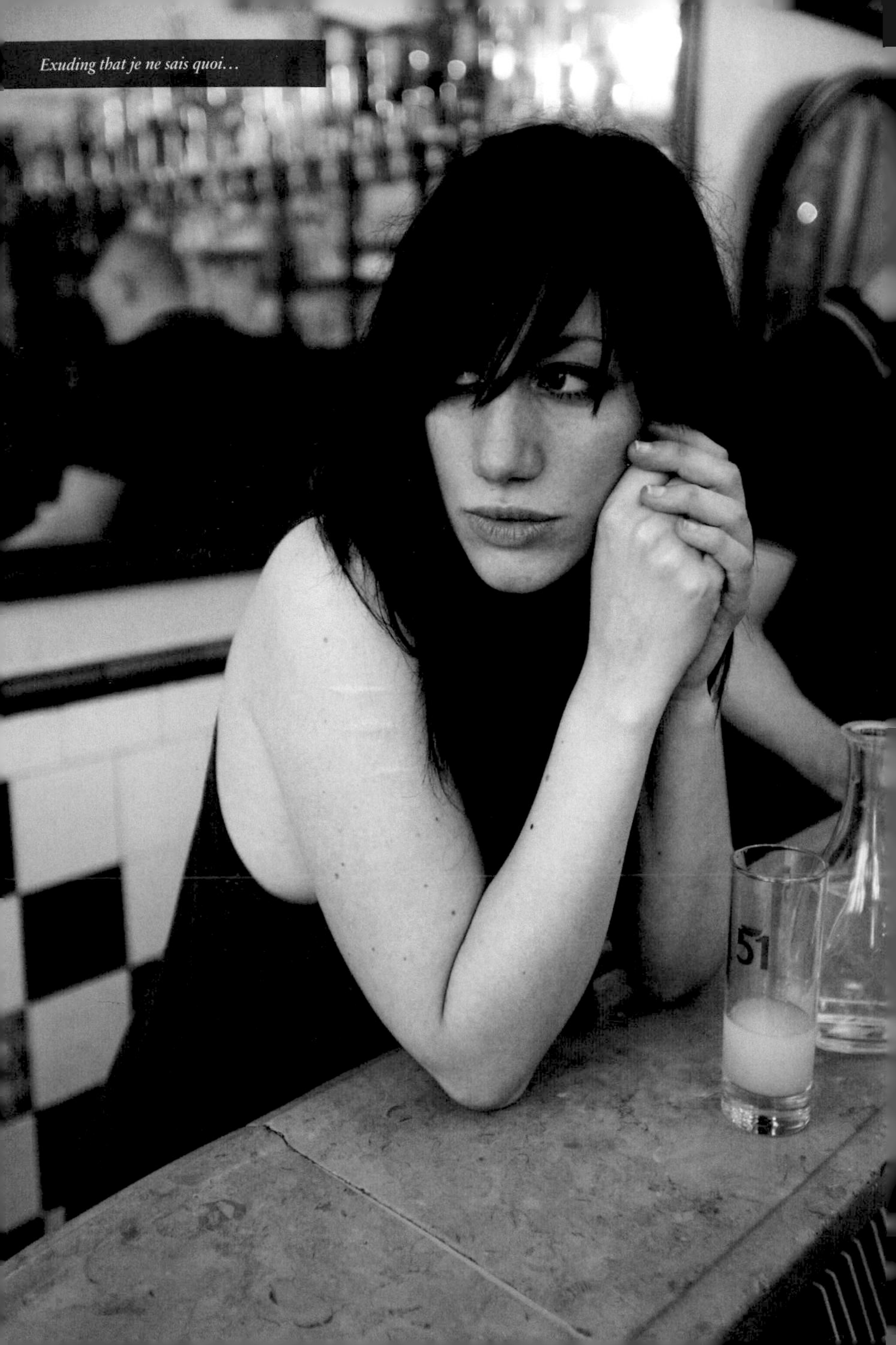

Exuding that je ne sais quoi…

PARISIENS, PARISIENNES

Everyone knows something about Paris, even without ever having visited. But the legends and stereotypes have more truth to them than you might think, and there are many exceptions that confound the rules.

Paris is divided by the Seine into two halves, with the Ile de la Cité and Ile St-Louis in the centre. According to an old saying, the Left Bank was where you did your thinking – the Sorbonne University has been located there since the Middle Ages – and the Right Bank was the place to spend money. Over time, the city was organised into arrondissements (districts), running outwards in a clockwise spiral from the Ile de France (1st arrondissement) to the northeast (20th arrondissement), all contained within the Périphérique (ringroad).

Within the various arrondissements there are recognised quartiers, or neighbourhoods, often worlds apart though linked by a short Métro ride. Each has its own shops, markets, cafés and local eccentricities. Parisians develop lifetime attachments to their quartier. Although supermarket chains are ubiquitous, residents still support local merchants and shop in specialist shops and local markets.

The east-west divide

The most important unofficial division in Paris is between the traditionally working-class east end and the mostly bourgeois west. In general, the further east you go, the further left you'll find its inhabitants on the political spectrum. Rents are exorbitant in the western arrondissements, but there's a substantial reservoir of affordable real estate in the east. City planners have been struggling for decades to improve the balance, hence the massive urban renewal projects at Bercy and the "new" Left Bank in the southeast.

Parisians have a real love affair with dogs.

The east-west dichotomy is rooted in recent history. When Baron Haussmann began to demolish the city's medieval slums in 1853, the middle classes tended to relocate to the west, whereas the working class moved east. The following decade was one of the most turbulent in the history of Paris and ended in the terrible events of the Commune.

Immigrants live on both sides of the Seine, east and west, from Chinatown in the 13th to the predominantly African Goutte d'Or in the 18th. However, the most diverse community of all is probably in the 19th arrondissement; in some schools half of the children speak Arabic

> Parisians topped a national survey on the most-hated people in France, above traditional targets such as civil servants, Corsicans and policemen; although many of the city's inhabitants were born and raised elsewhere.

as a first language, and there are nearly seventy other ethnic groups. Although the iconic rive gauche (Left Bank) still pulls millions of tourists south of the Seine in search of the literary vibe, there have been huge changes in the social geography of Paris since the days of Sartre and de Beauvoir. The Left Bank's Latin Quarter is one of the city's most expensive neighbourhoods, more notable for designer boutiques than it is for literary activity and bohemian lifestyles.

So, where do you go in Paris if you're young and adventurous? From the 1980s up until recently, the simple answer was Bastille. The labyrinth of cobbled backstreets around Place de la Bastille still has a great bar scene, trendy art galleries and cabaret theatre. However, nearby Rue Oberkampf and Rue Ménilmontant are

Business men heading out for lunch.

Browsing the Marché aux Fleurs.

now much cooler, particularly for clubbing. Belleville is also on the map, and for gay or lesbian hotspots, head straight for the Marais.

Outside the Périphérique

Paris proper has few ghettos to speak of. For the most part, they're beyond the Périphérique where many of the poor are housed in the cités (housing estates) of the banlieue (suburbs). Until recently, Paris seems to have turned a blind eye to the problems of its poorer suburbs, and most Parisians were rarely confronted with ghetto life unless they wanted to be.

The cités in the French suburbs were built in response to the housing shortage after World War II. Row upon row of ugly, grey rectangular high-rises were built to house French workers. Immigrants, encouraged to come to France during the economic boom of the 1960s, moved in later. With the oil crisis and recession of the 1970s, there was less and less employment. Crime and drug use soared.

Culture and multiculture

Paris considers itself to be the capital of everything French. Despite an official effort to promote regional development, there's still a

A balmy summer evening along the Canal St-Martin.

lot of one-way traffic to Paris for the best and the brightest provincials in almost every field of human endeavour. The tendency of the capital has long been to look down on the provinces. In return, many French people who live outside Paris are disdainful of its inhabitants: "Parigot, tête de veau" (which means "the Parisian is pig-headed" – or, literally, calf-headed).

> "If you are lucky enough to have lived in Paris as a young man, then wherever you go for the rest of your life, it stays with you, for Paris is a moveable feast." Ernest Hemingway, A Moveable Feast

But, as France moves gradually away from its rigidly centralised history, attitudes about the provinces are changing. The Paris press is full of stories about stressed-out Parisians who escape to a better life in the countryside. Regional development programmes are pumping a great deal of capital into cities like Bordeaux and Toulouse. And the new high-speed trains, that zap south in a flash, are worshipped not so much by provincials, but by Parisians who,

much as they love their city, can't get out of it fast enough.

Aside from the provinces, the largest con- tributors to the Parisian cultural and racial pot au feu are the former colonies of West and North Africa. Other, earlier waves of immigra- tion have brought an influx of Portuguese, Chinese, Vietnamese, Poles, Russians, Bosnians, Serbs, Armenians, Turks and Greeks. France has the largest Muslim population in Europe and its largest Jewish minority outside of Russia. If Paris on the whole displays genuine tolerance of other races and religions, "immigration" is still used as a code word – particularly by right- wing extremists – to express their fear of for- eigners. Legislation has been passed in recent years to beef up the country's security, expand the police force and make it harder for foreign- ers to move to the country.

The people who live here

Incredibly, Paris is more densely populated than Tokyo, London and New York, and Parisians' high stress levels can partly be put down to the fact that they live literally on top of one another, squeezed into small apartments, packed into the city's 100 sq km (40 sq miles).

Attending synagogue in the Marais.

There's intense competition for desirable living space. Moreover, high rents mean that many Parisians have neither the time nor the money to appreciate their city, being trapped in a routine they call Métro-boulot-dodo (commuting, working, sleeping). Nonetheless, for anyone fortunate enough to live in the city centre, the rewards far outweigh the demands. Human in scale, clean, safe, cosmopolitan and lively, Paris deserves its reputation as one of the best cities in which to enjoy the good life.

Parisians, as a whole, are such a diverse collection of races and cultures that it's virtually impossible to stereotype them. Still, there are ties that bind. Parisians are proud and often impatient, always complaining about their social services, yet often defending them, too. In general they are class-conscious and fashion-savvy, largely traditional when it comes to food and etiquette, refreshingly open-minded about art, politics and lifestyle. They're the most orderly people on the planet, and the most chaotic. They're forever in a hurry – and always late.

Appearances matter in a city where people-watching is a popular pastime. Almost everyone pays attention to le look (pronounced "louk"): an English word used to describe not only your wardrobe but also your "style". And if you change your style you are relooké(e).

A French sociologist once claimed that in his country there were not three social classes but 63. One entrenched classification is BCBG (bon chic, bon genre): the French equivalent of the British Sloane Ranger or the American preppy. The rich suburbs of the 16th and 17th arrondissements, Neuilly, Auteuil and Passy (known collectively as NAP), are their stamping grounds. If you are BCBG, your clothes are well

PARI-ROLLER

Every Friday night at 10pm hundreds of roller bladers meet at Place Raoul-Dautry in Montparnasse to head off on a three-hour, 30km (19-mile) tour around Paris; the route varies each week. Originally launched as an ad hoc gathering in 1993, Pari-Roller, a not-for-profit organisation, has now become part of the city's fabric thanks to a successful working partnership with the police, which ensures a safe and fun evening out for all; motorbikes lead the way and mobile officers mingle with participants. While Pari-Roller is for experienced skaters, there is a meeting more suited to beginners at 2.30pm on Sundays in Place de la Bastille. For further information see www.pari-roller.com.

Parisian waiter.

cut, but not daring or flashy. Another grouping is bobo (bourgeois bohème). These are the sort of bohemians who can afford the high rents of St-Germain-des-Prés or the Marais. They're just as bourgeois as the BCBG crowd, only they play up their informality with more youthful clothes.

Breaking the rules

Paris is riddled with rules and regulations, but Parisians have a special talent for breaking them. Things like building codes, labour laws or pollution will probably not come to the visitor's immediate attention. What will hit home, however, are things like clouds of cigarette smoke wafting through public spaces marked "no smoking". In theory, you can be fined for allowing your dog to leave its mess, yet dog dirt is by no means rare on Paris pavements.

La politesse

This is not to suggest the city is one big free-for-all. Parisian anarchy does not extend to etiquette, and their reputation for rudeness is largely undeserved. Good manners are considered essential to everyday life. Indeed, la politesse can often become outright chivalry. Visitors would be well advised to follow the same rules of courtesy. Whether you're buying a baguette or a Hermès scarf, starting any transaction with a "Bonjour Madame/Monsieur," and finishing with "Merci, au revoir" will make the world of difference to the service you receive.

If you forget, you may be reminded with an unspoken reprimand.

Taking to the streets

Somewhere in Paris, someone is on strike almost every day of the year. The expression for going on strike – faire la grève – refers to the still current practice of besieging Paris's Town Hall (located on what was once called Place de Grève) or marching from Nation and blocking streets all the way to Bastille. The strikes can involve many groups – transport workers, teachers, air traffic controllers, hospital staff, illegal immigrants, etc. These "social actions" might involve picketing school teachers, farmers dumping tomatoes on the Champs-Elysées or lorry drivers blockading roads. Perhaps going on strike is compensation for the decline of the trade unions and the weakening of political parties. But it can also seem rather more banal – a national sport in which Parisians are top of the league.

The protest march is part of the great Paris tradition of "the people" rising up. Parisians from all walks of life are willing to participate in street demonstrations for causes that matter to them. Several hundred thousand people packed the streets in 2003 to protest against the war in Iraq. In fact, there were so many marches and strikes that year, there was even a major protest march against strikes. In January 2015, 1.5-2 million people marched in a show of unity following the Charlie Hebdo terrorist attacks.

Santé!

DECISIVE DATES

The Gallo-Roman era

c.300 BC
A Celtic tribe, the Parisii, settle on the Ile de la Cité.

58–52 BC
Julius Caesar conquers Gaul; Lutetia is founded.

c.AD 250
Gaul converts to Christianity.

451
St Geneviève's troops fend off Attila the Hun.

The Dark Ages

486
Frankish king Clovis expels the last Romans. In 496, he is baptised at Reims; in 508, he makes Paris his capital.

751
The Carolingian dynasty: Emperor Charlemagne rules from 768 to 814.

845–80
Paris sacked by the Vikings.

Joan of Arc.

885
Eudes, Count of Paris, is chosen to be king of the Western Franks in 888.

The Middle Ages

Paris develops into a city of learning and political power. It spreads north of the river.

987
The Capetian dynasty starts.

1108–54
Paris becomes an important trading centre.

1163
Notre-Dame is started.

1190–1223
The Louvre fortress is built.

1242–8
Sainte-Chapelle is built.

1253
Sorbonne University created.

1340
Beginning of the Hundred Years War.

1358
Jacquerie peasant uprising.

1364
Charles V moves his court to the Louvre.

1380
The Bastille prison is built.

1420
English rule until 1436, despite Joan of Arc's military campaign of 1429.

Louis XIV, self-proclaimed Sun King.

The Renaissance

Wars with Italy expose the French to new ideas of art, wealth and luxury.

1469
First French printworks.

1516
François I brings Leonardo da Vinci to France; rebuilding of the Louvre starts in 1528.

1572
St Bartholomew's Day Massacre of Protestants.

1589
Henri III is assassinated.

1593
Henri IV becomes a Catholic.

1598
The Edict of Nantes ends the Wars of Religion.

1607
The Place Royale (now Place des Vosges) and Pont Neuf are finished.

"Le Grand Siècle"

Louis XIV spurs an age of extravagance by moving to Versailles and launching an opulent building programme.

1629
The Palais Royal is built.

1631
Launch of the first Paris newspaper, *La Gazette*.

1635
Académie Française set up.

1672–1705
The Grands Boulevards are built.

1678
Hôtel des Invalides finished.

1680
Comédie Française founded.

1682
Court moves to Versailles.

1686
The first café, Le Procope, opens in Paris.

Age of Enlightenment

The arts flourish, science develops and philosophers spread new ideas.

1715
Louis XIV dies and Philippe d'Orléans becomes regent.

1751
First volume of Diderot's *Encyclopédie* published.

1755
Place Louis XIV (now Place de la Concorde) is started.

1758
Panthéon is started.

Napoleon Bonaparte.

The First Empire

The French Revolution leads to a republic then an empire under Napoleon Bonaparte.

1789
Bastille stormed; Louis XVI leaves Versailles for Paris.

1791
Louis is caught fleeing Paris.

1792
The Republic is declared; the royal family is imprisoned.

The bloody St Bartholomew's Day Massacre.

1793
Louis and Marie-Antoinette are guillotined.

The execution of Queen Marie-Antoinette, 16 October 1793.

1794
The ensuing Terror claims more than 60,000 lives. The Directoire takes over.

1799
Napoleon seizes power and is crowned Emperor of the French in 1804.

1806
Arc de Triomphe started.

1814
Napoleon is defeated; the Russians occupy Paris.

1815
Napoleon briefly regains power before his downfall at the Battle of Waterloo; the Bourbon monarchy is restored with Louis XVIII.

The Restoration

Two more revolutions shake Paris, unseating the monarchy once and for all.

1830

Charles X is overthrown and Louis-Philippe d'Orléans becomes "the Citizen King".

1835

First French passenger railway service.

1848

Louis-Philippe is deposed. Louis-Napoleon Bonaparte is elected president of the Second Republic.

The Second Empire

Under Louis-Napoleon, Paris becomes the most efficient, modern city in Europe.

1852

Louis-Napoleon crowns himself Emperor Napoleon III; the Second Empire begins.

1853–70

Baron Georges Haussmann redesigns the city.

1852

Le Bon Marché, the first department store, opens.

1855

Paris's first World Fair.

1862

Hugo's Les Misérables published.

1863

Manet's Le Déjeuner sur l'herbe causes a scandal.

1867

Second World Fair.

1870

Franco-Prussian War.

The Belle Epoque

New inventions and a great artistic élan.

1871

Defeated France signs an armistice with Prussia. During the Paris Commune, 25,000 people are killed.

1875

The Third Republic begins.

Chemist and microbiologist Louis Pasteur.

1887

Louis Pasteur founds the Institut Pasteur.

1889

Gustave Eiffel completes his tower for the World Fair. The Moulin Rouge opens.

1894–1906

Dreyfus affair.

1895

Lumière brothers hold the world's first public film screening.

The Age of Anxiety

Social tensions multiply, and France is shaken by two world wars.

1900

The first Métro line opens. Pont Alexandre III, the Grand and Petit Palais are finished.

1914–18

World War I. Paris is saved from German attack by the Battle of the Marne.

1919

Versailles Peace Conference.

1924

André Breton publishes his Surrealist Manifesto.

1934

The Depression gives rise to riots and a series of strikes.

1939

World War II begins; France sides with Britain against Nazi Germany.

1940

Germany invades France.

1941–2

Mass arrest and deportation of Paris Jews.

1944

Paris liberated by the Allies. General de Gaulle in power until 1946, when the Fourth Republic is proclaimed.

1949

Simone de Beauvoir publishes The Second Sex.

1958

The Algerian crisis topples the Fourth Republic.

The Fifth Republic
De Gaulle returns as president of the Fifth Republic.

1958
Work begins on La Défense.

1962
End of the Algerian War.

1968
Strikes and student riots force de Gaulle to call an election. He wins.

1969
Georges Pompidou becomes president.

1972
The Tour Montparnasse is completed.

1973
The Boulevard Périphérique (ringroad) is opened.

1977
Centre Georges-Pompidou opens. Jacques Chirac elected mayor of Paris.

1981
Socialist François Mitterrand elected president. First TGV (high-speed) railway service.

1986
Chirac becomes prime minister in an unprecedented "cohabitation". The Musée d'Orsay and Cité des Sciences at La Villette open.

1988
Louvre Pyramid completed

1989
Bicentenary of the Revolution. Inauguration of the Grande Arche de la Défense and Opéra Bastille.

1995
Chirac elected president.

1998
France wins the football World Cup.

2001
Bertrand Delanoë elected mayor of Paris.

2002
The euro replaces the franc. Chirac is re-elected.

2003
Chirac opposes the war in Iraq and his popularity soars, then plummets with a reform of the French state pensions and benefit systems.

2005
French voters say *Non* to the European Constitution. Riots flare up in the *banlieues* (suburbs).

2006
New tram service in the south of the city.

2007
Right-wing Nicolas Sarkozy is elected president.

2009
65th D-Day anniversary in Normandy. "Grand Paris" proposals unveiled.

2011
Autolib' electric car sharing scheme launched.

2012
Socialist François Hollande is elected president.

2013
The second recession in four years. The far-right National Front party wins European elections.

2014
Unemployment reaches a high of 10.4 percent. Anne Hidalgo becomes the first woman to be elected Mayor of Paris.

2015
On January 7th, Islamist gunmen kill 12 people at the offices of *Charlie Hebdo*. Over the next two days, further attacks bring the death toll to 17 people. Between 1.5 and 2 million people joined the 'unity march' against terrorism and for freedom of speech. Sadly more terror was to come; on the night of Friday 13 November, Islamist gunmen launch a coordinated attack on multiple sites across the capital: several cafés, the national stadium and a concert hall, leaving 130 people dead and hundreds wounded.

Autolib' is an electric car sharing service launched in 2011.

Fourteenth-century peasants sowing in the shadow of the Louvre.

THE MAKING OF PARIS

The Parisii tribe discovered it, the Romans usurped it, the Franks invaded it and Napoleon ruled it. The city's refined culture and revolutionary politics changed the world.

Paris has been a site of human habitation since the Stone Age, and its history spans well over two millennia. A giddy whirl of invasion, uprising, murder, building, demolition, writing, painting, invention, song and dance; a past that's eternally present, reliably thrilling. And lucky too. Unlike many European cities in the 20th century, Paris almost entirely escaped wartime destruction.

The roots of the city

Paris has grown outwards, in fairly uniform rings from an island in the Seine, the Ile de la Cité. The foundations for the city as we know it today are deemed to have been laid down in around 300 BC by the Celtic tribe of the Parisii, who set up a trading settlement on the island. It was perfect for the transport of goods, from east to west by the river and from north to south along major overland routes that had converged there for centuries. The Seine was much wider then, and crossing it at the Ile de la Cité was easier than elsewhere.

Gallo-Roman pillar discovered in 1704 in a pylon of the Pont au Change.

> The author of a visitor's guide wrote, "One would be wrong if, seeing the vast number of books devoted to Paris, one imagined there was nothing more to be said." That was in 1765.

In 53 BC, some Gallic tribes failed to appear in Ambiani (Amiens) at the annual council convened by the Romans, who were in the process of colonising Gaul. Julius Caesar,

Roman commander in Gaul, sensed rebellion and transferred the council to the Parisii settlement. The Romans realised the advantage of the position, and developed the site for themselves, naming it Lutetia. A town grew up with all the hallmarks of Roman civilisation, and it spread to the Left Bank. Buildings were also scattered on the Right Bank, including a hilltop temple to Mercury where, in around AD 250, Christian missionary St Denis, the first bishop of Paris, was beheaded; according to legend, he picked up his severed head and walked 6,000 steps before being buried on the spot where the

St-Denis Basilica now stands. The hill subsequently acquired the name Mons Martyrum (Martyr's Mound), now Montmartre.

Lutetia soon fell victim to sackings by barbarians. In 358, Emperor Constantine sent his son-in-law, Julian, to Gaul to deal with them. Julian promptly fell in love with Lutetia and some say that it was he who renamed it Paris.

Geneviève, patron saint of Paris

Just under a century later, in around 451, the armies of Attila the Hun circled for the kill. The Parisians prepared to flee, but were assured by the pious 19-year-old Geneviève that the Huns would not harm the city, provided they stayed with her and prayed. The marauders passed southwest of the town and ran straight into the swords of a hastily raised army of legionaries. Geneviève later became the patron saint of Paris.

She was still alive when Clovis I, king of the Salian Franks and founder of the Merovingian dynasty, invaded much of Gaul, seeing off the Romans and sweeping into Paris. He promptly made it his capital and reconverted it to

Detail from a tapestry depicting the baptism of Clovis (c.1525).

St Geneviève as a shepherdess with the Butte Montmartre in the background.

Christianity. Later a basilica was built where he and St Geneviève were buried. The church was demolished; on its site now stands the Panthéon, the last resting place for France's great and good.

The Merovingian law of succession was simple: the empire was divided among the previous ruler's offspring. As a result, for the next 250 years, instead of serving as an administrative centre, Paris became a battleground for

---

CURRENT AFFAIRS

The Parisii tribe set up camp on the Ile de la Cité in around 300 BC but they were not the first people here: there's evidence of human habitation in these parts dating back to the Stone Age. In 1991, when archaeologists were working at Bercy in the 12th arrondissement, a mile or so from the site of the Parisii settlement, they unearthed several Neolithic dugout canoes, or pirogues, dating from 4500 BC – among the world's oldest known records of the use of canoes by hunter-gatherers. A nearby street was named Rue des Pirogues de Bercy in their honour and three of the craft are now exhibited in the Musée Carnavalet.

Sainte-Chapelle stained glass.

the murderous family bickering of Clovis's descendants.

Into the Middle Ages

The Carolingians, who ruled from 751, moved the political centre away from Paris, which was left in the charge of a count and his municipal guard. Charlemagne died in 814, leaving his son Louis – the first Louis of many – in charge.

The Norman (or Viking) invasions of the mid-9th century brought Paris back into the limelight. After several sackings of the city, in 885 Eudes, count of Paris, had fortifications built around the Ile de la Cité. The first siege of Paris lasted a year and almost bore fruit: the Carolingian army came to the rescue. But King Charles ("the Fat"), instead of attacking the siege-weary aggressors, let them sail up the Seine to pillage Burgundy. In defiance of the king, Eudes took the crown and Carolingian unity dissolved. A period of instability followed, as the French crown was passed from one dynasty to the next. The Saracens appeared in the south, Hungarians in the east, and the Vikings ran amok. Finally, the power struggle saw Hugh Capet, son of Hugh the Great, a descendant of Eudes, become king of all France

in 987. This marked the beginning of a new, long-lasting dynasty – the Capetians.

Paris prospered under the Capetians: new fountains were built to provide fresh drinking water, and armed *sergents de ville* walked a beat. With new churches and a cosmopolitan population, Paris soon became an intellectual hotspot. At the start of the 12th century, monks, scholars, philosophers, poets and musicians came to the city to learn, exchange ideas and teach.

Economic power rested in the hands of merchants and craftsmen, organised into guilds. The most powerful was the Water Merchants' Guild, which included all river workers and gave its coat of arms to Paris. Philippe-Auguste (1180–1223) built Les Halles for the guilds and improved the docks. The guilds took care of levying taxes, town-crying and other municipal duties. In 1200, Philippe-Auguste founded the University of Paris.

The first revolution

By the mid-14th century the Capetians had been replaced by the Valois dynasty, and the devastating Hundred Years War with England began.

Charlemagne, founder of the Carolingian dynasty.

Henri III, son of Catherine de Médicis.

Siege of Paris by Charles VI during the Hundred Years War.

In 1356, the English captured King Jean ("the Good") at Poitiers. Parisians, tired of incompetent leadership, rebelled; their leader was Etienne Marcel, a wealthy cloth maker and guild chairman. He also provided troop reinforcements to impoverished townspeople and peasants under Jacques Bonhomme, who chose the moment to start a revolt known as the *Jacquerie*.

For support, Marcel unwisely chose the king of Navarre, Charles ("the Bad"), an ally of the English. When the Parisians learned of the alliance, they turned on Marcel, who was killed in July 1358. Three days later, Jean's son entered the capital. The new regent, the future Charles V (1364–80), hammered out a truce with the English. But Parisians were seething. In 1382, during the reign of Charles VI (1380–1422), a group called the Maillotins rebelled against high taxes and were brutally repressed. Then, in 1407,

Most historians view the coronation of Hugh Capet (c.940–96), Count of Paris, as the beginning of modern France. The city flourished under his rule.

they were enmeshed in the struggle for power between the Burgundian Jean ("the Fearless") and his cousin Louis d'Orléans. Jean had Louis murdered and, in 1409, took control of Paris.

The advance of the English

While Louis's Armagnac son, Charles, raised a new army, Paris celebrated. Into the fray stepped a butcher named Caboche, demanding reforms. All hell broke loose as Jean's authority slipped into Caboche's hands. Profiting from the reign of terror, Charles's army re-entered the city. With France torn apart by civil war, the English resumed hostilities and, siding with the Burgundians, beat the Armagnacs at the Battle of Agincourt in 1415.

Four years later, Jean "the Fearless" was murdered, whereupon Henry V of England married Catherine, daughter of the mad King Charles, and occupied Paris in December 1420. The dauphin, the legitimate French heir, had some support in the capital, but could not keep out the English. Joan of Arc, a 17-year-old girl from Lorraine, came to his rescue in 1429 by defeating the English at Orléans; a year later, Charles VII was crowned at Reims. However, Paris remained English until 1436, when Charles recaptured his capital and drove the English back to Calais.

By the early 16th century, Louis XII (1498–1515) was embroiled in the Italian Wars. His successor, François I (1515–47), began the struggle against the Habsburgs but was captured at Pavia in 1525. The Parisians paid his ransom and he moved into the Louvre. In his wake came Italian architects, painters, sculptors and masons, whose task was to reshape the city's gloomy Gothic face.

The advent of the printing press underpinned the Renaissance and helped spread the new gospel of Protestantism through Catholic France. Paris, dominated by the conservative Sorbonne theologians, pushed for measures against the Protestants, known as Huguenots, often burning religious agitators at the stake. Henri II's sons and heirs, François II (1559–60), Charles IX (1560–74) and Henri III (1574–89), were not able to control France's religious factions; nor were they helped by the intrigues of the Queen Mother, Catherine de Médicis. The country was plunged into a religious war.

War between the Henris

King Henri III's concessions to the Protestants infuriated the Catholics, led by Henri de Guise and his Holy League. In 1584, the Protestant Henri de Navarre, a Bourbon, became heir to the throne, but had to fight de Guise for the right to accede to power. To this end, in 1589, Henri III had de Guise killed. Paris threw up its barricades, and the Holy League's Council of Sixteen took power and deposed Henri III, who joined forces with Navarre. His army, however, sided with the Catholics. That summer, Henri III was murdered and Henri de Navarre became Henri IV.

> In 1516, François I enticed Leonardo da Vinci to France. He lived in a manor house called Clos Lucé near the king's residence in Amboise and died there in 1519 at the age of 67.

Civil war dragged on for another five years. In 1593, Philip II of Spain, who had entered the war on the Catholic side, pressed to usurp the French throne. Henri IV chose that moment to convert to Catholicism, whereupon Paris welcomed him, and overnight the war-weary nation fell into line.

Henri IV patched up France spiritually and economically; in 1598, his Edict of Nantes set up guidelines for cohabitation between the religious groups. In 1610, Henri IV was murdered, and the young Louis XIII took to the throne.

Henri IV welcomed by Parisians on 22 March 1594 after converting to Catholicism.

The storming of the Bastille, 1789.

The Bourbons

In spite of the massive debts incurred by their foreign wars, the Bourbons lavished huge sums on Paris, while keeping it on a short political leash. Two marshy islets east of the Ile de la Cité were amalgamated to become the residential Ile St-Louis. New bridges crossed the Seine. Avenues cut through the dingy labyrinth. Architects built new houses, parks, palaces and schools and restored the old ones. Cardinal Richelieu, who largely governed on behalf of the young Louis XIII (1610–43), founded the

THE EDICT OF NANTES

The Edict of Nantes, signed by Henri IV on 30 April 1598, enshrined religious tolerance in French law, and was a significant step on the road to the secularism of the French state that holds today. The Edict's immediate purpose was to end the long-running French Wars of Religion by giving rights to French Protestants, also known as Huguenots, in what was a predominantly Catholic state. Once the Edict became law, all subjects of the French crown, with the exception of Muslims and Jews, were granted freedom of worship, the right to work in any sphere, including for the state, and the right to bring grievances directly to the king.

Académie Française. Under the Sun King, Louis XIV (1643–1715), the spending spree reached its zenith. His minister, Colbert, sanitised entire sections of the city and set up manufacturing plants. Louis XIV also had hospices constructed for the poor, and Les Invalides was built to house war veterans.

The influx of money and the proximity of the court attracted crowds to the capital. Theatres rang with the dramas of Racine and Corneille, and audiences roared at the comedies of Molière.

But trouble loomed. In 1648, Paris revolted, demanding greater political representation. The 12 provincial parliaments joined a body lobbying for change, as did a conspiracy of nobles under the Prince of Condé. This alliance, known as the Fronde, eventually collapsed, but Louis XIV later had his lavish palace built outside the city in Versailles, away from the Parisian mob.

The early 18th century was a time of great inequality in Paris. French high society enjoyed greater comforts and luxuries than ever before, and the court of the Sun King was a fertile breeding ground for debauchery and political intrigue. But the poor still had a raw deal. They were to make their displeasure felt with shattering consequences as the century drew to a close.

The revolutionary years

By the latter part of the 18th century, France's international renown rested increasingly on the writings of its intellectuals such as Voltaire, Rousseau and Diderot. But the poverty worsened; a bad harvest in 1788 caused the price of bread to soar and the people to become restless.

> "Society owes protection only to peaceable citizens; the only citizens in the Republic are the republicans. For it, the royalists, the conspirators are only strangers, or rather, enemies." Maximilien Robespierre

By 1789, France's debts had reached a critical level. King Louis XVI had to summon the Estates General, a legislative body of three estates: the Clergy, the Nobility and the rest of the populace, the Third Estate, to vote for reforms. Craftily, the king allowed only one vote per estate, so the huge Third Estate could be outvoted two to one by the smaller Clergy and Nobility. Eventually forced out, the Third Estate created a National Assembly to oppose the king. On 14 July, Parisians stormed the Bastille prison for weapons, proclaimed a Commune and formed a National Guard under liberal aristocrat and soldier Lafayette. The explosion of 1789 swept the past away. The First Republic was proclaimed and, in January 1793, Louis was guillotined in public, followed in October by Queen Marie-Antoinette. Paris was the epicentre of the French Revolution and its radical leaders Mirabeau, Danton and the fanatical Robespierre, egged on by Marat, whose murder in July 1793 pushed the Reign of Terror into top gear. Anyone suspected of stepping out of line got the chop; in July 1794, it was Robespierre's turn. The young brigadier-general Napoleon Bonaparte finally ended the Revolution, after quashing a royalist uprising in 1795. Four years later he was First Consul. In 1804 he crowned himself emperor of a totalitarian and military state.

The Napoleonic Empire

A masterful administrator, Napoleon drew up plans for a Bank of France, reformed the judiciary and local government, improved secondary education, instituted the Légion d'Honneur and restored the Church. He greatly strengthened France's power in Europe, and its trade links with the rest of the world.

Though he ruled supreme at home, he could not have things all his way on the battlefield for ever. His glorious empire ended with Paris occupied after the Battle of Waterloo in 1815. Bourbon Louis XVIII headed a constitutional monarchy, focusing on law and order and laissez-faire economics. In cultural circles, Romanticism was in the air; one of the movement's bearers was Victor Hugo (1802–85).

Boulevard Haussmann at the turn of the 20th century.

Inspired by the anti-establishment spirit of 1789, the Romantics railed against creaky academia and bourgeois respectability. In July 1830, Charles X revoked some electoral laws, sparking three days of rioting; he had to abdicate. His cousin, Louis-Philippe, Duke of Orléans, held power until 1848, when another revolution brought about his abdication in turn; the monarchy was finished.

The Second Empire

The first president of the Second Republic was Napoleon's nephew, Charles-Louis-Napoleon Bonaparte. The family traits didn't take long to show: he crowned himself Emperor Napoleon III in 1852, and arrested over 20,000 opponents to make his life easier.

The Commune

In 1870, Napoleon III went to war with Prussia. Two months later, he had been humiliatingly beaten, the Second Empire had become the Third Republic, and the Prussians were besieging Paris. In Bordeaux, the government of Adolphe Thiers waited for an uprising, which never materialised.

In January 1871, Thiers agreed to a ceasefire; the National Assembly ratified a peace treaty a month later. The Prussians marched through Paris, avoiding the eastern districts full of the starving and vengeful National Guard, which felt betrayed by the French government. Sensing trouble, Thiers moved his government to Versailles. In March, a Commune was proclaimed at the Hôtel de Ville after the bourgeoisie boycotted a municipal election. Civil war erupted and the Hôtel de Ville was burned. While the Communards hoisted red flags and argued over strategies, Thiers was busy raising a new army. The government forces succeeded where the Prussians had failed, and some 25,000 Communards were killed

> In Paris, Napoleon's architects and engineers improved the sewers and initiated a building boom. Paris wouldn't be the city it is today had it not been for Napoleon.

in the last weeks of May.

With the working class brutally tamed, Paris became host for the squabbles and plots of the Third Republic. The Republicans split into pro- and anti-clerical factions. In the 1890s, the left gathered around socialist Jean Jaurès. On the right were diehard monarchists and nationalists

The French army crosses the Isère River on improvised gateways under enemy fire, 1917.

Adolf Hitler visits occupied Paris in 1940.

Hitler being driven down the Champs-Elysées in 1940.

with a strong vein of anti-Semitism, as revealed by the Dreyfus Affair in the 1890s. This bitterly divisive scandal revolved around a Jewish army captain, Alfred Dreyfus, imprisoned on trumped-up spying charges. But amid the political acrimony, Paris hailed impressive new facilities: the first Métro lines were dug, the Eiffel Tower was built for the 1889 World Fair, and the first films were shown. Between 1880 and 1940, Paris was home to more artists than any other city.

World War I put a dampener on the high spirits, and in September 1914 the German artillery came within earshot. The city's military governor, Galliéni, rushed reinforcements (including the Paris taxi service) to the counter-offensive on the Marne, and the city was spared.

Normal life began to return after the armistice in 1918. From the east came Russian émigrés and from the west came American writers and composers. In the 1930s, Paris became a temporary haven to the refugees of fascism in Europe.

Between the wars

With 1 million dead, millions of others crippled and the agricultural north destroyed by shelling, France's part in the victory over Germany in 1914 was bittersweet. Conservative Republicans and left-wing coalitions, including the Communist Party (founded in 1920), tried to come to grips with the economic and social after-effects of the Great War. The extreme right, meanwhile, made some important gains.

Fascist-type groups had appeared in France in the late 19th century. In the 1920s and 30s they proliferated, fuelled by general discontent and

AN ERA OF GRANDEUR

The Second Empire was a grandiose era. New railway lines were built, and Paris hosted the World Fair in 1855 and 1867. Basking in financial ease, the city abandoned itself to masked balls, Offenbach operettas and salon conversation. Its prefet (director for public works), Baron Georges Haussmann, changed the face of Paris, demolishing most of the medieval city and gutting and rebuilding vast areas. Water mains and sewers were installed; parks were created and bridges built. Elegant boulevards and squares appeared, notably Avenue de l'Opéra and Place de l'Etoile, where all roads lead to the Arc de Triomphe; these served an aesthetic purpose, but also facilitated swift troop deployment and were hard to barricade.

fear of Bolshevism, and inspired by Mussolini and Hitler. They focused their efforts on Paris, parading and campaigning against the internationalists, the socialists and, above all, the Jews. On 6 February 1934, a coalition of fascist factions attempted a *coup d'état* in Paris. It failed, but the left was finally goaded into concerted action. In 1936, a front of radicals, socialists and communists, headed by the socialist Léon Blum, won the election. The so-called Front Populaire promised to fight fascism and improve the workers' lot, but the initial euphoria was short-lived. The Front disappeared after a series of wildcat strikes.

General de Gaulle, born in Lille and a veteran of both world wars, was the first president of the Fifth Republic, still in place today.

World War II

When war broke out against Nazi Germany in September 1939, France hunkered down behind its fortifications along its eastern border, the Maginot Line, mobilised its ill-equipped army and waited. In Paris, Louvre curators prepared paintings for transport to safety.

Chirac and Mitterrand, 1995.

On 14 June 1940, the Nazis marched into the City of Light after a lightning push through France from the Ardennes; the Germans had simply skirted the northern end of the Maginot Line. There was no siege, no National Guard, no *levée en masse*. Marshal Philippe Pétain, the 84-year-old hero of Verdun, became the head of a puppet regime in Vichy, in what was (at first) the unoccupied southern half of France.

While many Parisians were quiescent under the Nazi occupiers, and a number actively collaborated, there were those who bravely resisted, joining the Free French Movement led from London by General Charles de Gaulle. On 6 June 1944, Allied forces landed in Normandy and advanced on Paris. Dietrich von Choltitz, the German commander, received orders to blow up the city, but chose to surrender instead; for this action he was dubbed "the saviour of Paris".

On 24 August 1944, Paris was liberated and, two days later, General de Gaulle paraded down the Champs-Elysées. De Gaulle immediately formed a provisional government, which lasted until 1946. Tourists returned in droves. Bebop and rock 'n' roll arrived from across the Atlantic.

Post-war thought was dominated by the dark ideas of writers such as Jean-Paul Sartre and Albert Camus. In addition, France lost two major colonial wars, the first in Indochina (1946–54) and the second in Algeria (1954–62).

May 1968: the barricades are back

A wave of bombings hit Paris in the early 1960s, when it became clear that President de Gaulle, who had come out of retirement to head the Fifth Republic in 1958, wanted to pull out of the Algerian quagmire. His manner in dealing with internal matters was patriarchal and authoritarian.

The 1968 agitation began uneventfully enough in March, with a sit-in by students to revise the antiquated university system. But instead of initiating a dialogue with the students, the *ancien régime* called in the CRS (the riot police) to restore order.

On the night of 10 May 1968, the police stormed 60 barricades in the Quartier Latin. Unrest spread to the factories and other cities. France was soon paralysed and Paris was left in a state of siege. The state-run media broadcast heavily monitored programming,

Burned out vehicles testify to the riots in the Latin Quarter, May 1968.

while Parisians received the news from France's periphery. At the end of the month, de Gaulle announced new elections and warned against impending totalitarianism. The Parisian bourgeoisie awoke, and an hour later, over 500,000 supporters of de Gaulle were flowing down the Champs-Elysées.

The Gaullists won the election, but were not in power for long. Discontent continued, and the President resigned in 1969, leaving his Republic to his ardent disciple Georges Pompidou.

Mitterrand and Chirac

The 1970s were a time of relative stagnation, so when the Independent Republican president Valéry Giscard d'Estaing lost to socialist leader François Mitterrand in 1981, it felt like the dawn of a new era. However, the contrary Parisian character revealed itself again in 1986, during the legislative elections. Voters on the left were dismayed by what they viewed as Mitterrand's capitulation to business interests, and conservative forces, led by Paris mayor Jacques Chirac, swept in with a right-wing coalition; an unprecedented "cohabitation" was begun.

The 1993 elections maintained the swing to the right and two years later Chirac succeeded François Mitterrand as president. Mitterrand died in January 1996. His *grands projets* made an indelible contribution to the Paris landscape. By 1997, Chirac's popularity had plummeted, and when he made the disastrous decision to dissolve the National Assembly and call new legislative elections in June, the socialist Lionel Jospin was swept in on a flood of votes as prime minister.

The French presidential elections of 2002 produced a dramatic run-off between Chirac and the xenophobic far-right agitator Jean-Marie Le Pen. Parisians took to the streets in vast numbers to express their opposition to Le Pen. Chirac finally won 82 per cent of the vote, the largest in the country's history. His opposition to the war in Iraq saw his approval ratings soar. But the bubble soon burst with public protests against reforms to the state pension and benefit system.

Sarkozy comes to power

Perhaps Chirac's longest-lasting contribution will be the law he pushed through in 2000 to shorten the presidential term from seven to five years. His party's candidate to succeed him, Nicolas Sarkozy, won the presidency in 2007 with a clear six point lead over socialist Ségolène Royal.

Unfortunately, Sarkozy's taste for luxury and his marriage to former supermodel Carla Bruni, along with doubling his own salary, increasing

Nicolas Sarkozy, president from 2007 to 2012.

Faced with a downturn in the economy and two terrorist attacks in 2015, François Hollande has his work cut out.

the pension age from 60 to 62, his cosiness with Germany during the Euro crisis and public faux pas, made him France's most unpopular president ever. In May 2012 he was beaten at the polls by the Socialist François Hollande, surprisingly by just 3.2 percent. Sarkozy will be remembered on the world stage for strengthening France's ties with the UK and US, pledging to reduce his country's CO_2 emissions by 50 per cent and taking a lead role in Allied military action against Libya.

BERTRAND DELANOË

In 2001 Bertrand Delanoë became the first Socialist mayor of Paris for 130 years, elected by a populace who were disenchanted with the sleaze-ridden administration of his far-right predecessor. By the end of his second administration in 2014, the Tunisian-born mayor will probably be best known for bringing the beach – Paris Plage – to the banks of the Seine each summer since 2002, for introducing the *Vélib'* free bike scheme and for developing subsidised pre-school care for the city's toddlers. But his political ambitions may not end here – in 2008 openly gay Delanoë stood for (and lost) the leadership of his party with a view to becoming a presidential contender.

Enters Hollande

Drenched and then struck by lightning (at least his plane was) on the day of his inauguration, Hollande could only hope things would improve. This unassuming man, who has never held a ministerial post, is eschewing the grand ways of his predecessor, travelling by train and living in his own apartment instead of the Elysée Palace. Despite pushing through important reforms of the labour code and pension system, Hollande's popularity quickly plummeted to an embarrassing 20 percent. A stubborn unemployment rate of over 10 percent, an ailing economy and the embarrassing revelations of his private life did little to improve matters.

Paris's annus horribilis

The year 2015 was to be a very dark year for the French capital. On January 7th, Islamist gunmen stormed the offices of French satirical newspaper *Charlie Hebdo*, killing 12 people in retaliation for publishing cartoons of Prophet Mohammed. Over the next two days, further attacks brought the death toll to 17 people. The killings spurred a national and international movement of unity against terrorism. Only a few days after the killings President Hollande organised a 'unity march' against terrorism and for freedom of speech attended by 2 million people, including major European heads of state.

Sadly more terror was to come; on the night of Friday 13 November, Islamist gunmen launch a coordinated attack on multiple sites across the capital: the Stade de France national stadium, several cafés and the Bataclan concert hall in the east of Paris, leaving 130 people dead and hundreds wounded.

Both attacks, for which the so-called Islamic State have claimed responsibility, have brought Parisians together again in an act of defiance, determined not to be scared off by terrorism. The childish '*Même pas peur*' (Not even scared) became a rallying slogan, trending on social media. Inevitably, the attacks also fuelled the rise of the right and far-right. After thinking about retiring from politics altogether, Sarkozy has made a surprise political comeback and will likely stand against Hollande in the next elections in 2017. The growing popularity of Marine Le Pen, the leader of the far-right National Front Party, was further boosted by both attacks. Her party is now the third political party in France.

The Outsiders

Dictionaries translate banlieue as "suburbs", but whereas its English counterpart is relatively unproblematic, the French word is loaded.

Banlieue means "outskirts". Historically, it was the loop of land within a distance of one league ("lieue") from a city's perimeter; nowadays the word applies to any residential area on the edge of a large city or town. Some *banlieues*, like St-Germain-en-Laye, west of Paris, are affluent and picturesque; but out of context, "la banlieue" for most French people brings to mind high-rise estates like La Courneuve, Argenteuil or Aulnay-sous-Bois, with reputations for burned-out cars, delinquency and boiling-point tempers.

Long-term problems

Such estates have been an open sore for years, and not only on the Paris periphery: similar ghettos can be found elsewhere. Most were built in the 1960s and 70s, cheap housing for a growing workforce – in particular first- and second-generation immigrants from Algeria, Morocco and former French colonies in Africa. The effects of cack-handed urban and social engineering were compounded when industry slumped; and so began a vicious circle, whereby poor social facilities fuel local resentment, and chronic vandalism gives the state the perfect excuse not to invest.

Riots

In October 2005, the subject that many politicians and middle-class voters preferred to ignore punched its way to the top of the news. The trouble started in the Paris *banlieue* of Clichy-sous-Bois, where two teenagers, running from the police, climbed into an electricity substation and died. The resulting riots spread across the country; there were 23 nights of violence, 9,000 cars were torched, and a state of emergency was declared.

Cinematic inspiration

Still, not all of France was in denial. It's a measure of how heavy the topic weighs on the national conscience that there's even an established cinematic sub-genre, the "*banlieue* film", of which the best-known is Matthieu Kassovitz's incendiary 1995 hit *La Haine*; documentaries such as the Taverniers' *De l'autre côté du périph'* (1997) are frequent; and there's the occasional film made "from the inside", like *Wesh, qu'est-ce qui se passe?* (2001). Indeed, it's one of the ironies of the *banlieues* that their cultural scenes should be so vigorous and influential. In fashion, the "banlieue look" has entered the mainstream.

Hanging out at the entrance of a run-down block on an estate in the northeast suburb of Paris.

The future

Little has improved since 2005, yet the *banlieues* are at the heart of France's struggle to define and understand itself. They were in the news again in 2012 when random shootings took place in the suburbs of Paris and Toulouse and they will no doubt be in the spotlight again after the two terrorist attacks of 2015, when it transpired most gunmen had grown up in various *banlieues*. In spite of a €43 million renovation programme launched in 2003, the social problems remain deeply ingrained due to a lack of opportunities.

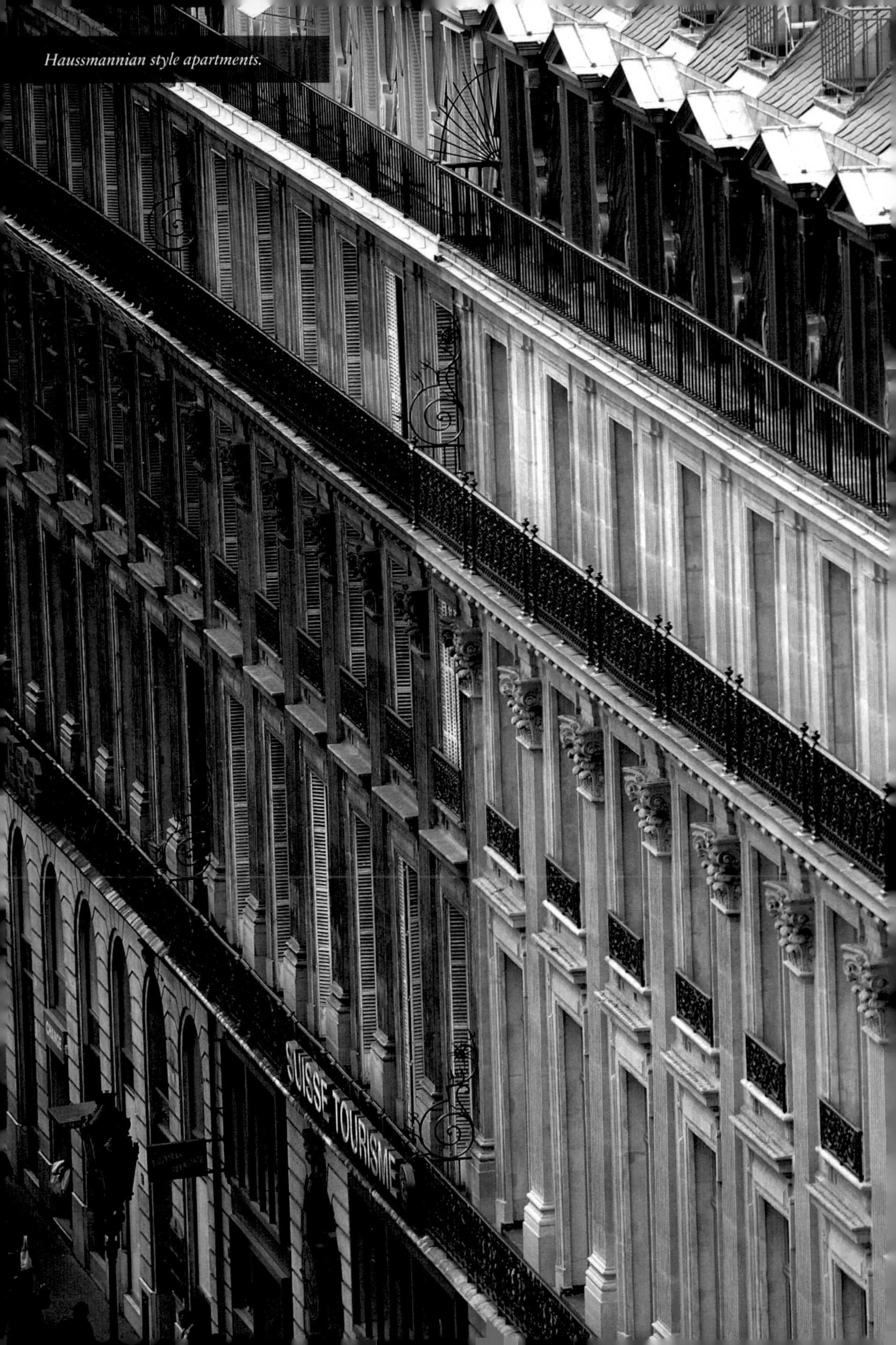

Haussmannian style apartments.

Old and new – the Louvre and its glass pyramid.

ARCHITECTURE

Paris is probably the loveliest and widest-ranging display of building styles in the world – and, with few exceptions, ancient and modern complement each other flawlessly.

Two thousand years of history and seven centuries of artistic brilliance have made Paris a city rich in architecture. Although invasions, sieges, insurrections and city planners destroyed a number of the capital's early masterpieces, fine examples remain, making modern-day Paris one of the most beautiful, fascinating – and intact – cities anywhere in the world.

Over time, the best architects have preserved this heritage, while looking forward and making room for the new. This explains the amazing juxtaposition of different architectural idioms.

Paris is a textbook of architectural history, boasting a full set of French architectural styles, especially from the 12th century and the beginnings of the Gothic era onwards.

Second-Empire style architecture on the Champs-Elysées.

Roman remains

Unsurprisingly, almost nothing remains of the wooden huts occupied by the Parisii. However, thanks to the Romans' development of a most durable concrete, their ruins can still be found in the Quartier Latin. Streets such as rue St-Jacques and boulevard St-Michel are built on ancient Roman roads. The vestiges of Roman baths can be seen in the garden of the Musée National du Moyen Age–Thermes de Cluny, and the ruins of the amphitheatre (Arènes de Lutèce) have also survived.

Unfortunately, nothing is left of the Merovingian and Carolingian eras (6th–9th centuries); the Vikings burned and pillaged Paris on several occasions during this period.

Romanesque and Gothic

The Romanesque era (10th–11th centuries), with its ponderous, gloomy structures, left hardly a trace either. The steeple of St-Germain-des-Prés church is a rare remnant. In the 12th century, Paris turned to the newest rage in religious architecture – Gothic, discerned by pointed arches and the use of ribbed vaults with flying buttresses, which allowed windows to replace walls and stone to soar towards the heavens.

Iraqi architect Zaha Hadid's Chanel Mobile Art Pavilion won the 2004 Pritzker Prize and has now found a permanent home at the Institut du Monde Arabe.

The most famous sacred building in Paris, Notre-Dame Cathedral, epitomises the perfection of Gothic style. Its construction began in 1163 on the site of a Romanesque church, which had been built on the foundations of a Carolingian basilica, which in turn had been built on the site of a Roman temple. It took 200 years to finish. The building began to decay in the 17th century, but restoration by 19th-century Gothic revivalist Eugène Viollet-le-Duc (1814–79) only started in 1841. The restoration took nearly 23 years.

Close by stands Sainte-Chapelle, a fragile-looking church in High Gothic style, which differs from Notre-Dame in that the vast stained-glass windows are supported by only a thin framework of stone. It was built by Louis IX in 33 months to shelter the Crown of Thorns.

The Renaissance

War in Italy, in 1495, brought the French into contact with Renaissance grandeur, and the style, characterised by contempt for all Gothic forms and a rediscovery of antiquity, was imported to France. In architecture, the ribbed vault disappeared in favour of flat ceilings with wooden beams. Medieval fortresses gave way to genteel palaces with Greek-style colonnades.

The Gothic splendour of Notre-Dame de Paris.

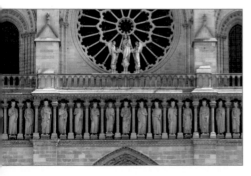

> *Lighter, more slender and luminous than previous styles, Gothic coincided with the strengthening of the French crown and a religious fervour inflamed by the Crusades.*

Among Paris's main exponents of the Renaissance were architect Pierre Lescot (1510–78), who's finest work is the west wing of the Louvre, and Jean Goujon (1510–68), who sculpted the reliefs on Lescot's Louvre facade and worked on the Hôtel Carnavalet (1544). Goujon's work can also be seen on Lescot's Fontaine des Innocents, an example of Renaissance sensuality.

Gateway to Place des Vosges, the most superb classical-style, royal square in Paris.

The Classical influence

While the Renaissance had succumbed to the Baroque in the rest of Europe at the end of the 16th century, a desire for strength and clarity born of rationalism dominated architecture. French architects were still looking towards sobriety and Classicism; the Classical style is based on symmetry, simplicity of line and great, wide-open perspectives. The Pont Neuf (1606), the first bridge to be built without houses on it, was one of the first examples. During this period, large squares were created, surrounded by uniform buildings and displaying a statue of the king in the middle of the large central garden. The Place des Vosges, commissioned by Henri IV in 1609, was the first and most elegant of the Classical-style royal squares.

The grand style

The Sun King, Louis XIV, left his mark on Paris and its surrounding region, but imposed his personality most forcefully on the palace of Versailles. Begun in 1668, the palace symbolised the absolute power of the monarch and employed the top talents of the time: architects Louis Le Vau and Hardouin-Mansart, painter Charles Le Brun and landscape gardener André Le Nôtre. Other fine examples of the Classical style are the Palais du Luxembourg (1631) and the Hôtel des Invalides (1677).

After Louis's death, building was kept to a minimum until the 1750s, when the neo-classical movement turned to forms lifted directly from antiquity, taking the utmost care to reproduce what recent progress in archaeology had brought to light. Jacques-Ange Gabriel laid out Place de la Concorde and built the Ecole Militaire, and Jacques-Germain Soufflot designed the Panthéon on the site of an older church.

With the coronation of a triumphant Napoleon and the installation of a new empire at the beginning of the 19th century came the triumphal arches (Arc de Triomphe du Carrousel and Arc de Triomphe) and the triumphal neoclassical Rue de Rivoli.

The Haussmann effect

Except for a few upper-class neighbourhoods, post-Revolution Paris was a squalid city. Poverty-stricken communities, in filthy, narrow alleyways and miserable, overpopulated shacks were constantly on the brink of revolt. For obvious sanitary reasons, but also to defeat riots, Napoleon III and the director for public works) Baron Georges Haussmann began a sweeping programme to redraw the city map in the 1850s. Medieval Paris all but disappeared:

THROUGH THE AGES

Architecture in Paris embodies a wide spectrum of styles. Here are a few examples:

Roman: Arènes de Lutèce (1AD)
Romanesque: The steeple of Saint-Germain-des-Prés (990–1014)
Gothic: Notre-Dame (1163–1345), Sainte-Chapelle (1245), Tour St-Jacques (1523)
Renaissance: Cour Carrée facade of the Louvre (1556), St-Eustache church (1532–1637)
Classical: Versailles (1668), Les Invalides (1677), Place Vendôme (1698)
Neoclassical: Ecole Militaire (1751–80), Panthéon (1790), Rue de Rivoli opposite the Louvre (1806–35), Arc de Triomphe (1806–36)
Second Empire: Gare du Nord (rebuilt 1861–65), Pont St-Michel (rebuilt 1857), Opéra Garnier (1875)
Modern: Institut du Monde Arabe (1981–87), La Défense, the Louvre Pyramid, Opéra Bastille (all three 1989), Bibliothèque Nationale François Mitterrand (1998), Louis Vuitton Foundation (2014).

whole quarters were razed, and wide, tree-lined avenues, harder to barricade than narrow alleys, cut through the maze of backstreets.

Paris still bears the indelible stamp of Haussmann's achievements. After clearing out slums and opening up the area around the Louvre, he concentrated on expanding the system of boulevards through the city centre begun by Louis XIV. A small hill then known as the Butte St-Roch, occupied by windmills, a gallows and a pig market, was intended to be their centre. It is hard to picture that today as you stand on the busy Place de l'Opéra, looking at Garnier's opera house, the Second Empire's most sumptuous construction.

Monsieur Eiffel's tower

The second half of the 19th century was rich in architectural creativity. Wrought iron made its debut with the Grand Palais, the Pont Alexandre III and, of course, the iconic Eiffel Tower. Panned by writers and critics during its construction for the World Fair in 1889, the tower is now the symbol of Paris. The tower embodied the uneasy relationship between science, industry and art in Paris. When the engineer climbed its 1,665 steps to plant the French

The Grande Arche at La Défense aligns with the Arc de Triomphe along the Axe historique which runs through Paris.

flag atop his iron latticework fantasy, crowds of ordinary Parisians who admired his vision cheered; the aesthetes stayed away.

It was an eclectic era. Having burned down during the Commune of 1871, the Hôtel de Ville (City Hall) on the Right Bank was rebuilt in Renaissance style, while Sacré-Cœur Cathedral fused neo-Byzantine and Romanesque styles. Numerous churches toed the neo-Gothic line. Reacting against these academic approaches and inspired by Japanese art, the Belgian Hector Guimard established the Art Nouveau movement. The graceful, organic forms and curving lines, natural and Baroque at the same time, were decried by some as "noodle style". Guimard designed several buildings in the 16th *arrondissement*, including the Castel Béranger (14 rue de la Fontaine), and also the city's Métro entrances, many of which, including those at Porte Dauphine and Abbesses, still remain.

The modern age

Both the modern movements of the 1920s and 1930s and Art Deco were born in the 16th *arrondissement*. Mallet-Stevens and Le Corbusier were the main exponents of the Cubic style of architecture, all pure lines and concrete. At the same time, a grandiose, neoclassical form of modernism appeared, as epitomised by the Palais de Chaillot.

From the 1960s, Paris underwent a transformation. Facades were cleaned, the Métro

The Eglise du Dôme in Les Invalides is also a fine example of the classical style.

was modernised and old parts of the city were demolished. New architectural projects were developed, keeping up with technical advances by building upwards (La Défense and the much-decried Tour Montparnasse), expanding indoor space (Centre Pompidou, Cité de la Villette, Palais Omnisports at Bercy) and experimenting with new materials that capture, reflect and admit light.

In the 1980s, Sino-American architect I.M. Peï designed a new entrance for the Louvre: a "landscape" of pyramids in stainless steel and specially made glass. Lauded for its beauty and efficiency, the central pyramid has undoubtedly earned its place on the city's architectural stage.

Like Peï's pyramid, the bankside Institut du Monde Arabe (designed in 1987 by Jean Nouvel) achieves a kind of harmony by reflecting the neighbouring buildings and the ever-changing Parisian sky.

> Amazingly, the Eiffel Tower was originally intended to be merely a temporary exhibit, to be dismantled after the 1889 World Fair. It is now the world's most visited paid monument.

Into the future

Innovation continues. The imposing 1997 Bibliothèque Nationale François Mitterrand, also known as the TGB (Très Grande Bibliothèque), is at the heart of the 'new' Left Bank, a vast renewal project in the 13th *arrondissement*. MK2 Bibliothèque, a cinema complex designed by Jean-Michel Wilmotte, opened nearby in 2003.

Two new footbridges have sprung across the river in recent years: the Passerelle de Solférino between the Tuileries and the Musée d'Orsay, in 1999, and the Passerelle Simone de Beauvoir the between the TGB and the Parc de Bercy in 2006. In the Parc de Bercy itself, a 1992 Frank Gehry building, became the new home for the iconic Cinémathèque Française in 2006. An even newer building, another Nouvel design, is the Musée du Quai Branly, a museum of art from Asia, Africa, the Americas and Oceania that opened in 2006 in the shadow of the Eiffel Tower.

In 2015, the Tour Triangle finally got a green light from the city authorities. This 180m (590ft) glass-and-steel pyramid is planned for

> Another Frank Gehry design is the Louis Vuitton Foundation, which opened in 2014 in the Bois de Boulogne, after 13 years in construction. This contemporary art museum is nicknamed "the iceberg" due to its billowing glass structure. This private museum was the brainchild of Europe's richest man, and CEO of LVMH luxury goods conglomerate, Bernard Arnault.

the Parc des Expositions, next to the Porte de Versailles. Hermitage Plaza is due to be completed by 2020 in La Défense and will be the tallest building in Paris, and indeed the European Union, at 323m (1060ft). These are two of several new skyscrapers planned by Mayor Delanoë on the outskirts of Paris after he successfully overturned a law restricting the height of new buildings to 37m/121ft.

To get a complete overview of the history of architecture in Paris, pay a visit to the permanent exhibition in Le Pavillon de l'Arsenal (21 boulevard Morland, 4th), itself a remarkable piece of 19th-century design, with natural light pouring through a superb glass roof.

The exquisite grand staircase inside the Musée Jacquemart-André.

The fabulous Belle Epoque interior of Le Train Bleu, which serves traditional fare.

PARIS ON A PLATE

This is a city that worships food – and recent years have brought plenty of notable new talents and intriguing new addresses to keep the dining scene alive.

The news of the death of French food has been greatly exaggerated. Critics hail Spain, or London, or Sydney, or New York, as the "new France" – whereas Paris, they whine, is stuck in a rut. But that's not an entirely fair evaluation. It's important to remember when you eat in Paris, where the cooking of the whole country converges, that you're sampling a long-established cuisine: a vast, yet coherent repertoire of dishes, ingredients and techniques that have stood the test of time. A new ingredient or dish won't be welcomed into the cuisine until it proves itself worthy.

For the traveller, if not for locals, such conservatism is a blessing. You want real French onion soup? You've got it. The menu says *steak au poivre*? That means it's *steak au poivre*: flat, rare, with creamy peppercorn sauce. This is not to say that contemporary and international experiences are not to be found. In recent years, a wave of young chefs has been opening snazzy yet relaxed restaurants serving French food with a fresh,

> French cooking may be slow to evolve, but it's because France is a country that truly knows its food. The French are incredibly protective, disciplined and judicious in this regard.

contemporary face, and integrating (ever so cautiously) more exotic flavours like ginger, peanut, coriander, curry and lime. Even stellar chefs like Joël Robuchon and Alain Senderens have taken a more unbuttoned approach to their trade by opening their own bistros.

Some Parisian bistros have small crêperie stands, like this one in Montmartre.

The international scene, although perhaps not as widespread as elsewhere, is also an integral part of the city's taste experience. Indeed, one thing that makes it exciting to eat in a country other than one's own is discovering the influences that immigrants from other places have brought to it. Paris has a lot of good North African, Vietnamese, Japanese, Lebanese and Afro-Caribbean cooking.

Street food and cafés

Street vendors are a welcome sight, especially in winter, with chestnuts roasting over beds of coal, waffle irons and crêpe grills ever at the

The much-loved baguette.

Charcuterie and cheese board.

ready. Falafels are sold through the windows on the Rue des Rosiers. Middle Eastern kebabs and savoury turnovers are sold throughout the city. Ice-cream stands abound on the Ile St-Louis.

To fill a picnic basket with traditional French fare, your best bet is a *charcuterie*, where you'll find ready-cooked dishes such as quiches, salads, pâtés, sausages, cheeses and prepared dishes like *poulet basquaise* (chicken with tomatoes

VEGETARIANS WILL SURVIVE

The vegetarian dishes of French cuisine are few and far between. In traditional restaurants, a solution is to order two meat-free starters instead of a main course. In an upmarket establishment, you can telephone ahead and request a vegetarian meal; this gives the cook time to concoct something just for you. Another option is to explore the city's ethnic restaurants, which serve meat-free snacks as well as elaborate three-course meals. However in recent years, vegetarian restaurants have been popping up all over Paris from Saveurs Végét'Halles (41 rue des Bourdonnais, 1st, tel: 01 40 41 93 95; www.saveursvegethalles.fr) to Tien Hiang (14 rue Bichat, 10th, tel: 01 42 00 08 23; www.tien-hiang.fr), whose menu consists solely of meat-free dishes from South East Asia.

and red peppers). Next, go to the bakery for a baguette or ready-made sandwiches.

If you're in a rush in the midst of shopping, traditional cafés will cater quickly while you give your feet a rest. Many will serve no more than simple baguette sandwiches. Others offer omelettes, or the quintessential café favourite, *croque-monsieur* (grilled ham and cheese on toast), or *croque-madame* (the same, but with a fried egg on top). Café salads are often hefty and filling, such as *Paysanne* (with potatoes, bacon and cheese) *Norvégienne* (with smoked salmon), *Landaise* (with duck breast), to name but three.

Bistros and brasseries

No restaurants are more popular – or more emblematic of Paris – than the neighbourhood bistros and brasseries. Brasseries (breweries) were introduced to the city in the 19th century, around the time when modern methods of brewing were being perfected. Many brasseries serve Alsatian specialities such as *choucroute* and *steins* of beer; others specialise in shellfish. Outside the latter, you'll spot heaps of clams, mussels and langoustines on beds of ice, and burly men in overalls shucking oysters from dawn until dusk. All brasseries serve a wide range of dishes, including standard bistro fare. They're a jolly experience: spacious, raucous and festive, usually decorated in Belle Epoque style.

> The name "bistro" supposedly derives from the days of the Allied occupation of Paris in 1814. Russian soldiers were forbidden to drink, so whenever they dived into a bar, they demanded their refreshments urgently – bystro – to avoid being caught.

For quieter, more intimate meals, opt for the bistros. These are smaller, more humble nooks, offering similar menus: *hareng pommes à l'huile* (smoked herring marinated in oil with warm potatoes), *œufs en meurette* (poached eggs with red wine sauce), *blanquette de veau* (veal in a white sauce), *coq au vin* (braised chicken in wine), *mousse au chocolat* (chocolate mousse) and *tarte Tatin* (caramelised upside-down apple tart). Some bistros have a regional bent,

proudly boasting their provincial specialities. In Auvergnat bistros, think blue cheese, potatoes, walnuts and superb beef; with Southwestern ones it's *foie gras* and duck; Basque flavours include hot pepper, salted cod and ham; and Provençal bistros guarantee ratatouille, lamb stew and *bouillabaisse* (*fish stew*).

The Michelin-starred experience

For those who want to dress up and splash out on dinner, there are countless prestigious restaurants in the city. A Michelin guide will point you in the direction of establishments that meet these exacting standards. Be ready to spend several hours at the table, to eat seven courses, and to have waiters attending to you every whim. The food in Michelin-starred restaurants (whether one star or three) should produce meals you'll remember for a lifetime, but some restaurants, unfortunately, rest on their laurels.

Contemporary French cooking

There is no single term for the sprouting of contemporary French restaurants: sleek, trendy, moderately priced, and with good, interesting

Cooking with panache.

food. Dinner usually consists simply of an *entrée*, *plat* and *dessert*. Dishes are lighter than in a bistro, less complicated than in Michelin-starred establishments; the wine list will probably include international bottles; the service is pleasant; and the crowds are *branché* (fashionable).

All in all, they're a good way to get a taste of the future of French food. The only drawback is that they don't feel particularly French.

> Part of the excitement of dining in France is having the option of – if not the appetite for – pig's ears, beef muzzle and blood sausage.

Food for thought

Not all visitors to Paris are as enthusiastic about certain French classics as the locals. Almost everyone knows that *escargots* are snails and *cuisses de grenouille* are frogs' legs, but many a tourist has unwittingly ordered calf's head *(tête de veau)*, expecting simply veal, or *andouillette* in hope of pork sausage only to discover tripe-filled concoctions. But dishes like these sound more frightening than

they really are: after all, millions of French people relish their taste.

Fish, of the truly excellent kind, is not especially easy to find in Paris, and where one does find it, it comes at a price. Brasseries usually have a promising array, for example on their *plateaux de fruits de mer* (shellfish platters). Of course, it's generally in the more expensive restaurants that it will be cooked best. In France, meats tend to be served at one extreme or another: at the one end, raw (for example, *tartare de bœuf* or beef tartare) or *saignant* (rare); and at the other, *confit* (preserved) or cooked tender until falling from the bone. If you order steak, it will come rare unless you specify "*à point*" (medium) or "*bien cuit*" (well done). Don't hesitate to send a dish back if the meat is not cooked to your liking. Fish is trickier. At mid-range restaurants it tends to be overcooked, so if you like it just done, it's important to ask for your fish cooked "*rose à l'arête*" (rare at the bone).

Cheese

Nowhere in the world is there a wealth of cheese to match that of France, where cheese is considered so important that an entire dinner

Contemporary cooking at Les Cocottes.

Andouillette and potatoes.

Coffee is served after dessert.

A tempting and colourful selection of French cheeses.

course is devoted to it alone. Between the main course and dessert, out comes the trolley or platter, laden with a delectably smelly array. The most pungent are generally cheeses such as Epoisses, Mont d'Or and Munster. If you prefer mild ones, steer instead towards goat's cheeses, young Comté or Mimolette. Blue cheeses vary greatly in creaminess and strength, but usually aren't too overpowering; Brie and Camembert are well known, mild and deliciously smooth. Try not to be overwhelmed by the number of options. It can take years to become familiar with French cheeses. Just remember two rules: in a cheese tasting, always start with the mildest cheese and work your way around to the strongest; and never steal the "nose" off a piece; always slice cheese in such a way as to preserve its shape, so the last person served won't be left with just the rind.

Drinks

It is usual to be offered an *apéritif* before a meal. A glass of champagne, white wine, or a *kir* (white wine with *cassis* – a blackcurrant liqueur) are most popular, but whisky and port are also common. Of course, you don't have to order an *apéritif*; you can jump straight to the wine list.

In the minds of the French, wine is the *de rigueur* accompaniment not only to French food, but to eating in general. In Michelin-starred restaurants, a deal of care is generally taken over which wine will go with what, but in most casual places, the rule is drink what you like.

Simple restaurants, in addition to bottles, sell wine by the glass or by the jug: *un pichet de rouge* (a jug of red) will get you an inexpensive, potentially rough but entirely drinkable red wine. Beer is usually only ordered with sandwiches, Alsatian meals or Asian lunches; cider accompanies Breton and Norman specialities (crêpes or mussels). Several mineral waters are on offer; request *pétillante* for sparkling, *plate* for still, or *en carafe* for tap water.

The French meal

Entrée (Americans, take note) means starter, not main course. *Plat* is the main dish. *Dessert* is, not surprisingly, dessert or pudding. All three are often included in *prix fixe* (fixed-price) menus, although a choice of either *entrée* and *plat* or *plat* and *dessert* is increasingly common.

In unpretentious places, nobody minds if you order two *entrées* instead of a full meal. What is often frowned upon, especially in upmarket restaurants, is passing dishes around the table to share, as chefs take pride in balancing the flavours on each plate. For a widely

North African fare is popular.

Couscous at Zerda Café in the Marais.

roaming meal, opt for a *menu dégustation* (tasting menu).

Coffee is served after dessert. *Café* means espresso, strong and black. If you like milk, order a *café noisette*. *Café crème* (coffee with milk) is considered a breakfast drink. Finally, if you're avoiding caffeine, ask for a *café décaféiné* (*déca* for short) or *une tisane* (herbal tea).

Last but not least, the *digestifs* (after-dinner drinks), ranging from Cognac to Armagnac to Calvados to other liqueurs. Beware: too many and you'll pay for it in the morning.

Due to the large American expat community, there are several places to get a decent brunch including Breakfast in America (17 rue des Ecoles, 5th and 4 rue Mahler, 4th) while Le Bal Café (6 impasse de la Défense, 18th), where apple crumble is usually on the menu, is a "must visit" for homesick Brits.

OTHER CUISINES

North African restaurants are probably the best-represented in the French capital, serving hearty dishes like *couscous* (steamed semolina topped with spicy meat or stewed vegetables) and *tagine* (braised meat stew, often cooked with preserved lemons and dried fruits).

Parisians have well and truly fallen in love with Japanese food, and dozens of restaurants have opened around the city in recent years, ranging from cheap noodle joints to more sophisticated, top Michelin-star establishments like Aida (1 rue Pierre-Leroux, 7th), where a menu can set you back €160. If your budget doesn't stretch that far,

head to the Porte d'Italie Chinatown neighbourhood, south of the Latin Quarter, for cheap and cheerful Vietnamese and Chinese eateries.

For Indian fare (not just restaurants, but also eclectic grocers), explore the 10th *arrondissement* around the Gare du Nord; this area is the place to look for Turkish restaurants too.

A good place to try out African food is the Belleville area, northeast of Place de la République, and Lebanese restaurants are dotted all over Paris, as are Thai establishments.

Chocolate and coffee éclairs aligned with precision at La Maison du Chocolat.

CHIC SHOPPING

From chic boutiques to mouth-watering food shops and from strutting-edge fashions to antique dealers and flea markets: welcome to the best collection of shops in Europe.

Though shopping abroad is an increasingly predictable affair, Paris can still claim to offer something different. It hosts an incredible variety of shops and has, by and large, retained its tradition of small specialist addresses and personal attention. Take a walk through the Passage des Panoramas (rue Montmartre, 2nd) to see some fine examples.

St-Germain-des-Prés is a great area for shoes, sensible or not.

Despite a tendency for fashion labels to aim for a citywide spread, there are fewer chain stores here than in most European capitals. With the exception of the Forum des Halles and a couple of small shopping centres, Paris remains largely free of the *centres commerciaux* (shopping centres) that disfigure its suburbs. Instead, boutiques ensure that Paris stays vibrant and alive.

The fashion industry is still a tangible presence in Paris; however, French designers no longer dominate the world fashion stage. But between the couture tags and the high-street chains, you can find boutiques with their own take on French style, retailers picking out exciting new talents, and the one-off boutiques of individual designers. And at some atelier-boutiques, in Bastille and Montmartre, you can buy direct.

Other aspects of French design are also worth exploring. Paris has a strong art and craft tradition, from the classic hallmarks of quality such as Lalique glass and Pierre Frey fabrics to contemporary design gurus such as Philippe Starck, and the rising talents Tsé & Tsé Associées and the Bouroullec brothers.

Then there's food, of course. Every *quartier* has its *chocolatiers*, *pâtisseries* and *boulangeries*, ripe-smelling cheese shops and bustling street markets.

Galerie de Valois, near the Palais-Royal, hosts luxury brands like Marc Jacobs, Stella McCartney and Jérôme L'Huillier.

Anne Fontaine, the queen of the white shirt.

Window shopping at the Dior store on Avenue Montaigne.

Under its stunning Art Nouveau glass dome, Galeries Lafayette offers a colossal fashion choice, from hip designer labels and classical womenswear to popular labels. There is an adjoining Lafayette Homme for men.

ART AND ANTIQUES

Vintage posters for sale in Passage Jouffroy.

As you'd expect from a city that has contributed significantly to the arts over the centuries, Paris has plenty to offer those looking to buy art or antiques. At the top end of the scale, Le Louvre des Antiquaires, housed in a beautiful 19th-century building on rue de Rivoli opposite the famous museum, has 150 galleries and showrooms selling everything from Old Masters to Art Deco dancer sculptures, while over in the Marais, the Village St-Paul has a more affordable, eclectic mix of galleries and designers.

Serious art collectors should head over to St-Germain as most of the major dealers are based on Rue de Seine and Rue des Beaux-Arts. Near here Librairie Taschen (2 rue de Buci) has dozens of books on the visual arts. For those on tighter budgets, a Marché de la Création takes place in Place de la Bastille on Saturday and in front of the Montparnasse tower on Sunday, where around 150 artists and craftspeople sell their wares from 10am to 7pm.

For iconic images of Paris, such as original posters by Toulouse Lautrec and photos by Henri Cartier-Bresson, the place to go is L'Ile aux Images (51-53 rue St-Louis-en-l'Ile, 4th) on Ile St-Louis.

Hip design store Merci in the Marais is a one-stop shop for a stylish life.

THE MARKET SCENE

The city's lively, colourful and breathtaking street markets are a vital part of life for many residents – all are different, which makes shopping endlessly interesting.

Visitors wanting a change from the cool chic of haute couture Paris should seek out a street market: there are more than 100. Foodies will be beguiled by the tantalising smells of the street food markets; photographers intrigued by the predominantly North African Marché d'Aligre; and browsers may prefer the *bouquinistes*, open-air booksellers whose stalls line the banks of the Seine. There are markets specialising in flowers, postcards and stamps; funky Left Bank markets selling second-hand designer clothes; rural markets overflowing with fresh farm produce and bargains; or genuine antiques to be had at the city's regular flea markets.

Non-French speakers need not worry too much. Items are usually marked clearly and many stall-holders speak English or are used to dealing with visitors from around the world; don't be afraid to barter when buying antiques or bric-à-brac. It's a good idea to have lots of change available, especially at food markets, as credit cards are not usually accepted. Markets can be a fun place to take children – just be sure to keep a close eye on them – due to the wide variety of produce and objects on offer, many of which are unlikely to be commonly found in other countries and which have a distinctly French or colonial feel.

Most of all, markets are one of the best opportunities for visitors to experience the real buzz of the various quartiers: whether rubbing shoulders with couture-clad grandes dames in the 8th or being serenaded by African drummers in brightly coloured tunics in Belleville.

A brocante stall near the Canal St-Martin.

At the Puces de St-Ouen, although a few of the markets remain shabby, much of what is on sale is classy and often quite pricey. Many of the stalls have the allure of shops, and stallholders are knowledgeable enthusiasts. The whole complex is now listed as a historic monument in an attempt to preserve its character.

Food markets provide a variety of produce not always found in supermarkets.

Food markets say a lot about the way Parisians live. The key to most is that they sell fresh, quality ingredients. Prices are not cheap, but the emphasis is on the best that is in season. There are two main types of food market: the roving street markets that appear a couple of mornings a week, and the historic covered markets.

Blooms for sale at the Marché aux Fleurs on Ile de la Cité.

THE BEST MARKETS

Old postcards for sale at the Puces de St-Ouen.

Paris is known for its many flea *(puces)* and food markets. Here are some of the best: **Marché de St-Ouen:** in the north of Paris (Métro Porte de Clignancourt). Reputedly the largest flea market in the world, with over 2,500 dealers spread over a dozen markets and arcades. Be ready to bargain. Mon 11am–5pm; Sat–Sun 9am–6pm.

Marché de Montreuil: tattier and more anarchic than St-Ouen, Montreuil (Métro Porte de Montreuil) sells car parts, tools and used clothes. Sat–Mon 7am–7pm.

Marché de Vanves: smaller than St-Ouen and Montreuil, Vanves (Métro Porte de Vanves) is a relaxed flea market within the Périphérique. Weekends 7am–2pm.

Marché d'Aligre: the oldest flea market in Paris, on the square next to the rue d'Aligre (Métro Ledru-Rollin) food market. Handful of stalls selling overpriced antiques and bric-a-brac. Tue–Sun 9am–12:30pm. Food Market: Tue–Fri 9am–1pm; 4–7.30pm; Sat 9am–1pm; 3.30–7.30pm; Sun 9am–1pm.

Marché Bastille on boulevard Richard-Lenoir (Thu 7am-2:30pm and Sun 7am–3pm; Métro Bastille) and **Marché Daumesnil** on boulevard de Reuilly (Tue and Fri 7am–2.30pm; Métro Daumesnil): are street markets with a great range of seasonal produce.

Rue Mouffetard: characterful food market in the Latin Quarter (Métro Censier-Daubenton). Tue–Sat (closed for lunch) and Sun am.

Marché St-Quentin: 85 boulevard Magenta, 10th (Métro Gare de l'Est), was built in the 1880s and remains the best-preserved cast-iron covered market. Stalls sell fresh produce and exotic snacks. Tue–Sat 8am–8pm, Sun 8am–1.30pm.

Vegetable-shopping at the Marché Saxe-Breteuil, Les Invalides.

PARIS AFTER DARK

The city's nightlife offers a multitude of options for drinking and dancing until the small hours, but live music and cabaret have their fans too.

Paris still isn't really a clubbing city, and stringent anti-noise laws mean most music venues can't stage late-night gigs. But there's no shortage of after-dark revelry if you know where to look. There has been an increase in the range and number of venues: upmarket clubs like VIP Room (188bis rue de Rivoli, 1st) and Neo (23 rue du Ponthieu, 8th) attract celebrities and the jet set. In 2005, an old warehouse on the bank of the Canal St-Martin was turned into Point Ephémère (200 Quai de Valmy, 10th), a giant arts and nightlife complex. In 2007, boat hangars beneath Pont Alexandre III were converted into glam club Le Showcase. And other stalwarts, like the live music venues La Flèche d'Or (102bis rue de Bagnolet, 20th) and Le Bus Palladium (6 rue Fontaine, 9th) have been given new leases of life. There's also a lot of jazz, blues, chanson and world gigs, and lively backroom gig spaces to complement the larger, more traditional music venues. The coolest bars are around Ménilmontant and Oberkampf while the Marais is the place to go for gay and lesbian venues. But going out in Paris isn't solely restricted to bars and dance clubs; the city has long been associated with cabaret, from the magnificent costumes of the Bluebell Girls at Le Lido (116 avenue des Champs Elysées, 8th) to the racy gyrations at adults-only Crazy Horse (12 avenue George V, 8th). Keep your ears to the ground and look out for flyers and free listings booklets in bars.

The bar at Le Milliardaire (8 boulevard de la Madeleine, 8th), whose red and black décor give a nod to the venue's theatrical days.

The Ducs des Lombards (42 rue des Lombards, 1st) is one of the main jazz clubs in the capital.

Located in an upbeat street in a trendy neighbourhood in the heart of the St-Michel quarter, the Caveau de la Huchette will have you dancing to salsa beats all night long.

La Flèche d'Or (102bis rue de Bagnolet, 20th) is an enjoyable anarchic music and clubbing venue housed in an old train station.

Le Kitch, in oh-so-trendy Rue Oberkampf, is a cosy, intimate bar, popular with the equally hip locals.

THE COCKTAIL HOTSPOTS

Glamorous Le Showcase boasts a great location under the Pont Alexandre III.

Parisian trendsetters still love Hôtel Costes (239 rue St-Honoré, 1st), which has a sleek bar and plays classic "lounge music". Kong, the super-stylish Asian-Fusion restaurant on the top floor of the LVMH building (1 rue du Pont Neuf, 1st), is a bar at weekends and offers wonderful views across the French capital from its Philippe Starck designed-home. Tucked away on a Marais backstreet, Candelaria is a Mexican restaurant with a cosy candlelit cocktail lounge where tequila rules, while gin reigns supreme in the G'Bar and Lounge at Renaissance Paris Le Parc Trocadéro Hotel (55–57 avenue Raymond-Poincaré, 16th). Harry's Bar (5 rue Daunou, 2nd), with its dark-wood pub-like interior, is the oldest cocktail bar in Europe and where the Bloody Mary was invented in 1920. For a more casual and exotic night, try Andy Wahloo to savour Moroccan tapas, funky decor and mint-and-vodka concoctions.

Another fashionable Oberkampf hangout is Café Charbon, where DJs spin their decks on Friday and Saturday nights.

PARIS AT THE MOVIES

In 1895, the first public film screening was held in Paris – and the city and cinema have been inseparable ever since.

If Paris feels eternally familiar, thank the movies. Indeed, you're in film-set Paris the second you get off the train at the Gare du Nord, filmed by, among others, Jean-Pierre Jeunet (*Amélie*) and more recently by Claire Simon for her 2013 film *Gare du Nord*. Next, naturally, you make your way to the Métro – an even more popular film location, used by everyone from Henri-Georges Clouzot to the Coen brothers. Perhaps you come out at the Champs-Elysées – another classic setting; as you walk up, imagine the Wehrmacht's daily parade coming the other way, as recreated to sobering effect in Jean-Pierre Melville's *L'Armée des Ombres*. The oldest bridge in Paris, the Pont Neuf, was the focus of a 1991 film, *Les Amants du Pont Neuf*, starring Juliet Binoche. And it's hard to miss the Eiffel Tower: not only filmed more times than it has rivets, it even starred in its own cartoon, *Bonjour Paris*. Hollywood has long been enchanted by the City of Light, from the 1950s films *An American in Paris*, starring Gene Kelly, and *Funny Face*, featuring Audrey Hepburn, to the controversial 1970s Marlon Brando movie *Last Tango in Paris* and Woody Allen's time-travelling 2011 offering, *Midnight in Paris*. More recently, Paris featured in such films as Michael Haneke's *Amour* and *Holy Motors* by Leos Carax (2012), as well as *Something in the Air* by Olivier Assayas (2013).

Vincent Cassel as a bad boy from the banlieue in Matthieu Kassovitz's ferocious 1995 agitprop drama La Haine, which won its director a major prize at the Cannes Festival that year. In its portrayal of the urban underclass, the film is still all too relevant.

Marlon Brando and director Bernardo Bertolucci on the set of Last Tango in Paris in 1972.

Woody Allen's 2011 time-travelling comedy Midnight in Paris, in which former First Lady Carla Bruni-Sarkozy plays a museum guide.

Jean Seberg and Jean-Paul Belmondo in probably the most famous Paris film, Jean-Luc Godard's Breathless (A Bout de Souffle).

GOOD OLD NEW WAVE

When people think of Paris movies, they often have in mind a small clutch of films – usually including *Breathless* and *The 400 Blows* – made by a small group of people in a short space of time. These Nouvelle Vague ("new wave") films were made between the late 1950s and mid-1960s, by a loosely affiliated group of directors opposed to what they saw as the stuffiness of cinema of the day; its leading figures were Jean-Luc Godard, François Truffaut, Claude Chabrol, Eric Rohmer and Jacques Rivette – only Godard and Rivette, now in their eighties, are still alive at the time of writing. The films brought international recognition to the actors Jean-Paul Belmondo, Jeanne Moreau and Jean Seberg, the late American actress who starred in *Breathless*. One of the movement's few women directors was Agnès Varda, whose 1962 film *Cléo de 5 à 7* is one of the best of the bunch.

Audrey Tautou as the eponymous heroine of Jean-Pierre Jeunet's 2001 smash hit Amélie (Le Fabuleux Destin d'Amélie Poulain). The Métro stop shown is not, in fact, Abbesses – but a disused station used exclusively for filming.

Christopher Nolan's visually innovative Inception (2010) features a memorable 'folding Paris' scene.

The awe-inspiring Arc de Triomphe at dusk.

A sweeping view over Paris from its most iconic landmark, the Eiffel Tower.

ORIENTATION

A detailed guide to the entire city, with principal sites clearly cross-referenced by number to the maps.

Paris is set in a natural basin, cut through the middle by the meandering River Seine and bordered by gentle hills. Situated on longitude 2° 20'W and latitude 48° 50'N, the city itself covers an area close to 100 sq km (40 sq miles), spanning 13km (8 miles) from east to west, and 9km (6 miles) north to south. On the map, 20 *arrondissements* (administrative districts) spiral out like a snail's shell, a pattern reflecting the city's historical development and successive enlargements. The Seine enters Paris close to the Bois de Vincennes in the southeast, and weaves gently past three small islands – Ile St-Louis, Ile de la Cité and, on its way out, Ile des Cygnes. Several hills rise up to the north of the river, including Montmartre, the city's highest point at 130 metres (425ft), Ménilmontant, Belleville and Buttes Chaumont; and to the south,

Postcards for sale at a bouquiniste with a view over to Paris's oldest bridge, the Pont Neuf.

The view from Paris's tallest building, Tour Montparnasse.

Montsouris, Montagne Ste-Geneviève, Buttes aux Cailles and Maison Blanche. Mont Valérien is the highest point on the outskirts at 160 metres (525ft), providing an immense panoramic view of Paris from the west. The lowest, at 25 metres (85ft) above sea level, is at Grenelle.

The city is contained by the *Boulevard Périphérique*, a ring road stretching 35km (22 miles). Built in 1973 to try to reduce traffic jams, the Périph' is invariably congested itself. Forming two concentric rings around Paris, the suburbs *(la banlieue)* are divided up into *départements* or counties. The inner ring incorporates Hauts-de-Seine, Val-de-Marne and Seine-St-Denis, and the outer ring consists of Seine-et-Marne, Essonne, Yvelines and Val-d'Oise. These counties, together with Paris, constitute the Ile-de-France region and are linked by eight major roads, five RER lines and an extensive rail network branching out from five stations in the capital. The city's calmest transport route is its river, barely ruffled by the daily flow of boat traffic. Barges and pleasure boats on their way to Burgundy use the St-Martin and St-Denis canals, cutting across the northeast of Paris.

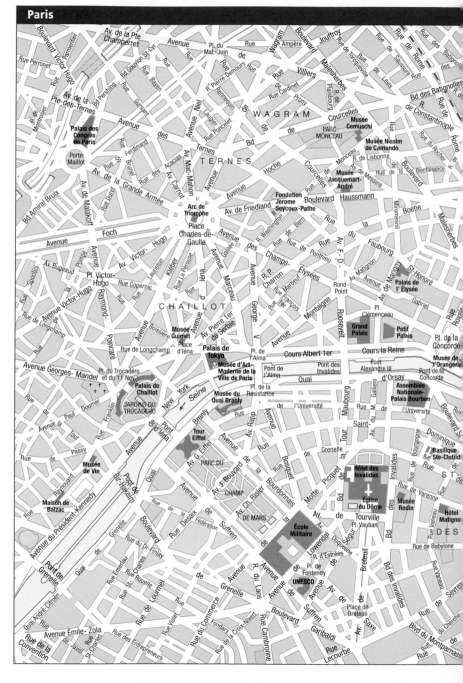

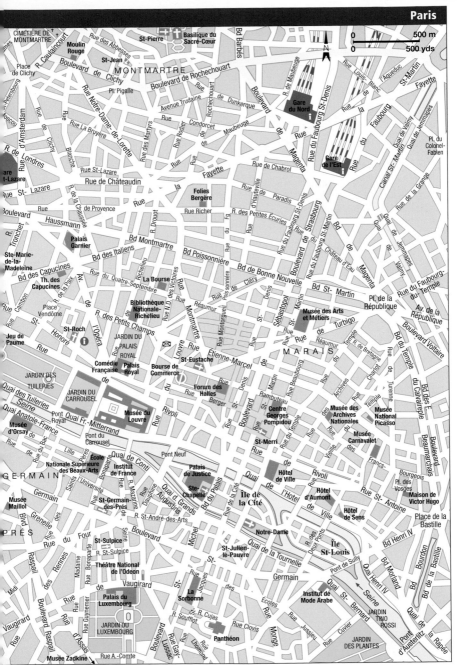

CIMETIÈRE DE MONTMARTRE
Moulin Rouge
R. Caulaincourt
Rue des Abbesses
St-Pierre
Basilique du Sacré-Cœur
Bd Barbès
St-Jean
Boulevard de Clichy
MONTMARTRE
Place de Clichy
Pl. Pigalle
Boulevard de Rochechouart
Rue des Martyrs
0   500 m
0   500 yds
N
Rue Louis- Blanc
L'Aqueduc
St-Martin
R. Caulaincourt
Rue des Abbesses
Avenue Trudaine
de Dunkerque
Rue de Maubeuge
Gare du Nord
Fayette
R. de Petersbourg
Rue Notre-Dame-de-Lorette
Rue
Rochechouart
Boulevard
de
Magenta
Rue du Faubourg St-Denis
Pl. du Colonel-Fabien
Rue La Bruyère
Rue
Rodier
Condorcet
Maubeuge
de
Gare de l'Est
Quai de Valmy
Quai de Jemmapes
Moscou
Rue d'Amsterdam
Rue
Blanche
des Martyrs
de
Canal St-Martin
Rue de Londres
de Clichy
St-Lazare
Fayette
Rue de Chabrol
Magenta
Rue de la Grange
are t-Lazare
R. de Londres
Rue St-Lazare
Rue de Châteaudin
Folies Bergère
Rue de Paradis
Rue d'Hauteville
Quai de Jemmapes
Ste-Marie-de-la-Madeleine
Bd Haussmann
Rue de la Chaussée
de Provence
Rue Richer
R. des Petites Écuries
Rue du Faubourg St-Denis
Boulevard
Rue
Tronchet
Palais Garnier
Bd Montmartre
Bd des Italiens
Bd Poissonnière
Bd de Bonne Nouvelle
Rue de Cléry
Château d'Eau
Magenta
Boulevard de Strasbourg
Quai de Valmy
Bd des Capucines
Th. des Capucines
Rue du Quatre-Septembre
La Bourse
Rue des Victoires
Richelieu
Poissonnière
Bd St- Martin
Rue du Faubourg-du-Temple
Av. de l'Opéra
Place Vendôme
R. de la Paix
Bibliothèque Nationale-Richelieu
R. des Petits Champs
Réaumur
Rue N.D.
Montmartre
Rue
Sébastopol
Musée des Arts et Métiers
Turbigo
Pl. de la République
Av. de la République
Boulevard Voltaire
Rue Cambon
St- Honoré
Jeu de Paume
St-Roch
JARDIN DU PALAIS ROYAL
Louvre
Étienne-Marcel
Réaumur
de
Rue
R. de Bretagne
Bd du Temple
Comédie Française
Palais Royal
Bourse de Commerce
St-Eustache
MARAIS
Bd des E.
Calvaireple
JARDIN DES TUILERIES
JARDIN DU CARROUSEL
Forum des Halles
Rue Berger
Rambuteau
Boulevard
Archives
Temple
Musée des Archives Nationales
Musée National Picasso
Boulevard Beaumarchais
Quai des Tuileries
Seine
Quai Anatole-France
Musée du Louvre
Rivoli
Rue
Rue
Centre Georges Pompidou
Rue Beaubourg
du Temple
Rue
Bourgeois
Pont Royal
Quai Fr.-Mitterrand
Pont du Carrousel
St-Merri
Musée Carnavalet
Francs-
Pl. des Vosges
Maison de Victor Hugo
Musée d'Orsay
Rue du Bac
Lille
Pont Neuf
École Nationale Supérieure des Beaux-Arts
Institut de France
Palais de Justice
Hôtel de Ville
Rivoli
Rue St- Antoine
GERMAIN
Germain
Quai de Conti
Quai des Grands
Ste-Chapelle
Île de la Cité
Hôtel d'Aumont
Hôtel de Sens
Place de la Bastille
Musée Maillol
Grenelle
Saints
l'Université
St-Germain-des-Prés
R. Mazarine
Augustins
Bd du Palais
Quai de l'Hôtel
Ville
Bd Henri IV
Raspail
Rennes
des
Boulevard
Dauphine
R. St-André-des-Arts
Notre-Dame
Quai de la Tournelle
Île St-Louis
Bd de la Bastille
PRÉS
Madame
Rue du Four
St-Sulpice
St-Sulpice
St-Julien-le-Pauvre
Germain
Pont de Sully
Quai St- Bernard
Rue Bonaparte
Théâtre National de l'Odéon
St-
Rue Jacques
Germain
Institut de Mode Arabe
Seine
JARDIN TINO ROSSI
Vaugirard
Vaugirard
Palais du Luxembourg
La Sorbonne
des
Écoles
Rue Clovis
Rue Monge
Jussieu
Pont d'Austerlitz
Quai de la Rapée
JARDIN DU LUXEMBOURG
Panthéon
JARDIN DES PLANTES
R. Cujas
R. Soufflot
Rue Gay-Lussac
Rue Lhomond
Rue Cuvier
Musée Zadkine
Rue A.-Comte

The Gothic towers of Notre-Dame.

ILE DE LA CITÉ AND ILE ST-LOUIS

Paris's Gothic heart, where the soaring towers and buttresses of Notre-Dame and the Sainte-Chapelle rise up next to the glowering fortress-prison of the Conciergerie, only a short walk from the 17th-century refinement of the Ile St-Louis.

The Ile de la Cité in the middle of the Seine is the birthplace and topographical centre of Paris, and has been its spiritual and legislative heart for more than 2,000 years. Invading the already established Parisii settlement in 53 BC, the Romans built a prefect's palace, law court and temple to Jupiter on the island. Across the river on the Right Bank, the Hôtel de Ville has been a cauldron of political debate since the Middle Ages (though the current building dates from the 1870s), while just to the north, the area of Les Halles fed the city's stomachs from 1110 until 1969. This is the core of the capital, an area which in many ways embodies the essence of Paris.

NOTRE-DAME ❶

Address: www.cathedraledeparis.com
Tel: 01 42 34 56 10
Opening Hrs: Mon–Fri 8am–6.45pm, Sat–Sun 8am–7.15pm; free guided tours in English: Wed–Thu 2pm, Sat 2.30pm
Entrance Fee: free
Transport: Cité

The Ile de la Cité is dominated by the soaring cathedral, Notre-Dame de Paris, which fills the eastern end of the island. Gazing up at its finely

Most brasseries and cafés on the island sell Berthillon ice creams.

sculpted facade, it's hard to imagine the building's condition when Victor Hugo (see page 91) wrote his novel *Notre-Dame de Paris* in 1830–1. He and fellow Romantics were appalled by the state of the building, and in 1841 succeeded in triggering a massive restoration programme, headed by Viollet-le-Duc. For 23 years, the meticulous architect repaired Notre-Dame from the foundations to the roof tiles, recreated stained-glass windows by copying extant ones and replaced sculptures destroyed in the

Main Attractions
Notre-Dame
Palais de Justice
Sainte-Chapelle
Conciergerie
Mémorial des Martyrs de la Déportation
Musée Adam Mickiewicz

Map
Page 74

Cité, Marais, Beaubourg and Les Halles

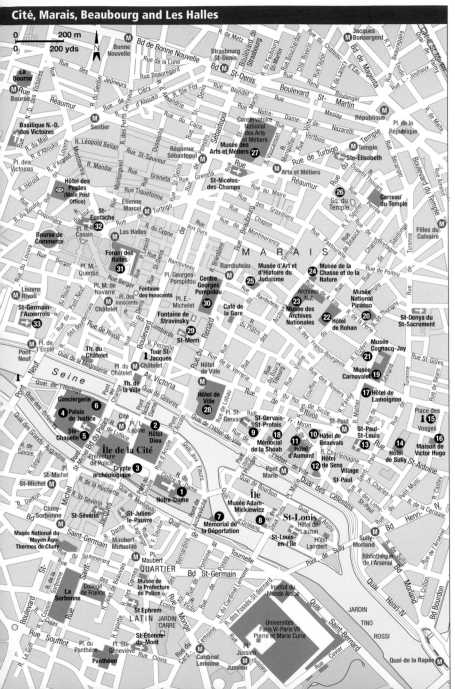

Revolution, such as the Gallery of Kings, by studying those of other Gothic cathedrals.

He also added a sacristy on the south side, now the Trésor de Notre-Dame (daily 9.30am–6pm; charge), housing the alleged Crown of Thorns, among other relics. For more on Notre-Dame, see page 84.

Royal shrine

The church of "Our Lady" was built on the site of earlier pagan fertility worship by Celts and Romans. In the 6th century, Clovis, the conquering Frankish king, erected a Christian basilica, which was replaced by a Romanesque church. In 1159, the young bishop Maurice de Sully decided that Paris deserved bigger and better. Work on the cathedral began in 1163 and took just under 200 years to complete, following plans by Pierre de Montreuil, also the architect of Sainte-Chapelle.

Even before it was finished, Notre-Dame had become the venue for state ceremonies, funerals and thanksgivings; in 1239 Louis IX deposited the Crown of Thorns and other relics acquired on Crusade here, while Sainte-Chapelle was being built. Since then Notre-Dame

has been witness to a string of historical events: in 1572, the cathedral's strangest wedding took place. The bride, Marguerite de Valois (a Catholic), stood at the altar, while bridegroom Henri de Navarre (a Protestant), called in his vows from the doorstep. Later, in 1589, Henri was crowned in the cathedral, having decided to convert to Catholicism. The famous comment attributed to him, "Paris is well worth a Mass" is almost certainly apocryphal.

The ascent of the towers rewards you with a glorious view of Paris.

The Portal of the Last Judgement.

"I find it hard to believe that other people who walk into Place Dauphine from the Pont Neuf aren't struck by its slightly curved triangular shape, and the line that runs through it… This is, no doubt about it, the sex of Paris."

André Breton

Riverside view of the cathedral

Come the Revolution, Notre-Dame was ravaged by looters, who melted down and destroyed anything that hinted of royalty, lopping off the heads of the kings of Judah along the top of the main portals. The cathedral was then turned into a "Temple of Reason", and by the end of the Revolution was being used to store wine.

By the time Napoleon decided to be crowned emperor in 1804, the cathedral was in such a shabby state bright tapestries were hung up to cover the crumbling decor. Pope Pius VII attended reluctantly, and when he hesitated at the altar, Napoleon took the crown and to cheers of *"Vive l'empereur!"* placed it on his head himself. Another dramatic event came in August 1944, at the thanksgiving ceremony for the Liberation of Paris, when the leader of the new government, General Charles de Gaulle, was shot at during the Te Deum.

Gothic architecture

Notre-Dame is magnificent from any angle, but its facade is particularly impressive. Viewed from Place du Parvis, the twin towers soar to the heavens with dramatic grace. The three porticoes each have a distinct design: an asymmetry typical of medieval architecture. Originally, the stone figures were finely painted against a gilt background, to illustrate Bible stories for an illiterate populace.

On the left, the Portal of the Virgin depicts the Ark of the Covenant and the coronation of the Virgin. The Portal of the Last Judgement, in the middle, shows the Resurrection, the weighing of souls and their procession to heaven or hell. The Portal of St Anne portrays the Virgin and Maurice de Sully. Above the doorways, the rose window, depicting the Virgin and Child in deep blues and rich reds, is a miracle of engineering. Picture the rickety scaffolding and the armies of stonemasons, who with simple measuring techniques constructed an intricate masterpiece that has lasted for 750 years. The glass, however, has been restored.

Towers of Notre-Dame

Tel: 01 53 10 07 00
Opening Hrs: daily Apr–Sept

10am–6.30pm (June–Aug Fri–Sat until 11 pm), Oct–Mar 10am–5.30pm, last admission 45 minutes before closing time
Entrance Fee: charge
Transport: Cité

The ascent of the towers (be prepared to queue) is a religious experience for those who love heights and a taste of hell for claustrophobics and vertigo sufferers. The ascent is long (387 steps) and narrow, but the reward is a breathtaking view over Paris. "Emmanuel", the 13-tonne bell, is rung only on state occasions. Legend has it that the purity of its tone is due to the gold-and-silver jewellery thrown into its heated bronze by the most beautiful women of Paris.

Cathedral interior

Inside, the cathedral is bounded by 37 side chapels. Supported by flying buttresses, the vault of the chancel seems almost weightless, with stained-glass windows distributing rays of coloured light into the solemn shadows. The exquisite 13th-century north and south rose windows are the two star attractions. The spectacular north window still retains most of its 13th-century glass, but the south rose had to be reconstructed completely by Viollet-le-Duc.

The 18th-century carved choir stalls, depicting the life of the Virgin Mary, were commissioned by Louis XIV, fulfilling a vow his father made 60 years earlier that he would devote the east chancel to the Virgin if he were to have an heir. Louis XIII's statue stands behind the high altar, with Guillaume Coustou's *Pietà*.

Hôtel-Dieu ❷

Address: 1 place du Parvis Notre-Dame 4th
Opening Hrs: courtyard daily
Entrance Fee: free
Transport: Cité

Just north of Notre-Dame is the Hôtel-Dieu, the oldest hospital in the city. Founded in 651 by Saint Landry, it was the recipient of generous donations from Louis IX during

Gothic perfection.

The superb rose window.

The entrance to the Palais de Justice.

the 13th century. Many famous doctors have worked here through the ages including Ambroise Paré (1510-1590) who is regarded as the father of prosthetics and forensic pathology. The hospital has remained in the same location despite several fires throughout the ages and the current building, which was constructed by Baron Georges Haussmann in the 1860s, was the scene of intense battles between police and the Germans in 1944.

Delicate statuary dot the exterior facades.

Crypte archéologique ❸

Address: www.crypte.paris.fr
Tel: 01 55 42 50 10
Opening Hrs: Tue–Sun 10am–6pm
Entrance Fee: charge
Transport: Cité

Underneath the parvis in front of the cathedral, inside the crypt, are excavations of buildings dating back to the Roman city of Lutetia in the 3rd century AD, including parts of a house inhabited by the Gallic Parisii, amid the remains of medieval cellars.

A short walk west of Notre-Dame are the imposing walls of the Palais de Justice and its wing, the Conciergerie.

Palais de Justice ❹

Tel: 01 44 32 50 50
Opening Hrs: Mon–Fri 9am–6pm
Entrance Fee: charge
Transport: Cité

At one time, the Palais de Justice was a royal palace, and Louis IX had his bedroom in what is now the First Civil Court. In the 14th century, the monarchy, in the person of Charles V, moved out, and parliament, with

full judiciary rights, moved in. A wander around the hushed building, past fleeting black-robed figures, might recall the tense days of the Revolution when the public prosecutor, Fouquier-Tinville, sent thousands of people to the guillotine. The present legal system is still based closely on the one founded by Napoleon Bonaparte. How the 4,000 people who work here find their way around the 24km (15 miles) of corridors is anyone's guess. But they won't have to for much longer as the Palais de Justice is due to move out in 2017 to swanky new premises designed by Renzo Piano on Boulevard de Clichy.

SAINTE-CHAPELLE ⑤

Address: www.monuments-nationaux.fr
Tel: 01 53 40 60 80
Opening Hrs: daily Mar–Oct 9.30am–6pm (15 May–15 Sept until 9pm Wed), Nov–Feb 9am–5pm
Entrance Fee: charge
Transport: Cité

Within the walls of the Palais de Justice, Sainte-Chapelle stands like a skeletal finger pointing heavenwards.

This miracle of High Gothic ingenuity is one of the most gorgeous buildings in Paris. Completed in just 33 months by Pierre de Montreuil and consecrated in 1248, the chapel was built to house the Crown of Thorns, bartered from the Venetians by Louis IX. Seemingly constructed without walls, the chapel's vaulted roof is supported by a thin web of stone, from which descend veils of richly coloured stained glass. A replica Crown of Thorns decorates the top of one of the pinnacles.

Built in two tiers, the lower chapel was designed for the palace staff, and is consequently smaller and gloomier. From the shadows, climb the spiral staircase into the crystalline cavern of the upper chapel. The soaring windows catch the faintest of lights, creating kaleidoscopes of colour that are still vivid, despite being nearly 800 years old. Depicted are 1,134 scenes from the Bible, which begin by the staircase with Genesis and proceed round the church to the 15th-century rose window. Regular concerts of chamber music are held in the chapel.

The delicate interior of Sainte-Chapelle, a masterpiece of High Gothic style.

Admiring tourists.

The flower market on Ile de la Cité is the oldest in Paris (1808).

The "veils" of stained-glass in Sainte-Chapelle.

THE CONCIERGERIE ❻

Address: www.monuments-nationaux.fr
Tel: 01 53 40 60 80
Opening Hrs: daily 9.30am–6pm
Entrance Fee: charge
Transport: Cité

In the northeast wing of the Palais de Justice, the Conciergerie looks like an intimidating castle, its four towers rising menacingly above impenetrable walls. It isn't hard to imagine this fortress as a merciless medieval prison – which it was (although much of the facade is 19th-century). It was originally built as a palace, administered by the Comte des Cierges or royal concierge – hence the name, Conciergerie – but after Charles Martel's revolt in 1358 King Charles V moved his main residence to his new palace of the Louvre.

The Comte was in charge of the king's seals, lodgings and taxes, until the Conciergerie was made a prison in 1391, when his job changed to that of chief gaoler. The Capetian palace came into its own during the Revolution, when it housed nearly 2,600 prisoners awaiting the guillotine, including Marie-Antoinette. Ironically, her prosecutor, Danton, resided in the next cell before his trip to the guillotine, as, in turn, did his nemesis Robespierre. In the merry-go-round of retribution, 1,306 heads rolled in one month at Place de la Nation. To the west is the Cour des Femmes, a rough courtyard where the women were allowed during the day.

The tower at the back is called Bonbec (the Squealer), for it was

here, from the 11th century, that torture victims told all. At the front is the 14th-century clock tower containing the first public clock in Paris, which is still ticking today.

Inside, the original kitchens are still intact. They were built to feed up to 3,000 people using four huge fireplaces and have a Gothic canopied ceiling supported by buttresses. The adjacent Salle des Gens d'Armes is a magnificent four-aisled Gothic hall where the royal guards, or men-at-arms, used to live.

EXPLORING THE ISLAND

Escape the shadows of the Revolution on Quai des Orfèvres, on the south bank of the island, where goldsmiths (orfèvres) once fashioned Marie-Antoinette's jewellery, but which is now home to the Police Judiciaire (the equivalent of the English cid). Beyond the Square du Vert-Galant and the statue of Henri IV, the river slides past the tip of the island. Pont Neuf, bisected by the island, is the oldest surviving bridge in Paris. It was made of stone, rather than wood, and was the first bridge

to be built without houses on it. In 1985, the artist Christo wrapped the whole length of the Pont Neuf in golden fabric. Between 1994 and 2007, the bridge underwent a major restoration project completed in time for its 400th anniversary, as a result of which it is looks particularly resplendent today. No small part of the Pont Neuf's charm, are the 385 grotesque faces below its cornices.

Relaxing in the autumn sunshine on the Square du Vert-Galant.

The Conciergerie, where Queen Marie-Antoinette spent her last days before her execution.

NOTABLE INMATES

A prison for five centuries, the medieval Conciergerie housed, among others, Captain Montgomery, a Scot, who fatally wounded Henri II during a tournament in 1559, and Ravaillac, assassin of Henri IV in 1610. During the Revolution, its big-name inmates ran from figures of the ancien régime such as Marie-Antoinette – whose cell has been carefully reconstructed – and Louis XV's favourite mistress, Madame du Barry, to Charlotte Corday, murderer of the Revolutionary leader Marat, and her defender the poet André Chenier, and finally the revolutionaries themselves, such as Danton, Camille Desmoulins, St-Just and even the architect of the Terror, Robespierre. In September 1792, more than 300 Revolutionary prisoners were killed here.

Café life on Ile St-Louis.

Charles Baudelaire, an Ile St-Louis resident.

small glasshouses selling flowers and plants underneath classical black street lamps. On Sunday, the stalls become a market for caged birds, and the jabbering of parakeets fills the air.

On the north side of Notre-Dame is the Quartier des Anciens Cloîtres (Ancient Cloister Quarter), home and study area for 12th-century monks and scholars who belonged to the cathedral chapter, including the theologian Pierre Abélard, famous for his love letters to the beautiful Héloïse. The area was once a warren of medieval churches and houses until Haussmann razed them to the ground, moving 25,000 inhabitants to the suburbs, to create the present vista. As you pass along Rue de la Colombe, note the remains of the Gallo-Roman wall in the pavement.

Mémorial des Martyrs de la Déportation ❼

Tel: 01 46 33 87 56
Opening Hrs: Tue–Sun Apr–Sept 10am–7pm, Oct–Mar until 5pm
Entrance Fee: free
Transport: Cité

On the eastern tip of the island lies this bleak but moving monument commemorating the 200,000 French deportees (Jewish, homosexual or

You can return to the east end of the island via the colourful Marché aux Fleurs in Place Louis-Lépine, opposite the Préfecture de Police and the Hôtel-Dieu.

In contrast to these forbidding structures, the market is an array of

THE URBAN NOMAD

One of the 19th-century's most towering literary figures, the poet Charles Baudelaire, lived on the Ile St-Louis, on the ground floor of the Hôtel de Lauzun from October 1843 to September 1845. While here, the young writer took hashish, fell obsessively in love with his mixed-race mistress and wrote several poems that were later to form part of *Les Fleurs du Mal*. Baudelaire had rarely lived at one address for such a long period of time: between his birth in 1821 and death in 1867 he lived at 45 different Paris addresses. The street named after him is in the 12th *arrondissement* – a part of the city he never called home.

resistant) sent to their deaths in Nazi concentration camps. The chambers of this prison-like structure are engraved with quotations and the names of concentration camps.

ILE ST-LOUIS

Away from the tourists and camcorders, across the pedestrian Pont St-Louis, Ile St-Louis is a privileged haven of peace and wealth. The island's elegance recalls the 17th-century, the era of Louis XIII and Cardinal Richelieu, and its mansions are home to Paris's elite.

Musée Adam Mickiewicz ❽

Address: 6 quai d'Orléans; www.bibliotheque-polonaise-paris-shlp.fr
Tel: 01 55 42 83 83
Opening Hrs: by reservation, Tue–Fri 2.15–6pm
Entrance Fee: charge
Transport: Pont Marie

Turning right along the south bank, you will come to this small museum.

Adam Mickiewicz (1798–1855) was a Polish poet, living in Paris from 1832–40, who devoted his work to helping oppressed Poles. The 17th-century building includes a Polish library and memorabilia of the Polish composer Frédéric Chopin, who often visited and played here.

Continuing eastwards round the island to the north bank, you will pass the private mansion Hôtel Lambert. Built in 1640 by Louis Le Vau, architect to Louis XIV, who built many of the houses on the Ile St-Louis and also worked on Vaux-le-Vicomte and Versailles, it is now owned by the Rothschilds. Further on is another mansion, the Hôtel de Lauzun, where the poets Théophile Gautier and Charles Baudelaire lived in 1843–5 and where Baudelaire wrote part of *Les Fleurs du Mal*.

The building now belongs to the City of Paris, and is reserved for official guests. Behind, the Rue St-Louis-en-l'Ile is full of chic gift shops, bars, restaurants and quaint tearooms. Also on this street is the church of the same name. Built between 1664 and 1765, the **Eglise St-Louis-en-l'Ile** (www.saintlouisenlile.catholique.fr) has a classic Baroque interior and hosts popular classical concerts.

EAT

The Ile St-Louis's most popular attraction (except on cold days) is edible: the famous ice creams of Berthillon (www.berthillon.fr), 29–31 rue St-Louis-en-l'Ile, in over 100 delicious flavours. The shop is open Wed–Sun 10am–8pm.

Berthillon boasts some unusual ice cream flavours – all delicious.

The streets of Ile St-Louis are surprisingly tranquil.

NOTRE-DAME DE PARIS

On the eastern tip of the Ile de la Cité stands the Gothic cathedral of cathedrals, "parish church of the history of France".

Notre-Dame cathedral's fortunate position – at one end of an island, with river to its north and river to its south – has meant it never got hemmed in by urban clutter: visitors are better able to appreciate its beauty due to the vast open space around it. It has had an eventful history. It stands on the site of a former Gallo-Roman temple to Jupiter, and was damaged by rioting Huguenots in 1548. It was sacked during the Revolution, then turned to new use as a "Temple to Reason" and a warehouse; it remained in poor repair – some city planners even propounded its demolition – until an extensive renovation programme was begun in the mid-19th century, after a campaign led by Victor Hugo. In 1965 the late decorative artist and glassmaker Jacques Le Chevallier was commissioned to design stained-glass windows for high up in the nave. In 1991 another programme of restorations got under way, with a timetable that was expected to run for a decade; the primary job was to clean the western facade. Work is still going on, most recently to renovate the organ. Amazingly, the architect of this awe-inspiring monument is unknown.

The Essentials

Address:
www.cathedralede
paris.com
Tel: 01 42 34 56 10
Opening Hrs: Mon–Fri
8am–6.45pm, Sat–
Sun 8am–7.15pm
Entrance Fee: free
Transport: Cité

Angels flanking the Portal of the Last Judgement.

HUGO, THE HUNCHBACK AND HISTORY

Notre-Dame's north and south rose windows are both masterpieces of stained glass.

Notre-Dame's largest bell weighs 13 tonnes and was cast in the 14th century; it was recast in 1631, and is famous for the purity of its F-sharp tone. The bells, of course, are a distinguishing element in one of the great love stories of literature: the love of the cathedral's hunchbacked bell-ringer, Quasimodo, for the beautiful Esmeralda, in Victor Hugo's 1831 novel *Notre-Dame de Paris*. There have been numerous film adaptations of the story over the years starting with *Esmeralda*, a ten-minute silent short film in 1905; to the contemporary French comedy *Quasimodo d'El Paris* (1999); Lon Chaney Jr (1923), Charles Laughton (1939) and Anthony Hopkins (1982) have taken the lead role in Hollywood versions; while Disney released an animated adaptation in 1996. Hugo had a special regard for the cathedral, then a tatty place seen by most as a leftover from a barbaric age; he said he was inspired to write the book by an ancient graffito– *"FATE"* – he found etched on one of the towers.

The cathedral is a superb venue for sacred music. As well as amazing free organ recitals held Saturdays at 8pm, prestigious vocalists and ensembles perform here at various times in the year. Services are in French, but the 11.30am Mass on Sunday is the international Mass with part of the readings and prayers said in English.

The south tower is home to Notre-Dame's largest bell, known as the Emmanuel Bell. It is sounded for major holidays like Christmas and Easter, or for more important events, like the death of a pope.

Charles Laughton as Quasimodo (1939).

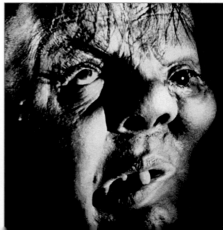

*One of the elegant archways leading off
the 17th-century Place des Vosges.*

3ᴱ Arrᵗ

PLACE
DES VOSGES

THE MARAIS

Left behind by history for three centuries but now restored to vibrant life, this charming quarter offers elegant *ancien régime* mansions, trendy bars and boutiques, a whole array of intriguing museums and the city's oldest and most beautiful square.

There's nowhere quite like the Marais, an elegant district that oozes charm and character. There's so much to recommend it: mansions and museums, chic boutiques and kosher grocers, gay bars and cosy cafés, all bundled together in a labyrinth of narrow streets and alleyways. Stretching west to east from Beaubourg to Bastille, straddling the 3rd and 4th *arrondissements*, with the Rue des Francs-Bourgeois pulsing across it like a central artery, the Marais offers a wonderfully compact package of history, local colour and plain fun. Few parts of the Right Bank have so much in so little space.

It's hard to believe that for many centuries the area was a mosquito-infested swamp ("marais" means marsh), cut right through the middle by Rue St-Antoine, the old Roman road. The marshes were drained in Philippe-Auguste's reign, and when Charles V moved his royal court from the Ile de la Cité to the area around the Tuileries in 1358, a royal influx to the Right Bank began.

In 1609, Henri IV had sumptuous accommodation built for his court all around the Place des Vosges,

thereby shifting the political and financial focus from the Louvre. As a result, the finest architects and stonemasons in Europe descended on the Marais, building countless grand residences, or *hôtels particuliers*, for the nobility, each more spectacular than the last.

The Place des Vosges itself, initially known as the Place Royale, was the first planned square in Paris, and, with its red brick-and-stone facades tapering into arched walkways, remains as beautiful as ever.

Main Attractions

Hôtel de Sens
Place des Vosges
Maison de Victor Hugo
Jewish Quarter
Musée Carnavalet
Musée National Picasso
Musée Cognacq-Jay
Musée des Archives
  Nationales

Map

Page 74

The archways are lined with restaurants and art galleries.

The Marais is one of the few Paris quarters where a large number of shops open for business on a Sunday, its busiest and most crowded day of the week.

The Used Book Café inside hip design concept store Merci (111 boulevard Beaumarchais, 3rd).

Rue des Francs-Bourgeois is a busy shopping street.

THE MARAIS'S FALL AND RISE

The pendulum of fashion swung away from the Marais after Louis XIV moved his court to Versailles in the 1680s, and the nobility moved to the Ile St-Louis, then westwards to the Faubourg St-Honoré and the Boulevard St-Germain. During the Revolution, the area was abandoned to the people, and the Marais's graceful *hôtels particuliers* fell into disrepair.

In the 19th and 20th centuries, the quarter became a centre for small industries and craftwork, and successive developers dug up and widened its picturesque streets. In 1962, André Malraux, President de Gaulle's arts minister, set wide-scale renovation work in motion to preserve what had by then become a very run-down area. By the 1990s, the Marais had regained its status as one of the most fashionable – and costly – places to live in Paris.

The Jewish and working-class communities that once occupied the area have been marginalised by the relentless gentrification process. The character of the Marais is now

defined by its designer boutiques, trendy bars and cafés, and a thriving gay community.

A TOUR OF THE OLD *HÔTELS*

Most of the *hôtels particuliers* have been converted into luxury apartments or offices, but several have been left intact and now house museums. A good place to begin a Marais tour is at the Hôtel de Ville (City Hall), on Rue de Rivoli, which marks its western boundary. Behind it is the 17th-century church of **St-Gervais-St-Protais ❾** (daily; free) with a triple-tiered facade, Italianate steps and monstrous-looking gargoyles. The church is renowned for its 18th-century organ, and concerts are held here frequently.

Rue François-Miron leads from Place St-Gervais into the heart of the Marais. By the 1950s the houses here were practically derelict, but they have been carefully restored. At the

corner of Rue Cloche-Perce is a half-timbered medieval house, and at No. 68 stands the **Hôtel de Beauvais** , built by Catherine Beauvais in 1654 with money from Louis XIV, who had greatly enjoyed her favours. She is also said to have entertained arch-bishops here. A more innocent young Mozart stayed here on his first visit to Paris, at the tender age of seven.

Neighbouring Rue de Jouy con-tains **Hôtel d'Aumont** ⑪, designed by the Versailles architect Louis Le Vau, renovated and enlarged by François Mansart (1598–1666) and decorated by Charles Le Brun (1619–90). With a formal garden by Le Nôtre, the mansion now functions as the city's administrative court.

Hôtel de Sens ⑫

Address: 1 rue du Figuier
Tel: 01 42 78 14 60
Opening Hrs: Tue, Fri, Sat 1pm–7.30pm, Wed, Thu 10am–7.30pm
Entrance Fee: free
Transport: Pont Marie

Built in the late 15th century for the Archbishop of Sens, this tur-reted mansion is one of Paris's few surviving medieval residences, with immaculate gardens. Henri IV lodged his first wife Marguerite de Valois (Reine Margot) here when he could no longer stand her promiscu-ity. She continued to leave a trail of broken hearts, and when a jealous ex-lover killed her current beau, she had him beheaded. It now houses the Bibliothèque Forney, devoted to graphic and applied arts.

THE VILLAGE ST-PAUL

Opposite the Hôtel de Sens, the Rue de l'Avé-Maria intersects with the Rue des Jardins St-Paul, a block away. This leads into the Village St-Paul past two towers and ramparts, the remnants of the city wall built for King Philippe-Auguste around the year 1200, and which now shadow the antics of local school children. The restored "village" consists of a series of small courtyards and fountains, sheltering bustling antique shops and second-hand stalls. At night, it is tranquil beneath the halo of old street lamps.

On Rue Charlemagne, wooden walkways running between the buildings have been restored to the way they were in the Middle Ages.

EAT

Place des Vosges is a good place for a pit stop. Those looking for something special should head to Michelin-starred L'Ambroisie (9 place des Vosges; tel: 01 42 78 51 45; www.ambroisie-paris.com) while cosy Ma Bourgogne (tel: 01 42 78 44 64; www.ma-bourgogne.fr) at No. 19 is renowned for its *steak tartare* (raw minced beef). Upmarket *pâtissier* Carette (tel: 01 48 87 94 07; www.carette-paris.fr) has a stylish tearoom at No. 25.

Relaxing in the delightful Place des Vosges.

Left along Rue St-Paul is an ancient passageway leading to the church of **St-Paul-St-Louis** , an amalgamation of two parishes, constructed by Jesuits in 1627 copying the Gesù church in Rome. Here, the hearts of Louis XIII and Louis XIV were kept as embalmed relics until the Revolution, when they were removed and sold to an artist, who crushed them to mix with oil for a varnish for one of his pictures. Later he gave what was left of Louis XIII's heart to the newly installed King Louis XVIII, in return for a golden snuffbox.

PLACE DES VOSGES

Rue St-Antoine is the ancient Roman road that led east out of the city. Built wide and straight in typical Roman fashion, it became a site for jousting tournaments until, in 1559, Henri II was fatally injured by a sliver from the shattered lance of Gabriel Montgomery, his Scottish Captain of the Guard. In a drastic bid to save his life, Henri's physician, Ambroise Paré, ordered the immediate decapitation of every prisoner awaiting execution and had their heads rushed to the surgery so that he could experiment on them in a bid to rescue his king. Needless to say he didn't succeed, and Henri died 10 days later. The unfortunate Montgomery lost his head, too.

At 62 rue St-Antoine, roughly halfway between Métro St-Paul and Place

Equestrian statue of Louis XIII.

Victor Hugo lived on Place des Vosges.

A MAN OF MANY WORDS

Poet, dramatist, novelist and politician, Victor Hugo (1802–85) lived at 6 place des Vosges from 1832 to 1848. His salon – now a museum – drew great luminaries of the day, including Balzac and Dumas. The museum traces Hugo's life: before exile, during exile and after exile. In 1841 he was elected to the Académie Française, and accepted political posts under King Louis-Philippe. During the 1848 Revolution, he became a leader of democratic opposition to Louis-Napoleon. In 1851 he went into exile in the Channel Islands, where he wrote much of *Les Misérables* (1862). At the fall of the Second Empire in 1870 Hugo returned to Paris.

de la Bastille, stands the **Hôtel de Sully** ⑭ (www.monuments-nationaux. fr; courtyards open daily 9am–7pm) one of the finest mansions in the Marais, and which is appropriately the HQ of Monuments Nationaux, the public organisation that looks after the country's most important historical buildings. Under the courtyard's grumpy statues, Voltaire was beaten with clubs by followers of the Count of Rohan, following a slanging match between the two at the Comédie Française. The cosy garden with clipped privet hedges à l'anglaise is an unexpected surprise. A door in the back right corner leads to the **Place des Vosges** ⑮. Initially called the Place Royale prior to the Revolution, this enchanting 17th-century square, with a garden surrounded by 36 arcaded residences, was built by Henri IV as a showcase for his court. Here courtiers paraded, preened and pranced. After the Revolution, when the melted-down

statue of Louis XIII had been recast and replaced, the square was named after the Vosges, the first French *département* to have paid Napoleon's war taxes promptly.

Today, this is the most beautiful square in Paris, and one of the capital's most sought-after addresses. The arcades house chic cafés and boutiques, and in summer play host to classical music concerts – in the same place that Mozart gave one of his first recitals in 1763.

Maison de Victor Hugo ⑯

Address: 6 place des Vosges
www.maisonsvictorhugo.paris.fr
Tel: 01 42 72 10 16
Opening Hrs: Tue–Sun 10am–6pm
Entrance Fee: free
Transport: St-Paul

In the southeast corner of the square stands the house that was the Romantic writer's Paris home for 15 years. It's now a museum to the great man, containing portraits of his family, manuscripts, accomplished pen-and-ink drawings and pieces of furniture made by Hugo in his spare time.

Try Sacha Finkelsztajn for its cheesecake, strudel and poppy-seed cakes.

Librairie du Temple in Rue des Rosiers specialises in Jewish publications.

Jewish population was depleted by the Holocaust. Numbers swelled again with an influx of Sephardic Jews from North Africa following the independence of Algeria in the 1960s, giving the area a Middle Eastern feel. Among the restaurants and bookshops around the synagogue, look out for Chez Marianne (tel: 01 42 72 18 86), the perpetually busy restaurant for Jewish specialities such as rollmops and falafels. Jewish history and decorative arts are treated in the Jewish Museum (see page 95). A few minutes south, behind St-Gervais-St-Protais, is the Mémorial de la Shoah.

Mémorial de la Shoah 🅒

Address: 17 rue Geoffroy l'Asnier
www.memorialdelashoah.org
Tel: 01 42 77 44 72
Opening Hrs: Sun–Fri 10am–6pm,
Thu until 10pm
Entrance Fee: free
Transport: Pont Marie

The memorial has a permanent exhibition on the concentration camps, in which documents, photographs and personal artefacts are used to present an overview of Nazi deportation and extermination, and moving

Old signs at the Musée Carnavalet.

Madame de Sévigné.

THE JEWISH QUARTER

Between the northwestern corner of Place des Vosges and Rue Vieille-du-Temple runs the Rue des Francs-Bourgeois, a shopper's paradise crammed with boutiques and curiosity shops, many of which have retained the shop signs from their previous incarnations as butchers or bakers. A left-hand turning just past the Musée Carnavalet leads to Rue Pavée and the **Hôtel de Lamoignon** 🅒, built in 1584 for the Duchesse d'Angoulême. Sixty people were murdered here during the massacres of 2 September 1792. The *hôtel particulier* now houses the city's historical library.

Rue des Rosiers, a little further on, is the hub of what remains of the Jewish Quarter. As the area has become increasingly popular with bar and boutique owners, the Jewish community has retreated to a small pocket centred on this narrow street lined with kosher delis, falafel stands and tiny shops packed with religious artefacts. Originally an Ashkenazi community, with its origins in Eastern Europe, the local

personal stories. As the most important centre in Europe devoted to the Holocaust, it also contains a research centre, archive and auditorium. In the crypt, within a black marble Star of David, an eternal flame burns for the Mémorial du Martyr Juif Inconnu (Memorial to the Unknown Jewish Martyr).

Rue des Rosiers leads on to the **Rue Vieille-du-Temple**, with one of the best and liveliest stretches of cafés and bars in Paris.

CARNAVALET AND PICASSO

Musée Carnavalet ⑲

Address: 23 rue de Sévigné
www.carnavalet.paris.fr
Tel: 01 44 59 58 58
Opening Hrs: Tue–Sun 10am–6pm
Entrance Fee: free
Transport: St-Paul

This is one of the most fascinating of the many Marais museums. Occupying two mansions, the main 16th-century Hôtel Carnavalet and the neighbouring 17th-century Hôtel Le Peletier, it covers the history of Paris chronologically from its beginnings as a Gallo-Roman settlement to its transformation into a modern-day metropolis. The evolution of the

capital is traced through paintings, objets d'art, sculpture and costume. Madame de Sévigné, whose celebrated letters provide an insight into 17th-century Paris high society, lived in the Hôtel Carnavalet between 1677 and 1696, and there is a gallery here devoted to her life.

Rue de Thorigny leads to one of the Marais's finest mansions, now home to the Musée National Picasso.

On his way to the synagogue.

The Hôtel de Sens, the oldest mansion in the Marais.

CURIOUS CANNONBALL

Stand at the junction of Rue du Figuier and Rue de l'Hôtel-de-Ville, look up at the Hôtel de Sens and you'll see, buried in the gable stonework, next to the left-hand turret, a cannonball the size of a fist with a date (28 July 1830) written underneath it. The iron sphere was fired on day two of the July 1830 revolt, in which 600 rioters and 150 soldiers died, from a besieged army barracks on nearby Rue Charlemagne. Was it a warning shot? Was it aimed at the second-storey window just below? And when the fighting was over, did no one ever think to dig it out?

Ancient relief at the Musée Carnavalet.

Ofr system Bookshop and Gallery (20 rue Dupetit-Thouars, 3rd).

Musée National Picasso ⑳

Address: 5 rue de Thorigny
www.museepicassoparis.fr
Opening Hrs: Tue–Sun 9.30am–6pm
Entrance Fee: charge
Transport: St-Paul

The Hôtel Salé was constructed with the booty of a 17th-century tax collector. Three centuries later, the French tax authorities scored another coup. Following his death in 1973, Pablo Picasso's family was faced with an enormous inheritance tax bill, and so, in lieu of payment, they donated to the French nation a vast collection of his works: 200 paintings, over 3,000 drawings and 88 ceramics, along with sculptures, collages and manuscripts, as well as Picasso's own collection of works by other artists like Cézanne, Matisse and Modigliani.

The museum shows all Picasso's periods, in chronological order, including the Blue, Pink, Cubist, classical and Post-Cubist phases. The famous beach pictures of the 1920s and 1930s are here, as well as remarkable portraits of his model mistresses, Marie-Thérèse and Dora Maar. There is also a lot of sculpture made of driftwood, scrap iron and bicycle parts, a reminder of Picasso's motto: "I do not seek, I find."

The museum has also a collection of furniture designed by the Swiss sculptor Diego Giacometti for the Hôtel Salé, including bronze benches, chairs and tables. After the recent renovation the museum has better exhibition spaces, a great rooftop café and is fully accessible for disabled people.

A CLUSTER OF MUSEUMS

Musée Cognacq-Jay ㉑

Address: 8 rue Elzévir
www.cognacq-jay.paris.fr
Tel: 01 40 27 07 21
Opening Hrs: Tue–Sun 10am–6pm
Entrance Fee: free
Transport: St-Paul

The exquisite Hôtel Donon houses the art and antiques collection of Ernest Cognacq and his wife Louise Jay, founders of La Samaritaine department store. The collection, which includes works by Rembrandt and Canaletto, is displayed in a succession of salons and small rooms, which are furnished to give the feel of a private house.

Hôtel de Rohan 🉒

Address: 87 rue Vieille-du-Temple
Opening Hrs: during exhibitions,
times and details as for Musée des
Archives Nationales
Further west, this stunningly restored
mansion is part of the National
Archives and hosts exhibitions relating to history. Even if you don't go
inside, take a look in the courtyard at
the superb sculpture of the horses of
Apollo over the stables.

Musée des Archives Nationales 🉓

Address: 60 rue des Francs-Bourgeois
www.archives-nationales.culture.gouv.fr
Tel: 01 40 27 60 96
Opening Hrs: Mon, Wed–Fri
10am–5.30pm, Sat–Sun 2–5.30pm
Entrance Fee: charge; gardens free
Transport: Rambuteau
The Hôtel de Soubise is an exquisite 18th-century mansion, with a
superb arcaded courtyard and exuberant Rococo decor. It now houses the
National Archives, in which over 6 million of France's most important historical documents are kept, on 290km (180
miles) of shelving. Also here is a collection of historical objects including a

small replica of the Bastille and furniture from Soubise and Rohan. Across
the street is the Crédit Municipal (www.
creditmunicipal.fr), the state pawnbroker.
Nicknamed *"Ma Tante"* (My Aunt), it
opened in 1777, and still functions.

Musée de la Chasse et de la Nature 🉔

Address: 62 rue des Archives
www.chassenature.org
Tel: 01 53 01 92 40
Opening Hrs: Tue–Sun 11am–6pm;
Wed until 9.30pm
Entrance Fee: charge
Transport: Rambuteau
The Hôtel Guénégaud houses a display of stuffed animals and hunting-related objects with enjoyably quirky
touches, such as "hunted species" that
include unicorns. It also has a collection of arms, furniture, sculptures
and ceramics.

Musée d'Art et d'Histoire du Judaïsme 🉕

Address: 71 rue du Temple
www.mahj.org
Tel: 01 53 01 86 60
Opening Hrs: Mon–Fri 11am–6pm,
Sun 10am– 6pm

Pablo Picasso.

PICASSO - A SPANISH GENIUS

Born in Málaga in Spain, Pablo Picasso (1881–1973) settled in Paris
at the age of 23, having studied art in Barcelona and Madrid. His
career began to take off thanks to the patronage of wealthy American
art collector Gertrude Stein and the promotion of his work by highly
respected dealer Daniel-Henry Kahnweiler. However, he never lost
touch with his Spanish roots: his works ooze life, humour and sex, in
a career that could never be separated from his personal life. The
leading figure in 20th-century art, he passed through many phases,
including his early Blue Period, as in the 1901 Self-Portrait, and Les
Demoiselles d'Avignon, painted in 1907, which is often regarded as
the first work of Cubism. In the 1920s and 1930s he produced his
most abstract work, but in 1937 he painted Guernica, on the Spanish
Civil War. He stayed in Paris, in Rue des Grands-Augustins, during
World War II, moving to the south of France afterwards. His last paintings
were long considered a splashy, crude decline, but they have
been rehabilitated as proof of his continuing inventiveness up to his
death in 1973, in Mougins. He left behind a massive collection of
paintings, sculpture, drawings and ceramics.

DRINK

Rue Vieille-du-Temple is the epicentre of the Marais's cosmopolitan café culture. Trendy young types frequent the Café La Perle, the picturesque Petit Fer à Cheval, wine bar-cum-bookshop La Belle Hortense and artfully distressed cocktail bar Les Etages. During early-evening happy hour, the gay community heads to Le Cox and the Open Café on nearby Rue des Archives.

The Marais teems with hip bars and cafés, including La Belle Hortense, a literary wine bar (31 rue Vieille-du-Temple, 3rd).

Entrance Fee: charge
Transport: Rambuteau

The grand Hôtel St-Aignan is now a fascinating museum of Jewish art, culture, history and heritage. As well as the permanent and temporary exhibitions, there are often music concerts.

QUARTIER DU TEMPLE

To the north of the Marais, the Quartier du Temple was once the headquarters of the Knights Templar. A medieval order of soldiers, originally formed to protect pilgrims in the Holy Land, the Templars owned large properties in France and were in charge of the royal treasury until 1307, when Philippe the Fair burned their leaders at the stake, and the order was disbanded. During the Revolution, the Temple Tower was a prison for the royal family; it was from here that Louis XVI went to the guillotine. It was razed by a superstitious Napoleon, and Haussmann replaced it with a wrought-iron covered market, the Carreau du Temple, which still sells second-hand clothes and cloth by the metre.

Along Rue Perrée lies all that remains of the Temple fortress, the **Square du Temple** ㉖, a tree-lined garden that echoes with the gentle sound of table tennis balls on its two outdoor tables. Not far from the Temple

district, another 10 minutes along Rue Réaumur, is France's most prestigious technical college, the **Conservatoire National des Arts et Métiers**, and its museum, the oldest dedicated to science and technology in Europe.

Musée des Arts et Métiers ㉗

Address: 60 rue Réaumur
www.arts-et-metiers.net
Tel: 01 53 01 82 00
Opening Hrs: Tue–Sun 10am–6pm, Thu until 9.30pm
Entrance Fee: charge
Transport: Arts-et-Métiers

The best part of this fascinating museum of technology is the converted 11th-century chapel that houses, among other innovations, Foucault's pendulum (a copy of which hangs in the Panthéon, see page 190). There are also ancient cars and flying machines set on glass floors, and hands-on exhibits for children.

To end a visit to the Marais, head down Rue du Temple to No. 41 and its courtyard. Once the headquarters of the Aigle d'Or, the last stagecoach company in Paris, it is a bustling corner, where the **Café de la Gare** theatre (www.cdlg.fr; tel: 01 42 78 52 51) puts on alternative comedy and musical performances.

Café Society

If you've never nipped into a café to make a phone call or met your lover on a *terrasse*, you are not a true Parisian.

The neighbourhood café is the Parisian's decompression chamber. It offers a welcome pause in which to savour a *p'tit noir* (espresso) or an *apéritif*, empty the mind of troublesome thoughts and people watch. The café is also the place to meet friends, have a romantic tryst or even do business in a relaxed atmosphere.

The first café in France was Le Procope in 1686, and the literati soon began to congregate there, keen to exchange ideas. More sprang up all over the country, and it wasn't long before there was at least one in every village. In the 19th century, the neighbourhood *zinc*, named after its metal counter, became part of the fabric of French life. In Paris, each café developed its own character, and with the widening of the boulevards, their tables spilled out onto the pavements. By 1910 there were 510,000 *zincs* in France.

Ups and downs

But today café life is waning. While the invasion of fast-food restaurants is partly to blame, changes in the French way of life are also culpable. When customers move out to homes in the suburbs, they tend to "cocoon", staying in to watch TV, and the local café eventually has to close. Then there are the ageing proprietors to consider: a café is traditionally a family business, but today fewer sons and daughters are prepared to take on gruelling 16-hour days.

Sadly, even the atmosphere of remaining cafés is not what it was. There is formica where once there was marble. Piped muzak and the beep of video games have replaced accordionists and the furious volleys of players on *baby-foot* machines. Only the Gauloise-fed haze (attitudes to the 1992 smoking ban are casual) and the hazards of the lavatories (some still holes in the ground) are the same.

Yet all is not lost. Authentic zincs can still be found in Paris, and many are thriving. Try stylish Café de l'Industrie on rue St-Sabin (www.cafedelindustrieparis.fr), La Palette on rue de Seine (www.cafelapaletteparis.com) or the tiny but lovingly restored Le Cochon à l'Oreille on rue Montmartre. For literary atmosphere there's Les Deux Magots (www.lesdeuxmagots.fr), home to almost every Paris intellectual from Rimbaud to André Breton. At nearby Café de Flore, Sartre and Simone de Beauvoir wrote by the stove. "My worst customer, Sartre," recalled the *patron*. "He spent the entire day scribbling away over one drink."

A lifestyle under attack

On 13 November 2015, Islamist gunmen targeted a handful of Parisian cafés during their murderous rampage. The following days, Parisians tweeted their defiance by posting photos under the hashtag #Je SuisEnTerrasse ("I am on the terrace").

Having a coffee en terrasse.

BEAUBOURG AND LES HALLES

One of the world's most popular venues, the "inside-out" Pompidou Centre has given this area its modern identity. But nearby around Les Halles – though blighted by failed 1960s redevelopment – there remain many traces of Paris's historic market district, one of the most pungently atmospheric parts of the city.

Sandwiched between the Louvre and Palais Royal to the west, and the Marais to the east, this central chunk of the Right Bank is one of the city's most hyperactive commercial and cultural areas. Its epicentre is the Forum des Halles, a vast and unlovely shopping and leisure complex undergoing a thorough reconstruction to be completed in 2018. The other landmark building here is the Pompidou Centre, Paris's modern art museum. This hulking mass of pipes, ducts and scaffolds painted in primary colours is strangely alluring, and one of the world's most visited sites.

Place du Châtelet, by the Seine, is a good starting point for exploring the area. Flanked by two theatres (Théâtre de la Ville and Théâtre du Châtelet, for opera and modern dance), it lies above one of Paris's biggest Métro and RER stations. To the northeast rises the Gothic **Tour St-Jacques**, a lone belfry once attached to a church that was destroyed during the Revolution. Look out for the statue of scientist and philosopher Blaise Pascal (1623–62), who carried out pioneering experiments on atmospheric pressure from the top.

Shoppers on Rue Montorgueil.

HÔTEL DE VILLE

Address: www.paris.fr
Tel: 01 42 76 54 04
Opening Hrs: regular guided tours but must be booked two months in advance.
Entrance Fee: free
Transport: Hôtel de Ville

Opening out at the eastern end of avenue Victoria is the wide esplanade of the Hôtel de Ville (Mairie de Paris), ornate home of the city council. In medieval times, the square was the site of hangings and macabre

Main Attractions
Hôtel de Ville
Centre Georges Pompidou
Les Halles
Rue Montorgueil
Eglise St-Eustache
Eglise St-Germain-l'Auxerrois

Map
Page 74

The Auberge Nicolas Flamel promises an "alchemy of flavours" (51 rue de Montmorency, 3rd).

Watching the French Open on a big screen in front of the Hôtel de Ville.

Such grandeur and opulence are a fitting backdrop for the city's governing powers, and the grand halls are often used for banquets and ceremonial receptions.

At most times only an exhibition space is open to visitors, but the rest of the building can be seen on free guided tours, available by arrangement, tel: 01 42 76 54 04. It's worth skirting around to Rue de Lobau at the rear of the Hôtel to see the two monumental bronze lions either side of the eastern entrance. These noble beasts are by the late 19th-century animal sculptor Alfred Jacquemart, who also made the colossal rhino in the square just west of the Musée d'Orsay (see page 228).

executions. No traces of its horrific past remain; today, the pedestrianised Place de l'Hôtel de Ville, which overlooks the Seine, is a pleasant place to stroll through, especially in the evening, when the fountains and Town Hall are floodlit.

The elaborate neo-Renaissance building, with its splendid mansard roofs, carved facade and army of statues, was rebuilt after the original 17th-century Town Hall was burned down in the 1871 Commune. The majestic Salle des Fêtes (ballroom), a magnificent staircase and chandeliers are the most notable features inside.

QUARTIER BEAUBOURG

This area may, thanks to the Centre Pompidou, be synonymous with avant-garde architecture, but it's also one of the oldest parts of the city. In fact, what is said to be the oldest house in Paris is at 51 rue de Montmorency; on the ground floor is the Auberge Nicolas Flamel (tel: 01 42 71 77 78; www.auberge-nicolas-flamel.

fr), a restaurant named after the house's original occupant, the famous alchemist who took in the poor and homeless here. Beaubourg's parish church of St-Merri was at the centre of a local building boom in the 16th century, as the old medieval houses were steadily replaced by grand private mansions; the district remained a seat of nobility until the Revolution. Little of this architectural heritage remains today, however: many of the historic residences were pulled down in the 1930s, and the quarter was transformed further by the renovation of Les Halles in the 1960s and 1970s.

St-Merri ㉙

Address: 76 rue de la Verrerie
www.saintmerry.org
Tel: 01 42 71 93 93
Opening Hrs: daily
Entrance Fee: free
Trasnport: Châtelet

Off Rue St-Martin stands this richly adorned 16th-century church, built in Flamboyant Gothic style. Its bell dates from 1331 and the organ was played by the composer Camille Saint-Saëns (1835–1921).

Between the church and the Centre Pompidou, the playful waterworks of the **Fontaine de Stravinsky** were inspired by the composer's ballet *The Firebird*. Created by artists Niki de Saint-Phalle and Jean Tinguely, the forms and figures in the fountain represent the story – a heart, a snake, a bare-breasted torso, pursed red lips and the firebird in the middle all spin and spit water in every direction. In fine weather, this square is a favourite picnic spot. Alternatively, take a seat at one of the handful of cafés looking out at the colourful ensemble.

CENTRE GEORGES POMPIDOU ㉚

Address: www.centrepompidou.fr
Tel: 01 44 78 12 33

Opening Hrs: Wed–Mon 11am–9pm; Thu until 11pm
Entrance Fee: charge
Transport: Rambuteau

Known locally simply as Beaubourg, the Centre National d'Art et de Culture Georges Pompidou welcomes more than 6 million visitors a year. The basic idea was first mooted in 1969 by the cultivated president of the day, Georges Pompidou; the

Homage to the great composer Igor Stravinsky.

The Fontaine de Stravinsky.

Exterior tube escalators add to the "inside-out" allure of the Centre Pompidou.

The imposing Fontaine des Innocents.

initial tender was put out in 1972. No fewer than 681 designs were put forward by architects around the world, but the winning partnership was Italian Renzo Piano and British Richard Rogers. The Centre opened to the public on 31 January 1977.

Rogers and Piano had placed the infrastructure – escalators, lifts, ducts, etc. – on the outside: this high-tech design caused uproar when it first opened, but its popular appeal soon silenced the critics.

As well as housing one of the world's most important modern art collections, the cavernous interior accommodates a large public library, an educational area, a performance space, auditorium, cinemas and the IRCAM, an avant-garde music institute. There's also an excellent art bookshop on the ground floor,

FONTAINE DES INNOCENTS

The Fontaine des Innocents, a Renaissance fountain decorated with water nymphs by Pierre Lescot and Jean Goujon, stands in the square des Innocents, between place du Châtelet and Forum des Halles, formerly the site of the notorious Cimetière des Innocents. In use since the 12th century, the graveyard, encircled by a high wall and covering just 130 metres x 65 metres, had become a public health hazard by the 18th century, as the dead – mostly paupers – were carried there among produce bound for the market at Les Halles. Gruesome tales are told about how people ground up bones for bread when Paris was under siege in 1590, and used the skeletons for firewood. By 1780, corpses were overflowing above street level and the area was teeming with rats, which started to gnaw their way into people's homes. It was recognised that something had to be done, so the cemetery was finally closed and its contents moved to the Catacombs, where the remains can still be seen. (see page 205).

Today, the square and fountain are a meeting place for the city's youth, and the pedestrianised Rue des Lombards is a centre for nightlife with bars, restaurants and jazz clubs.

and the swish restaurant **Georges** (see page 107) on the roof. The fifth-floor balcony and roof terrace enjoy magnificent views of the city, right across to Montmartre. On place Igor Stravinsky, there are colourful mechanical sculptures by Tinguely.

Exhibits and activities

The **Musée National d'Art Moderne** is on the fourth and fifth floors. Incredibly, the works on display represent only a small proportion of the 50,000-strong collection, which is why the museum has regular rehangs, in order to rotate the works of art and give the public access to as many of them as possible.

The museum's permanent collection is arranged thematically, suggesting interesting confrontations and parallels between different periods and styles. Architecture and design are displayed alongside painting, sculpture and video installations. Thus modern masterpieces by Matisse, Picasso, Kandinsky, Delaunay, Dalí and Grosz can be seen with post-war masters like Dubuffet, Johns, Warhol, Bacon and Merz, and works by contemporary artists like Boltanski, Sherman and Viola.

In recent years the Centre has boosted its cinematic presence, acting as another Cinémathèque, with comprehensive retrospectives of the likes of Martin Scorsese and Jacques Rivette. Hand in hand with such seasons is an active publishing programme, which produces attractive and scholarly books on the directors under examination.

Outside there is a reconstruction of Constantin Brancusi's studio, a bequest to the French state, **l'Atelier Brancusi** (Wed–Mon 2–6pm; free). Look out for American sculptor Alex Calder's work *Horizontal*, which is recognisable by its black triangular base. Place George Pompidou itself is a bustling space popular with street performers, buskers, barrel organists and portrait painters.

LES HALLES

The Les Halles quarter gets its name from the historic food market that stood from 1183 to 1969 on the spot now occupied by a vast shopping complex. Large-scale construction has been a feature of the area since 1851, when Napoleon III ordered architect Victor Baltard to design 10 colossal cast-iron hangars to go over the market. "Iron, nothing but iron" and "Make me some umbrellas" were the emperor's two instructions, and the resulting construction was an elegant masterpiece of 19th-century design, widely copied throughout France and abroad.

Stallholders, restaurant owners, pickpockets, artists, prostitutes and police inhabited this vast market, which novelist Emile Zola called "the belly of Paris". Unsurprisingly, the market had a strong presence in the literary output of the time. Zola set an entire novel here; Hugo described it in some detail in *Les Misérables*; and the area was a regular haunt of the Romantic poet and tormented bohemian Gérard de Nerval, who was born here and eventually ended his own life by hanging himself in a nearby cellar.

FACT

The Pompidou's primary-coloured pipes are not just for show: the blue convey air, the green transport water, the yellow contain electricity and the red conduct heating.

The east facade of the Centre and its colour-coded tubes.

SHOP

When it comes to fashion, the eternally crowded Forum des Halles is something of a wash-out: mostly chain stores like H&M. Far richer pickings are to be had in the much nicer setting of Rue Etienne Marcel, a major *mode* thoroughfare of labels like Sandro, Diesel, Replay and smaller, seriously hip labels.

Gateway to Rue Montorgueil, a foodie's haven.

The foyer inside the Centre Pompidou.

By the 1960s the site, already expanded in 1936, had become impractical – not least owing to traffic problems associated with bringing vast quantities of provisions to a site in the centre of the city. The market decamped to the suburbs of Rungis and the hangars were thoughtlessly pulled down, leaving a gaping hole that became a national joke. It was filled in the 1980s by the **Forum des Halles** ㉛ (www.forumdeshalles.com), an underground shopping mall with shops, a multiplex cinema, the Forum des Images film archive and cinema and an Olympic swimming pool. Combined with a massive RER/Métro interchange, the Forum has acquired a dodgy reputation as a hang-out for gangs of youths from the suburbs. In 2004, the Mairie de Paris launched a competition for redeveloping the Forum and relandscaping the squares and gardens. The works began in 2010 and are to be completed in 2018.

Paris's modern underbelly

Surrounding the market area are some remnants of a bygone age, with brasseries staying open around the clock (the early-hours clientele no longer formed by hard-working market porters, but exhausted partygoers) and sleazy Rue St-Denis, the age-old domain of prostitutes, albeit only in its northern reaches; the section adjacent to Les Halles is instead packed with small independent clothes

Greengrocer on Rue Montorgueil.

shops, selling largely tacky streetwear and trainers.

The best place for a glimpse of the old Les Halles is **Rue Montorgueil**, a narrow, pedestrianised street packed with romantic cafés, wine and cheese merchants, garrulous butchers and colourful fruit and vegetable stalls.

The street also contains the venerable *pâtissier* **Stohrer** (www.stohrer.fr), purveyor since 1730 of delectable cakes and tarts; its founder Nicolas Stohrer is said to have invented the rum baba. This short, attractive strip makes it easy to linger – even if you end up buying nothing more than a coffee.

Ribbons for sale.

RAG TRADE

Like any area not enshrined in administrative ink, Sentier has fuzzy boundaries: however, to most Parisians it is the top-right of the 2nd *arrondissement*, north of Rue Réaumur. This maze of narrow streets is the stronghold of the wholesale clothes industry. Most buildings are taken up by workshops and storerooms, and windows pour out a constant buzz of machinery. Sentier makes clothes and it makes fortunes: the secret of its success is not just its low-paid, often immigrant workforce but the ability of its workshops to take in the latest couture trends almost overnight. Check out Rue Réaumur with its architectural collage and the Egyptian Revival architecture of Place du Caire (see page 137).

The Renaissance interior of St-Eustache.

The Gothic gaze of St-Eustache.

St-Eustache ㉜

Address: rue du Jour
www.saint-eustache.org
Tel: 01 42 36 31 05
Opening Hrs: Mon–Fri 9.30am–7pm, Sat 10am–7pm, Sun 9am–7pm
Entance Fee: free
Transport: Les Halles

North of the Forum des Halles, this colossal, beautiful church is a rose among thorns. Modelled on Notre-Dame (note the flying buttresses), it took over a 100 years to build (1532–1637). The interior is a Renaissance feast of majestic columns, arches and stained-glass windows. Berlioz and Liszt played here in the 19th century, and concerts are held regularly – often for free – using the church's 8,000-pipe organ; now it has an electronic equipment allowing the organ to be played from ground-level consoles. St-Eustache also has a prestigious choir, and is the burial place of French composer Jean-Philippe Rameau, and another personage with a musical connection – Mozart's mother.

Outside the church, a sculpture of a giant head and cupped hand by Henri de Miller attracts both children and pigeons to its benign seat.

During Paris-Plage, the Voie Georges-Pompidou is shut to traffic and the beach takes over.

The stretch of gardens between Les Halles and St-Eustache is peopled by dog-walkers, loitering teenagers and down-and-outs. The green space features glass pyramids full of palms, papayas and banana trees. Metal walkways pass through them to the **Bourse du Commerce** (tel: 01 55 65 55 65; Mon–Fri 9am–6pm; free), a circular building erected in the 18th century as a corn exchange, and now a seat of the Paris Chamber of Commerce.

LES HALLES TO THE BEACH

Head back towards the Rue St-Honoré, south of Les Halles, an elegant street with a rich history and upmarket shops. A little further on, facing the eastern facade of the Louvre, is the church of **St-Germain-l'Auxerrois** ❸ (tel: 01 42 60 13 96; Tue–Sat 9am–7pm, Sun 9.30am–8.30pm, summer Tue–Sun 9.30am–7pm; www.saint-germainauxerrois.fr). At midnight on 24 August 1572, the church's bells rang as the signal to start the St Bartholomew's Day Massacre, when thousands of Protestants were butchered on the orders of the Catholic Catherine de Médicis. Behind the church on the banks of the Seine is the historic La Samaritaine department store, which has been closed for major safety modifications since 2005 and is still closed.

Immediately in front of La Samaritaine is the voie Georges Pompidou, the river front roadway that hosts much of the Right Bank portion of the annual **Paris-Plage** festivities. Every summer since 2002, the road has been shut to traffic, covered with tonnes of fine golden sand and kitted out with palm trees, deckchairs, refreshment kiosks, beach volleyball courts and a free lending library. The highly popular city-beach concept has been copied in other big cities, including Lyon, Toulouse, Berlin and Budapest. And in Paris, the holiday fun has now expanded to the Bassin de la Villette in the 19th arrondissement and Port de la Gare on the Left Bank.

Controversial colonial fresco on Rue Montorgueil.

CENTRE POMPIDOU

The inside-out museum of modern art is a world icon of contemporary architecture. Its escalators, outside sculptures and roof-top restaurant add to its charm.

Georges Pompidou, the President of France from 1969–74, was a moderniser – and had a lasting fondness for the arts. He compiled an anthology of French poetry and it was he who proposed the building of a major cultural centre in Beaubourg. The chosen design, by the then-unknown duo Richard Rogers and Renzo Piano, put the air-conditioning ducts and escalators on the outside, which made for an adaptable space within. When Rodgers was awarded the prestigious Pritzker Architecture Prize in 2007 for designing the Lloyd's Building in London, the jury said that his Pompidou Centre "revolutionised museums, transforming what had once been elite monuments into popular places of social and cultural exchange, woven into the heart of the city". When the centre opened in 1977 its multi-disciplinary set-up – the largest museum of modern art in Europe, plus a public library and cinemas – was an instant hit. It had a revamp at the end of the 20th century, which included the opening of the fashionable Georges rooftop restaurant (see page 107). Entrance to the forum and library is free, but you have to pay to go up the escalators.

Georges, the Centre's swish rooftop restaurant.

The Essentials

Address: www.centre pompidou.fr
Tel: 01 44 78 12 33
Opening Hrs: Wed–Mon 11am–9pm, Thu until 11pm.
Entrance Fee: charge
Transport: Rambuteau

The view from the panoramic roof walkway covers a huge swathe of the city, including Montmartre.

The vast and cavernous atrium.

The Centre has an avant-garde music institute (IRCAM).

INSIDE AND OUT

The escalators are contained in glass tubes.

The collection at the Pompidou is far too large to be displayed, even in such a cavernous setting: there are 50,000 works of art in all, and only 600 or so can be exhibited at once. Level four contains post-1960s art: here you'll find architecture, design and sections on movements like Arte Povera and Anti-Form. On level five is work produced between 1905 and 1960 by Matisse, Picasso and Braque, as well as Klee, Kandinsky, Magritte, Miró, Ernst and more. Art isn't confined indoors; the outdoor terraces showcase various sculptures and on the plaza is Alexander Calder's *Horizontal*, a kind of giant mobile with a black triangular base supporting a silver arm with coloured "petals" dangling off it. While to the south of the Centre is the *Fontaine de Stravinksy* by Niki de Saint-Phalle and Jean Tinguely. On Place Georges Pompidou, the studio of Paris-based Romanian sculptor Constantin Brancusi (1876–1957) has been recreated exactly as it was on the day he died.

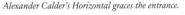

Alexander Calder's Horizontal graces the entrance.

Louvre and Grands Boulevards

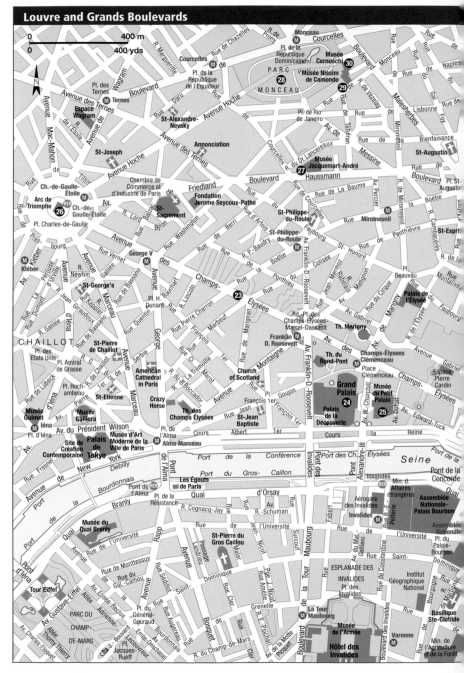

0   400 m
0   400 yds

R. de Prony
Monceau
M Courcelles
Courcelles
Boulevard
R. de Chazelles
R. de Naples
Rue
Rue
de
Rue
de Monceau
Pl. de la
République
Dominicaine
Courcelles
Pl. de la
République
de l'Equateur
M de
Musée
Cernuschi 30
Malesherbes
Lisbonne
Rue
de Vézelay
PARC 28
Musée Nissim
de Camondo
MONCEAU 29
Espace
Wagram
Pl. des
Ternes
Ternes
Daru
Avenue Hoche
Rue
de
de
Pl. de Rio
de Janeiro
Av. de Téhéran
Rue
Foy
Avenue des Ternes
Avenue de Wagram
Av. de
Messine
R. du Dr Lanceréaux
St-Alexandre-
Nevsky
St-Joseph
Annonciation
R. de Courcelles
Bienfaisance
St-Augustin
St-Augustin
Avenue Hoche
Chambre de
Commerce et
d'Industrie de Paris
Boulevard
Haussmann
Musée
Jacquemart-André 27
Boulevard
Pl. St-
Augustin
Ch.-de-Gaulle-
Étoile
M
Arc de
Triomphe
26 RER
Ch.-de-
Gaulle-Étoile
Pl. Charles-de-Gaulle
Friedland
Fondation
Jerome Seycoux-Pathé
St-
Sacrement
Rue de La Baume
Av. Percier
R. de Miromesnil
Boétie
St-Espri
R. Cambacérès
St-Philippe-
du-Roule
Miromesnil M
Av.
R. Lord
Byron
Rue Washington
R. d'Artois
St-Philippe-
du-Roule
Faubourg
St-Honoré
Penthièvre
Kléber M
Av. Kléber
R. Newton
George V M
Rue de Berri
R. P.-Baudry
Boétie
Colisée
Pl.
Beauvau
R. de la
St-George's
Pl. H.
Dunant
Rue Pierre Charron
Rue Marbeuf
Rue de Ponthieu
du
Franklin-D.-Roosevelt
Rue Jean-Mermoz
R. Matignon
R. du Cirque
Palais de
l'Élysée
CHAILLOT
Pl. des
États Unis
St-Pierre
de Chaillot
Rue Quentin
George
Rue Clément Marot
Champs- 23 Élysées
Rond-Pt. des
Champs-Élysées-
Marcel-Dassault
Th. Marigny
Franklin
D. Roosevelt
Th. du
Rond-Point
Champs-Élysées
Clémenceau
Espace
Pierre
Cardin
American
Cathedral
in Paris
St-Etienne
Church
of Scotland
Avenue Montaigne
Place
Clémenceau
Grand
Palais 24
Musée
du Petit
Palais 25
Crazy
Horse
Th. des
Champs Élysées
Rue François 1er
St-Jean
Baptiste
Palais
de la
Découverte
Av. Edward-Tuck
Musée
Guimet
Musée
Galliera
Av. du Président Wilson
Musée d'Art
Moderne de la
Ville de Paris
Pl. de
l'Alma
Alma Marceau
Cours
Albert 1er
Reine
Site de
Création
Contemporaine
Palais
de
Tokyo
York
Pont
de
l'Alma
Port
de
la
Conférence
Port des Ch.
Élysées
Pont
des
Invalides
Pont
Alexandre-III
Seine
Pont de la
Concorde
Les Égouts
de Paris
Quai
d'Orsay
Min. d.
Affaires
étrangères
Assemblée
Nationale-
Palais Bourbon
Musée du
Quai Branly
Rue de l'Université
St-Pierre du
Gros Caillou
Assemblée
Nationale
Pl. du
Palais-
Bourbon
Tour Eiffel
PARC DU
CHAMP-
DE-MARS
ESPLANADE DES
INVALIDES
Pl. des
Invalides
La Tour
Maubourg
Musée
de l'Armée
Hôtel des
Invalides
Varenne
Basilique
Ste-Clotilde
Institut
Géographique
National
Min. de
l'Agriculture
et de la Forêt

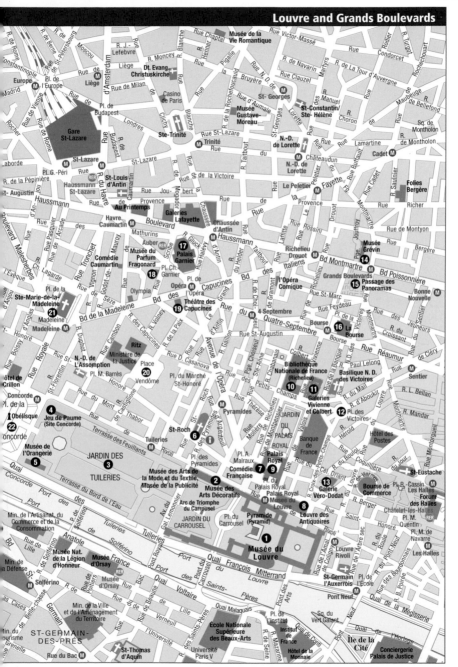

THE LOUVRE AND QUARTIER DES TUILERIES

Royal Paris: the queen of all art museums, the gracious Tuileries gardens, a fascinating mix of smaller museums, the urban oasis of the Palais Royal and, tucked away, the world's most charming shopping arcades.

On the Seine's Right Bank beautifully laid-out gardens stretch into ostentatious squares, and wide tree-lined boulevards overflow with upmarket restaurants and designer boutiques. There are royal palaces, an opulent opera house and the world's most famous museum. Meticulously planned by Haussmann, the elegant buildings, boulevards and open spaces engulf the visitor in 19th-century grandeur.

This area covers the royal heart of Paris, from the Louvre and Palais Royal westwards to the Jeu de Paume gallery and the Musée de l'Orangerie at the far end of the Tuileries gardens. The grand squares – Place de la Concorde, Place Vendôme and Place de la Madeleine – with the Champs-Elysées, the Grands Boulevards and the Opéra are covered in the next chapter.

MUSÉE DU LOUVRE ❶

Address: www.louvre.fr
Tel: 01 40 20 53 17
Opening Hrs: Wed–Mon 9am–6pm, Wed, Fri until 9.45pm
Entrance Fee: charge
Transport: Palais Royal-Musée du Louvre

Once the seat of royalty, the Musée du Louvre has been the home of fine art since a colony of painters and sculptors moved into the empty halls after King Louis XIV left for Versailles in 1682. The Louvre's art collection goes back even further, to 1516, when François I invited Leonardo da Vinci to be his royal court painter, and he brought with him his masterpieces the *Mona Lisa* and *Virgin of the Rocks*.

Originally built as a fortress in 1190 by Philippe-Auguste to protect a weak link in his city wall, the Louvre

Main Attractions
Musée du Louvre
Louvre Pyramid
Jardin des Tuileries
Musée de l'Orangerie
Rue de Rivoli
Comédie Française
Palais Royal
Galerie Vivienne
Place des Victoires

Map
Page 110

The old palace seen under one of the smaller pyramids.

Daniele da Volterna's two-sided David killing Goliath (c.1555) takes pride of place in the centre of the Grande Galerie.

was transformed into a royal château in the 1360s by Charles V, who established his extensive library in one of the towers. Successive monarchs demolished, rebuilt and extended various sections until Louis XIV moved out. The squatters who consequently took up residence in the palace included Guillaume Coustou, sculptor of the Marly Horses, now one of the Louvre's most prized exhibits. A fine artistic reputation grew out of the decaying passageways and galleries and, in the 18th century, the fine arts academy, which had joined the Académie Française and other academic bodies in the royal apartments, set up salons for artists to exhibit their work, a tradition which lasted for more than 120 years.

From palace to museum

After the Revolution, in a moment of creative fervour, the new regime decided to open the palace as a museum, thereby fulfilling the plans of Louis XVI, the king they had just beheaded. Opened in August 1793, the museum benefited from the collection of royal treasures, augmented by Napoleon's subsequent efforts to relocate much of Europe's artistic wealth, following his victorious military campaigns in Italy, Austria and Germany. After Napoleon was defeated at Waterloo in 1815, a large number of the stolen masterpieces were reclaimed by their rightful owners. But many more remained.

In 1981, the newly elected President Mitterrand commissioned a massive renovation of the Louvre, one of his *grands projets*, transferring in the process the Finance Ministry from the Richelieu Wing to Bercy, in eastern Paris, in order to free up more space for the vast collection. When it was finally finished, the *Grand Louvre*, already a vast museum, had doubled in size, making it the worlds' biggest.

The Pyramid

In 1989 the emphatically modern Louvre Pyramid, designed by Chinese-American architect I.M. Pei, opened above the Louvre's new main entrance. A celebration of angles, the pyramid's 666 panes of glass are held together by stainless-steel nodes and cables. The glass reflects and too many minds complements the lines of the surrounding building; however, to traditionalists, such modernism amid such historic beauty is a heresy – the same criticism that was levelled against the now-beloved Eiffel Tower when it was first erected. The Pyramid stands on the Axe Historique, an alignment of monuments, regal and triumphal, leading from the Louvre's Cour Carrée all the way to the Grande Arche at La Défense.

Of course, it was not just designed to dazzle. The Pyramid also serves an important practical purpose, as it allows light to flood into the sunken court where you buy your ticket, along with three smaller pyramids that illuminate the area where a cluster of shops, restaurants, cafés and an exhibition area are situated. This exhibition area, called the Medieval Louvre, shows the palace at different stages of its development. It is also a location for the twice-yearly Paris fashion shows.

Mix style, culture and cuisine at the Louvre's Café Marly.

The Pyramid is the main entrance to the museum.

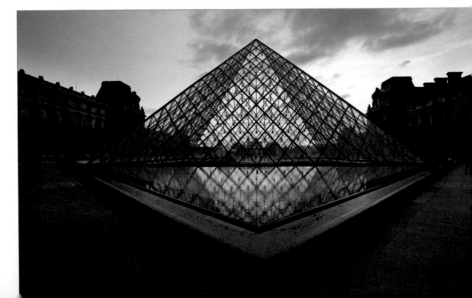

The Louvre's massive Wedding at Cana (1563), by Paolo Veronese.

The Louvre's vast covered courtyards make a nice change from the crowded galleries.

However, the Pyramid entrance gets very congested, so try to avoid peak times such as Sundays. There's an alternative entrance at 99 rue de Rivoli, which takes you in via the swanky Carrousel du Louvre shopping centre, or you can enter directly from Palais Royal-Musée du Louvre Métro. There are special queues for museum pass-holders, who can also use the Porte des Lions entrance.

A tour of the treasures

From the central Hall Napoléon, escalators whisk visitors off to various parts of the complex, divided into three separate sections: Sully (east wing), Denon (south wing) and Richelieu (north wing), with the exhibits on three levels. Although star attractions are well signposted, the free map provided is essential.

A good exhibition to start your visit with is the Medieval Louvre, en route to the Crypte Sully under the Cour Carrée, where the remains of Philippe-Auguste's fort and keep, as well as some of the artefacts discovered in the excavations to build the underground complex, can be seen. Pieces of Charles VI's parade helmet were found at the bottom of the well in the keep in 1984, and a replica of the helmet is on display in the Salle St-Louis.

Up on the ground floor of the Sully and Richelieu wings are

Oriental Antiquities, including the Mesopotamian prayer statue of Ebih-il (dating from approximately 2400 BC), with its striking lapis lazuli eyes, as well as the black basalt Babylonian *Code of Hammurabi* (1792–1750 BC), which is one of the world's first legal documents.

Greece to the Renaissance

On the south side of the Sully Wing you will find the graceful Hellenic statue *Venus de Milo* (2nd century BC), bought by the French government for a thousand francs in 1820 from the Greek island of Milos. Head on into the Denon Wing to see the Etruscan sarcophagus of a *Reclining Couple* (5th century BC). Continuing along the ground floor, you will reach the Italian Sculpture section and its famous masterpieces, such as Michelangelo's *Slaves* (1513–20), sculpted in marble for Pope Julius II's tomb but never finished, and Canova's neoclassical *Psyche Revived by the Kiss of Cupid* (1793).

In the Denon Wing, on the first floor, is the work of art that everyone wants to see for themselves, the *Mona Lisa* (1503) – *La Joconde* in French. The first incumbent in the Louvre, Leonardo da Vinci's small painting of a Florentine noblewoman rests securely behind bulletproof glass since her knife assault in the 1980s. It now hangs in pride of place in the restored Salle des Etats, along with Veronese's superb *The Wedding Feast at Cana* and other Venetian paintings by Titian and Tintoretto. The €4.7 million cost of the refurbishment was met, believe it or not, by Japan's Nippon Television Network, which also forked out €1.7 million to upgrade the gallery housing the *Venus de Milo*. Other Italian masterpieces include works by Fra Angelico, Raphael and Caravaggio.

Delacroix to Rembrandt

On the same floor is the Grande Galerie, starting at the top of the Escalier Daru opposite the *Winged Victory of Samothrace* (2nd century BC), a Hellenistic stone figure commemorating a sea victory. Here hang 19th-century French paintings, with Delacroix's *Liberty Leading the People*, Géricault's *Raft of the Medusa*

The Department of Islamic Art under Cour Visconti.

ISLAMIC ART GETS A NEW HOME

In the autumn of 2012 the Louvre opened a new exhibition space, which is the museum's most ambitious project since I.M. Pei's Pyramid. The Department of Islamic Art, previously confined to a section of the Department of Near Eastern Antiquities, now has its own special home in (or rather, underneath) Cour Visconti. The courtyard was excavated to a depth of 12 metres (40ft) and the exhibition space, covering 2,800 sq metres (30,000 sq ft), is spread over two floors. With around 3,000 works in its collection, which span the globe from Spain to India, the first floor focuses on Islamic artworks from the 7th to 10th century while the ground floor, or basement, takes visitors on a journey through the Islamic civilisation from the 11th to 19th century. The most striking aspect of this new "wing", designed by Rudy Ricciotti and Mario Bellini, is its undulating roof that is made up of 2,350 glass triangles each measuring 2.4 metres (8ft) wide. Visitors can get a shimmering view of the courtyard buildings from underneath the roof while those looking down from Galerie Daru and Salle des États will see what the has been described as "a golden, iridescent cloud".

The exquisite Pavillon Richelieu.

Louis-Auguste Levêque's Diane the Huntress, in the Tuileries.

and David's *Sabine Women*. Spanish Paintings, with masterpieces by El Greco and Goya, are close by.

The second floor of Richelieu and Sully Wings are entirely given over to paintings, including Rembrandt's masterly portrait of his second wife, *Bathsheba Bathing* (1654), and his Dutch compatriot Vermeer's telling portrayal of domestic life in the 1660s, *The Lacemaker*. The beautifully renovated Richelieu Wing houses a vast collection of French sculpture on the ground floor and is focused around two splendid sculpture courts, dominated by Guillaume Coustou's two large marble Marly Horses.

Musée des Arts Décoratifs ❷

Address: 107 rue de Rivoli
www.lesartsdecoratifs.fr
Tel: 01 44 55 57 50
Opening Hrs: Tue–Sun 11am–6pm, temporary exhibitions Thu till 9.30

Entrance Fee: charge
Transport: Palais Royal-Musée du Louvre

In a separate wing of the Louvre are three other museums that complement the main collection. This one is concerned with interior design and applied art from medieval tapestries to extravagant Empire furniture and

Up the stairs to the headless Winged Victory of Samothrace.

20th-century design, including Art Nouveau and Art Deco. There are medieval and Renaissance galleries, a jewellery collection and period rooms such as the lavish bedroom of Baron William Hope.

Musée des Arts de la Mode et du Textile

It's part of the Musée des Arts Décoratifs.

In the same wing on Rue de Rivoli, this museum covers Paris fashions and textiles from the 16th century until today. Each year it mounts a big display focusing on a different aspect of its collection (which comprises 16,000 costumes, 35,000 fashion accessories and 30,000 textile pieces) from the earliest existing dresses to the ground-breaking designs of big-name couturiers of the 20th century, such as Schiaparelli and Christian Dior.

Musée de la Publicité

Address: www.museedelapub.org; other details as for Musée des Arts Décoratifs

Upstairs in this wing, the "Advertising Museum" was designed for the millennium celebrations by French architect Jean Nouvel, who turned to the city for inspiration. It is home to a comprehensive collection of posters – around 100,000 in all, starting from as early as

The enigmatic Venus de Milo.

the Middle Ages. Press, TV and radio adverts and promotional memorabilia, are complemented by interactive displays, slide shows and videos. Only a fraction of the vast collection can ever be exhibited at one time.

A WALK IN THE TUILERIES

The **Jardin des Tuileries ❸** offers shade, statues, fountains and a place in which to relax and pretend to read *Le Monde*. Once a rubbish tip and a clay quarry for tiles (*tuiles*, hence the name), the garden was initially created in 1564 for Catherine de Médicis in front of her palace, to remind her of her native Tuscany. Louis XIV's celebrated gardener André Le Nôtre redesigned it in 1664, giving free rein to his predilection for straight lines and neatly clipped trees.

Louis XIV, however, was far more interested in Versailles, and the Tuileries gardens were, surprisingly, opened to the public. They quickly became the first fashionable outdoor area in which to see and be seen, triggering the appearance of Paris's first deckchairs and public toilets. One of

The Arc de Triomphe du Carrousel.

Sitting by the hexagonal pool in the Jardin des Tuileries.

the earliest hot-air balloon flights was launched from here, in 1783.

The Tuileries Palace for which the gardens had been created – which "closed off" the two wings of the Louvre – burned down in 1871,

during the Paris Commune, leaving the gardens as a permanent park.

Sculpture, paths and ponds

The Tuileries were renovated in the 1990s, restoring Le Nôtre's original design and incorporating a sloping terrace and enclosed garden. The Passerelle de Solférino footbridge across the Seine, opened in 1999, provides a quick route from the gardens to the Left Bank and Musée d'Orsay.

Approaching the gardens from the Louvre, you pass through the Arc de Triomphe du Carrousel, the smallest of the three arches (the others being the Arc de Triomphe and the Grande Arche at La Défense) on the Triumphal Way. Erected in 1809 by Napoleon to commemorate his Austrian victories, this arch is a garish imitation of the great triumphal arches built by the Romans, and the four horses galloping across its top are copies of four bronze horses that were stolen by Napoleon from St Mark's Square in Venice to decorate his memorial. After his downfall in 1815, the originals were returned.

In front and a little to the right of the arch, where the Tuileries Palace once stood, is a collection of sculptures of sensuous nudes, produced between 1900 and 1938 by Aristide Maillol, adorning ornamental pools and hedge-lined pathways. More

Relaxing in the Jardin des Tuileries.

Old-fashioned carousel in the Tuileries.

Under the arcades of Rue de Rivoli.

Tempting window display at Angelina's.

works by sculptors such as Rodin and Le Pautre, along with copies of ancient works and a selection of modern sculpture by, among others, Dubuffet, Etienne-Martin, Ellsworth Kelly, Laurens and David Smith, can be found scattered around the park.

Continue westwards along the Terrasse du Bord de l'Eau, where Napoleon's children played under the watchful gaze of their father, to the hexagonal pool – still a favourite spot for children with boats, and seagulls with attitude. Here, facing each other, are the twin museums of the Jeu de Paume and the Orangerie. These buildings are all that remain of the Palais des Tuileries, after the fire that engulfed the royal residence during the 1871 Commune.

Jeu de Paume (Site Concorde) ❹

Address: www.jeudepaume.org
Tel: 01 47 03 12 50
Opening Hrs: Tue 11am–9pm, Wed–Sun 11am–7pm
Entrance Fee: charge
Transport: Concorde

Once the real tennis court of the Tuileries Palace, the Jeu de Paume is now a light, airy exhibition space, which is the main base of France's national photography centre. Its approach is multi-disciplinary, featuring video, installation and film, documentary and art photography.

Musée de l'Orangerie ❺

Address: www.musee-orangerie.fr
Tel: 01 44 77 80 07
Opening Hrs: Wed–Mon 9am–6pm
Entrance Fee: charge
Transport: Concorde

The list of canvases here is impressive: 22 Soutines, 14 Cézannes – including one of *The Bathers* that was cut in three, then stuck back together again (look for the joins) – 24 Renoirs, 28 Derains and a pile of Picassos, Matisses and Utrillos. The highlight, though, is the unforgettable, extraordinarily fresh series of water lilies by Claude Monet, conceived especially for two oval rooms upstairs. Donated by the artist in 1918, the eight vast curved panels hover between abstraction and decoration.

The entrance to the Musée de l'Orangerie.

During extensive renovations at the Orangerie, workers uncovered a wall dating back to Charles IX's reign (c.1566).

RUE DE RIVOLI

The long Rue de Rivoli starts in the Marais and then runs past the Louvre and along the Tuileries – where its north side becomes a pedestrian arcade topped with Haussmannian apartments – to Place de la Concorde. It was built to commemorate Napoleon's victory over the Austrians at Rivoli, north of Verona, in 1797, but was completed well after the emperor's demise. Amid the souvenir shops, the presence of two English-language bookshops (Galignani and an outpost of WH Smith) and shirtmaker Hilditch & Key are a legacy of the English, who often stayed here in the 19th and early 20th centuries, notably at the Hôtel Meurice. Nearby is Angelina (see margin).

Parallel to Rue de Rivoli is the ancient Rue St-Honoré. Once full of noble residences, it still has some elegant facades and ornate shop fronts, but the area, long considered staid and straight-laced, has been transformed by the arrival of influential designer boutiques and so-called concept stores, of which the first and still the best-known is Colette.

DRINK

Refreshments in the Tuileries gardens can be had at Café Diane (tel: 01 42 96 81 12; www.cafe1diane.com), on the northeast side of the gardens. In fine weather, it is almost always packed, even though it seats 200 people.

Claude Monet's Water Lilies.

The Palais-Royal métro entrance, as transformed by contemporary French artist Jean-Michel Othoniel.

The palatial dining room at Le Meurice.

St-Roch ⑥

Address: 296 rue St-Honoré
www.paroissesaintroch.fr
Tel: 01 42 44 13 20
Opening Hrs: Tue–Sun 8.30am–7pm

Entrance Fee: free
Transport: Pyramides

This Baroque church contains the tombs of royal landscape gardener Le Nôtre, the playwright Corneille

HOTEL WITH HISTORY

The sumptuous Hôtel Meurice (228 rue de Rivoli) is one of Paris's grandest hotels, with a spa, Michelin-starred restaurant, supremely elegant cocktail bar and sumptuous decor. During the Nazi Occupation, however, it was the German headquarters. It was here on 25 August 1944 that General Dietrich von Choltitz, military governor of Paris (he was only promoted to the job on 7 August 1944), received direct orders from Hitler to blow up most of the city in advance of the Allied liberation. Von Choltitz famously refused – an act of disobedience that earned him the sobriquet "saviour of Paris" and the presence of French generals at his funeral 22 years later.

and philosopher Diderot. In 1795, Royalist insurgents were shot dead on the church steps on the orders of a young general named Napoleon Bonaparte (the bullet holes are still visible). The church's spotlessly clean, honeyed stone facade is particularly fine.

On nearby Place des Pyramides is a shiny equestrian statue of Joan of Arc (one of four statues of her in the city), wounded here in battle when fighting against the English in 1429.

Comédie Française ❼

Address: 1 place Colette
www.comedie-francaise.fr
Tel: 01 44 58 15 15
Transport: Palais Royal-Musée du Louvre

The French national theatre overlooks two squares named after the writers Colette and Malraux. The company that started life with Molière and his acting troupe, was confirmed by royal decree in 1680 by Louis XIV. It has been in the present building since 1799,

A game of pétanque in the Palais Royal garden.

and the plays of Racine, Molière, Corneille and Shakespeare continue to form the backbone of its classical repertoire.

Louvre des Antiquaires ❽

Address: 2 place du Palais-Royal
www.louvre-antiquaires.com
Tel: 01 42 97 27 27
Opening Hrs: Tue–Sun 11am–7pm
Entrance Fee: free
Transport: Palais Royal-Musée du Louvre

On Place du Palais-Royal, now a popular spot for daredevil rollerbladers, is this massive building, built as a department store and now home to some 150 upmarket antique dealers. Specialists take in everything from fine art, porcelain and furniture to Chinese and Japanese ivories, antique jewellery and scientific instruments. The area was cleared by a paranoid Napoleon following an attempt on his life in 1800, when two Royalists planted

Buren's Columns has turned the Palais Royal courtyard into a modernist playground of sorts.

Lunch at Galerie Vivienne's Le Bougainville café-restaurant.

The graceful Fontaine Louvois.

explosives in a cart, but the bomb missed his carriage.

PALAIS ROYAL ❾

The Palais Royal is a timeless and tranquil spot. The palace was built on the site of a Roman bathhouse for Cardinal Richelieu, Louis XIII's chief minister from 1624. On Richelieu's death in 1642, it was passed to the Crown, and became the childhood home of Louis XIV. At the beginning of the 18th century, the dukes of Orléans, descendants of Louis XIV's younger brother, took up residence, and the palace turned into a den of debauchery, with the infamous "libertines' suppers" thrown regularly by the Regent, Philippe d'Orléans.

In 1780, to compensate for his family's profligate spending, Louis-Philippe of Orléans, known as "Philippe-Egalité" due to his liberal ideas, enclosed the gardens at the back of the palace with an elegant three-storey arcade, spaces in which were let as shops, theatres, restaurants, cafés, sideshows and brothels. The Jardins du Palais Royal became a focal point of Parisian life, as a place where all classes could mingle freely; the duke forbade the police entry to the palace precincts, and gambling and prostitution were rife.

Birthplace of revolution

It was also a hotbed of radical ideas, and it was famously from a café table in the Palais Royal that Camille Desmoulins made an impassioned speech on 12 July 1789 calling on the people of Paris to take arms against the royal government, which led directly to the storming of the Bastille two days later. After the Revolution the complex continued to be one of the social hubs of Paris, until the Palais was reclaimed by the Orléans family after the demise of Napoleon. The Palais Royal was seriously damaged during the Commune (1871), but was faithfully reconstructed in the following years.

Today, the Palais Royal houses the Ministry of Culture. In the main courtyard (daily 8am–7.30, Jun–Sept till 11pm) stand 250 black-and-white-striped columns of varying heights, erected by artist Daniel Buren in 1986. At weekends it echoes with the squeals of delighted children, who love to play around them. The garden, once a meeting place for revolutionaries, is now a tranquil oasis – with some fine restaurants – while the eccentric mix of shops ranges from old-fashioned specialists in medals and lead soldiers to make-up, vintage couture and upmarket interior design. In more recent years some seriously glam fashion labels

SHOP

If you ever get invited to the Oscars, Didier Ludot at 25 galerie Montpensier (tel: 01 42 96 06 56; www.didierludot.fr), in the Palais Royal, is the place to go for a one-of-its-kind dress; this boutique primarily sells vintage couture. Opposite, at 125 galerie Valois, his other shop, La Petite Robe Noire (tel: 01 40 15 01 04), deals solely in "little black dresses".

Browsing at the Louvre des Antiquaires.

Molière, one of the most famous French playwrights.

MASTER OF COMEDY

Born Jean-Baptiste Poquelin in Paris in 1622, Molière, playwright, actor, director and stage manager, wrote 12 enduring comedies, including *Tartuffe* (1669) and *Le Bourgeois Gentilhomme* (1671). After studying law, he formed an acting troupe with the Béjart family (including his lover, Madeleine Béjart). He also changed his name to Molière, perhaps to spare his father the embarrassment of an actor in the family. The troupe had an unsuccessful start, but after Molière polished up his act in the provinces, they became Louis XIV's court entertainers.

In 1673, at 51, Molière collapsed on stage with a haemorrhage while playing *Le Malade Imaginaire*, in which an old man feigns death; he died hours later. In 1680 the king merged his company with a rival's, creating the Comédie Française, which was originally situated at 14 rue de l'Ancienne Comédie on the Left Bank but later moved to the theatre, now known as the Comédie Française, in Rue de Richelieu near the Palais Royal where his plays are still produced. The great thespian lived at 40 rue de Richelieu, and is commemorated by a fountain close by. The giant chair in which he was sitting when he died is in a case in the theatre's foyer.

The upmarket lingerie boutique Chantal Thomass on Rue St-Honoré, right next to the historic Hôtel de Noailles.

The entrance to Galerie Vivienne on Rue des Petits-Champs.

have boosted the arcades' pulling power considerably: newcomers include Marc Jacobs, Rick Owens and Didier Ludot.

Bibliothèque Nationale de France (Richelieu) ⑩

Address: 5 rue Vivienne
www.bnf.fr
Tel: 01 53 79 59 59
Opening Hrs: exhibitions Tue–Sat 10am–7pm, Sun 1–7pm

Entrance Fee: charge
Transport: Bourse
North of the Palais Royal is the former mansion of Cardinal Mazarin, which became the royal library and so the foundation of France's national library. Most of the collection has been transferred to the massive building at Tolbiac (see page 207) – last (and least successful) of Mitterrand's *grands projets*. The book collection is one of the biggest in the world, and includes Charlemagne's illuminated Bible, as well as manuscripts by Rabelais, Hugo and Proust. The Richelieu building now houses the collections of prints, drawings, maps, music and manuscripts. The main reading room, designed by Henri Labrouste in 1863, is an architectural masterpiece. Downstairs, the **Cabinet des Médailles** contains coins and objets d'art from the royal collections that were seized during the Revolution. A vast renovation of the building began in 2011 and is due to finish in 2019, so some parts may be temporarily closed.

GALERIE VIVIENNE

Opposite the library, across Rue de Richelieu, the charming **Square Louvois** contains one of the most beautiful fountains in Paris, which represents the four "female" rivers of France – La Loire, La Seine, La Garonne and La Saône.

GLORIOUS *GALERIES*

The area between the Palais Royal and Rue du Faubourg-Montmartre is laced with picturesque covered shopping arcades. The 20 or so *galeries* represent a fraction of the number that existed in the early 19th century. By the 1840s there were over 100 such *passages*, built by speculators who snapped up the land of the dispossessed aristocracy that came onto the market after the Revolution, and making imaginative use of the new technologies of the era with their combination of iron and glass to create a light, airy, and yet enclosed space. They became the ideal places in which to discover novelties, inventions and the latest fashions, while keeping out of the city's mud-splashed, carriage-laden thoroughfares.

Galeries Vivienne and Colbert

The best-preserved and most elegant of these shopping arcades is **Galerie Vivienne** ⓫, (www.galerie-vivienne. com) first opened in 1826, which has a fine mosaic floor, intricate brass lamps, graceful glass canopies and restored wooden shop fronts. It has been colonised by art galleries, upmarket clothes designers, restaurants and a very pretty tearoom, A Priori Thé. The adjoining **Galerie Colbert** has a spectacular glass dome. Formerly an annexe of the Bibliothèque Nationale, it houses art institutions such as the Institut Nationale d'Histoire de l'Art (INHA) and the Institut National du Patrimoine (INP).

Adjacent to these arcades is the **Place des Victoires** ⓬, an archetypal royal square designed in 1685 by Louis XIV's architect Jules Hardouin Mansart as a backdrop for the equestrian statue of his patron the Sun King. The square became a model for squares across France. It was designed to give the impression of an entirely enclosed space, but this effect was destroyed by the opening up of Rue Etienne Marcel in 1883. Nowadays a large number of its surrounding mansions are occupied by designer boutiques (Apostrophe, Mercadel, Kenzo and more).

Heading south down Rue Croix-des-Petits-Champs for about five minutes, you reach the most beautiful and atmospheric passageway in Paris, **Galerie Véro-Dodat** ⓭ (opposite Rue Montesquieu), with polished mahogany facades, brass lamps and skylights all beautifully preserved. It is named after the duo of wealthy pork butchers who financed the arcade's construction in 1826, fitting it with the new technology of the day: gas lighting. One of its main attractions is the picture-perfect brasserie the Café de l'Epoque.

EAT

A Priori Thé (tel: 01 42 97 48 75; www.apriorithe. wordpress.com), in the Galerie Vivienne, is an elegant *salon de thé* that spills out into the gallery's main passageway. As well as teas and coffees, it serves light snacks and a very good cheesecake.

The Delamain bookshop has been in its current location in front of the Comédie Française since 1906.

THE LOUVRE

The largest museum in the world is a matchless treasure trove of paintings, sculpture, decorative art and antiquities – with an architecturally stunning new wing.

The most famous painting of all: the Mona Lisa.

The Musée National du Louvre has something for everyone. The palace that houses it is in itself a building of breathtaking beauty, and its galleries form a labyrinth of corridors. Getting lost may be a good way to find unexpected gems, but wander for too long without direction and you might miss even the major collections. Use the map on the right, or pick up one showing current exhibitions at the information desk on your way in. If it all gets too much, you can leave the museum and return on the same day, or you can rest and get a bite to eat at one of the Louvre's cafés and restaurants (one of the best is Café Marly, with a terrace overlooking the pyramid). The museum also has some excellent shops selling souvenirs – but don't try to see everything in one day; go back again, and get lost in a different place.

The Essentials
Address: www.louvre.fr
Tel: 01 40 20 53 17
Opening Hrs: Wed–Mon 9am–6pm, Wed, Fri until 9.45pm; closed Tues
Admission Fee: charge
Transport: Palais Royal-Musée du Louvre

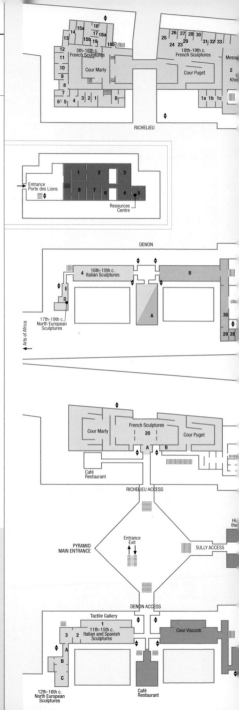

Ground Floor

Near Eastern Antiquites

Islamic Art

Sculptures

Egyptian Antiquities

Greek, Etruscan and Roman Antiquities

History of the Louvre, The Medieval Louvre

Arts of Africa, Asia, Oceania and the Americas

Lower Ground Floor

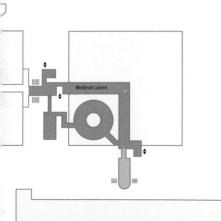

THE HIGHLIGHTS

The Martyrdom of St Sebastian (c.1495), by Pietro Perugino.

The Seated Scribe (2500–2350 BC) This Ancient Egyptian figure is made from painted limestone and alabaster, with eyes of rock crystal (Sully, 1st floor).

Persian Winged Bull glazed tiles (c.500 BC) A glazed, moulded relief from the palace of the Persian king Darius I at Susa (present-day Iran).

The Venus de Milo (c.2nd century BC) The iconic Greek marble statue is on display in a gallery parallel to the Galerie des Antiquités.

Virgin and Child in Majesty (c.1270) by Cimabue This Early Renaissance masterpiece was acquired by Napoleon (Denon, 1st floor).

Venus and the Graces Presenting Gifts to a Young Woman (c.1483) by Sandro Botticelli One of a pair of frescoes from the Villa Lemmi near Florence, thought to have been commissioned for a wedding (Denon, 1st floor).

Mona Lisa (1503–6) by Leonardo da Vinci The most famous Renaissance smile is better-displayed than ever, in a purpose-built new gallery.

The Rebellious Slave (1513–5) by Michelangelo One of a pair of unfinished sculptures intended for the tomb of Pope Julius II (Denon, ground floor).

The Card Cheat (c.1635) by Georges de la Tour A rich but unworldly young man falls in with a gang of card-sharps (French 17th-century painting; Sully, 2nd floor).

The Astronomer (1668) and *The Geographer* (1668–9) by Vermeer Painted by Vermeer to celebrate the progress of science in Europe in the 17th century (Richelieu, 2nd floor).

The Bather (1808) by Ingres This celebrated figure was reused by Ingres 50 years later for his painting *The Turkish Bath* (French 19th-century painting; Sully, 2nd floor).

Raft of the Medusa (1816) by Géricault A stirring vision of suffering based on a true story of shipwreck and cannibalism (Denon, 1st floor).

Liberty Leading the People (1830) by Delacroix Iconic painting of the July Revolution by the leader of Romanticism (Denon, 1st floor).

Egyptian antiquities

The collection spans the period from the 4th millennium BC to the 4th–6th centuries AD.

Oriental antiquities and Islamic arts

The collection is mainly from the eastern Mediterranean, and holds the oldest item in the museum – a 7,000-year-old Neolithic statue from Ain Ghezal.

Greek, Roman & Etruscan antiquities

A comprehensive collection that includes the mythical *Venus de Milo* and the *Three Graces*.

French painting 17th–19th century

Works are arranged in chronological order, from the Late Gothic period to the mid-19th century.

French sculpture

French sculpture dominates the collection in the courtyards of the Richelieu wing.

Italian and Spanish painting

The Italian galleries contain early masterpieces, but the Spanish collection is patchy.

Northern Schools

Six new rooms show Northern European paintings of the 18th and 19th centuries.

Decorative arts

One of the least-known aspects of the Louvre is the extensive decorative arts collection.

Graphic arts

The Louvre has a vast stock of drawings and engravings by Michelangelo, Raphael, Dürer and more, which are shown in changing exhibitions.

An Egyptian relief.

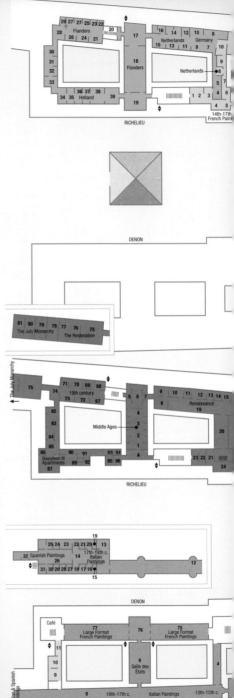

Second Floor

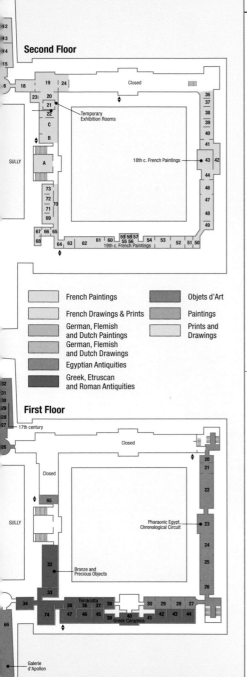

19 24   Closed   ‖‖‖‖

18   23| 20
21
22   Temporary
C   Exhibition Rooms

B

SULLY   A   18th c. French Paintings

73
72   70
71
69

67 66 65
68   64 63 62 61 60 59 58 57   54 53   52 51 50
55 56
19th c. French Paintings

French Paintings	Objets d'Art
French Drawings & Prints	Paintings
German, Flemish and Dutch Paintings	Prints and Drawings
German, Flemish and Dutch Drawings	
Egyptian Antiquities	
Greek, Etruscan and Roman Antiquities	

First Floor

17th century

Closed

Closed

65

SULLY   Pharaonic Egypt,
Chronological Circuit

32   Bronze and
Precious Objects

33
34   35 36 37 38   30 29 28 27
Terracotta   42 43 44
74   47 46 45 39 40 41
Greek Ceramics

66

Galerie
d'Apollon

EGYPTIAN ANTIQUITIES AND ISLAMIC ARTS

The museum's spectacular Egyptian collection is very popular. Its core originates from the victory spoils of Napoleon's Egyptian campaign of 1798. The collection was subsequently expanded, largely through the efforts of the famous Egyptologist Jean-François Champollion (1790–1832), the first person to decipher hieroglyphics. Beyond the pink granite *Giant Sphinx*, insights into Egyptian life and the Nile culture are given through a thematic presentation on the ground floor, followed by a chronological presentation on the first floor. The later rooms follow religion and funerary rites.

The oriental antiquities collection (essentially from the eastern Mediterranean) may be overshadowed by the Egyptian collection, but it is no less important. The most spectacular items are the reconstructions of palaces at Susa and Khorsabad. The palace of Persian King Darius I at Susa (in present-day Iran) was constructed in around 510 BC. Other highlights include Cypriot terracotta figures and stag-shaped vessels, Mycenaean pots with geometric decoration, carved ivory, chalcolithic vessels from the Negev and the Neolithic statue from Ain Ghezal, discovered in 1985.

Dating probably from the 2nd century BC, the marble Venus de Milo with its serene gaze, soft curves and naturalistic drapery rivals the Mona Lisa as an icon of female beauty. She was discovered, minus her arms, on the island of Melos in 1820 and promptly purchased by the French government for 6,000 francs. Various authorities have suggested that her left hand might have been holding the golden apple that was presented to Venus by Paris of Troy.

GRANDS BOULEVARDS AND CHAMPS-ELYSÉES

This area is a paradise for shoppers and strollers, with giant stores and grand fashion houses, glittering gourmet palaces and chic modern cafés, celebrated monuments and intimate mansion-museums, all amid some of Paris's most magnificent vistas.

N orth of the Palais Royal lie the Grands Boulevards, a string of wide avenues running from east to west. Their oldest sections date from the 17th century, when Louis XIV tore down the medieval walls around Paris and created wide, open spaces bordered with trees for his subjects. In the 19th century, Baron Haussmann extended the string westwards along Boulevard Haussmann. The western boulevards became the preserve of the rich, while the east was the playground of the city's industrial workers, lined with vaudeville theatres, restaurants, bars, brothels and, later, cinemas. Today the boulevards are dominated by mass-market clothing chains and discount outlets, but if you look up, traces of Second Empire extravagance can be seen in the ornate balconies and facades.

THE GRANDEST AVENUE

To the west, at a haughty distance from the populist strip, is the grandest of Parisian avenues, the Champs-Elysées, begun by Le Nôtre in 1667 as an extension of the Tuileries. Initially the promenade reached only as far as the Rond-Point des Champs-Elysées; over 100 years passed before the rest, stretching up to the Arc de Triomphe, was completed. Its reputation has ebbed and flowed with the centuries: today, chic restaurants, cafés and nightclubs are joining the fashion and luxury goods shops that appeared there through the 1990s, heralding the monumental avenue's comeback as one of the world's premier shopping destinations.

ALONG THE BOULEVARDS TO THE OPÉRA

Traces of the Grands Boulevards' early pomp can be seen in one of

Main Attractions

Palais Garnier
Grands Magasins
Place Vendôme
La Madeleine
Place de la Concorde
The Champs-Elysées
Grand Palais
Petit Palais
Arc de Triomphe

Map

Page 110

Ladurée tearoom, a true Parisian institution.

A short walk from the Palais Garnier is another, smaller opera house, the Opéra Comique (closed for renovation till December 2016, www. opera-comique.com). This very pretty venue hosts a mixture of chamber orchestras and musicals.

The opulent Opéra Garnier.

the easternmost sections, Boulevard St-Denis (around Strasbourg St-Denis Métro), in the two triumphal arches erected by Colbert in the 1670s in honour of Louis XIV's military victories, the **Porte St-Denis** and **Porte St-Martin**. When they were built they stood on the very edge of the city, and greeted new arrivals from the north.

Musée Grévin 🕙

Address: 10 boulevard Montmartre www.grevin.com
Tel: 01 47 70 85 05
Opening Hrs: Mon–Fri 10am–6pm, Sat–Sun 9.30am–7pm, but opening times vary throughout the year
Entrance Fee: charge
Transport: Grands Boulevards

Heading westwards, the first place of interest, especially if you have kids in tow, is Paris's venerable wax museum. It's full of cheerfully incompatible figures – from Marie-Antoinette and Gandhi to virtual heroine Lara Croft, Elton John and of course national football hero Zinédine Zidane – and a hall of mirrors. The lavish decor of this

century-old establishment is a confection of Venetian Rococo, rosewood and marble, and the staircase by Rives is an architectural gem.

To the left of the Grévin is the **Passage Jouffroy** (www.passagejouffroy.com) with a shop selling cinema books (many in English and/or out of print) and memorabilia, antique silver and the old-fashioned, affordable Hôtel Chopin. Next door is the soothing **Café Zephyr**, one of few cafés with style on the Grands Boulevards.

Across the busy boulevard is the **Passage des Panoramas** 🕕 (www.passagedespanoramas.fr), one of the earliest of the covered arcades. It was opened in 1800 on the site of a former aristocratic mansion, and Parisians flocked here to see the giant painted panoramas of different cities that were exhibited in two great rotundas. The shop **Stern Graveur** (www.sterngraveur.com) has been engraving fine notepaper and wedding invitations since 1840; other shops sell lingerie, floaty clothes, vintage vinyl and old postcards, but above all this *passage* is a

Place du Caire.

haven for philatelists, with half a dozen specialist stamp dealers.

La Bourse 🔟

Address: place de la Bourse
www.palaisbrongniart.com
Tel: 01 83 92 20 20

Emerging from the arcades, head south to Paris's imposing former stock exchange, also known as **Palais Brongniart** after its architect Alexandre Brongniart. Built in 1808, the grand colonnaded building is one of the most distinctive neoclassical constructions of the Napoleonic era. It now hosts events and conferences and is not open to the public.

Rue du Quatre-Septembre leads from here to Place de l'Opéra. This broad square is lined by elegant shops, luxury hotels and cafés, notably **Café de la Paix** (www.cafedelapaix. fr), where you can join the chic clientele enjoying coffee and croissants, or a glass of wine and oysters later in the day. Just remember, the prices match the luxurious setting.

Palais Garnier – Opéra National de Paris 🔟

Address: place de l'Opéra
www.operadeparis.fr
Tel: for visits 01 71 25 24 23
Opening Hrs: daily 10am–5pm, 15 Jul–Aug till 6pm, guided tours for groups
Entrance Fee: charge
Transport: Opéra

Soaring above the square is Paris's celebrated, beautifully restored opera house, the Palais Garnier. It is now only part of the Opéra National de Paris with the Opéra Bastille, which has taken charge of larger, more ambitious opera and ballet productions, but the newcomer can never challenge the original "Paris Opera" in the style stakes. In 1860 architect Charles Garnier was commissioned by Napoleon III to build an opera house for the imperial capital, and his lavish designs were wholly in tune with the pomp and opulence that characterised the Second Empire, creating a style in themselves.

FACT

When it was built, the Palais Garnier was the largest performance venue in the city. It has 1,991 seats, 334 boxes, 1,606 doors, 7,593 keys, 450 fireplaces and 6,319 steps.

EGYPT-SUR-SEINE

Place du Caire, in the Sentier garment district – just north of Sentier Métro, up Rue d'Aboukir – is one of Paris's curios, off the tourist trail. This was the site of the so-called *Cour des Miracles* in the 1600s, home to beggars who spent their days around the city, apparently disabled, blind or deaf. At night they returned here, and immediately shed their wooden legs and eye patches – hence the "miracles". Not until 1667 did Louis XIV's police chief La Reynie clean up this notorious den of iniquity of all kinds. Today the square is notable for the bustle of multiracial porters lugging rolls of cloth or racks of finished clothes between workshops, as well as its mementoes of Napoleon's campaign in Egypt: the north side is covered with sphinxes and hieroglyphics. On the facade of 2 place du Caire are three sculpted heads of Hathor, the goddess of love, music, dance and fertility, who is remarkable by her cow's ears; and in the middle of the panel of hieroglyphs just below the roofline is the face of a man with an enormous nose – not Gérard Depardieu, but a local 19th-century scoundrel called Bouginier; Hugo mentions him in *Les Misérables*.

Rue St-Honoré, and its even more elegant continuation west of Rue Royale, Rue du Faubourg St-Honoré, form the traditional heartland of Parisian high fashion. St-Honoré, beginning at the Palais Royal, has cutting-edge boutiques as well as big names like John Galliano; the really grand fashion houses (Dior, Guy Laroche, Hermès) are clustered together on Rue du Faubourg. The concentration of chic is just dazzling.

Fashion emporium Galeries Lafayette.

The facade and exterior are covered in sculptures of great composers and allegorical figures representing spirits of music and dance, including voluptuous nudes that caused a scandal when first unveiled. The profusion of marble and gilt inside is almost oppressive in its excess, but the glamour of the Opéra's foyers is undeniable. The grand staircase was conceived by Garnier as the ultimate celebrity catwalk: "Everything is designed so that the parade of spectators become themselves a performance." The five-tiered auditorium, dripping in red velvet and gilt, is dominated by a 6-tonne chandelier, which famously crashed down on the audience during a performance in 1896. The auditorium ceiling was painted by Marc Chagall in 1964, commissioned by André Malraux. The visit also takes in the **library** and **museum**, with scores, portraits, costumes and sets.

Behind the Opéra is the **Musée du Parfum Fragonard** ⑱ (9 rue Scribe; www.fragonard.com; tel: 01 47 42 04 56; Mon–Sat 9am–6pm, Sun until 5pm; charge), a compact museum tracing 5,000 years of perfumery. A

Pomp and lavishness at the Opéra.

heady fragrance permeates the air, in a beautifully restored 19th-century townhouse. Nearby at 39 boulevard des Capucines is the **Théâtre des Capucines** ⑲ (Mon–Sat 9am–6pm),

where legendary music-hall singer and actress Arletty began her career in the 1930s, and which is now also owned by Fragonard and has a perfume museum.

Printemps, along with its rival Galeries Lafayette, are the two behemoth department stores on boulevard Haussmann.

Grands magasins

The area just behind the Opéra, along Boulevard Haussmann, is dominated by the *grands magasins* (department stores). **Galeries Lafayette** and **Printemps** both established in the late 19th century, have remained rivals ever since. Galeries Lafayette is especially famed for its splendid Art Nouveau central hall, topped with a vast stained-glass dome.

THE LUXURY QUARTER

One essential side of Paris: the streets and squares southwest of the Opéra are the number-one home of the fine foods, high fashion and exquisite jewellery that have made the city world capital of luxury for two centuries.

Place Vendôme 20

Centre of a grand vista between Palais Garnier and Rue de Rivoli, octagonal Place Vendôme is perhaps the smartest square in Paris. Laid out in 1699 by Colbert to glorify Louis XIV – whose equestrian statue was subsequently replaced in the centre by an imitation

The Opéra's five-tiered auditorium, decked out in velvet and gilt.

The glitzy Ritz hotel on Place Vendôme.

of Trajan's Column, glorifying Napoleon's exploits – it is now home to luxury jewellers and designers such as Boucheron, Van Cleef & Arpels, Bulgari, Cartier, Chaumet and Dior. Here, too, are big financial institutions such as the J.P. Morgan merchant bank, and of course the Ritz, at No. 15. The luxury hotel is now most famous as the place where Princess Diana had her last meal before her fatal car crash in August 1997. The legendary hotel, once home of Coco Chanel, is due to reopen in spring 2016 after a €200 million refurbishment.

Eglise de la Madeleine ㉑

Address: place de la Madeleine
www.eglise-lamadeleine.com
Tel: 01 44 51 69 00
Opening Hrs: daily 9.30am – 7pm
Entrance Fee: free
Transport: Madeleine

From just south of Place Vendôme chic, boutique-laden Rue St-Honoré leads to the church of **Sainte-Marie-de-la-Madeleine**, rising up amidst roaring traffic and expensive shops. This giant neoclassical temple was commissioned as a self-aggrandising

exercise by Napoleon, but more recently has become a favourite venue for celebrity weddings and funerals. In the square around it the mouth-watering displays at food stores **Fauchon** (www.fauchon.com) and **Hédiard** (www.hediard.com) are tourist attractions in their own right.

Place de la Concorde ㉒

Rue Royale runs from La Madeleine to place de la Concorde, designed for Louis XV by Jacques-Ange Gabriel as a hub of spectacular vistas to north, south, east and west. The square has been the site of many historical events since its completion in 1763, notably the decapitation of Louis XVI by the Revolutionaries in 1793. Majestic in the middle of the traffic chaos, the central obelisk was a gift from the Viceroy of Egypt in 1829; the 3,300-year-old column, weighing 220 tonnes, took four years to reach Paris. On the north side of the square is a pair of grand neoclassical mansions, flanking the Rue Royale: the one on the right is the French Navy Ministry, the other is the opulent Hôtel de Crillon (www.crillon.com), where Benjamin

The stunning Art Nouveau stained-glass dome of the Galeries Lafayette.

Franklin signed the Treaty of Amity and Commerce between the newly formed United States of America and King Louis XVI in 1778.

THE CHAMPS-ELYSÉES ㉓

Initiated by Louis XIV in 1667, the Champs-Elysées was originally laid out by landscape architect Le Nôtre to create a visual extension of the Tuileries gardens running west from the Louvre. The broad avenue, lined with elegant gardens and rows of trees, was continued after the completion of the Arc de Triomphe in 1836. By the 1900s the Champs, in contrast to the rather downmarket Grands Boulevards, had reached a zenith of popularity and elegance, attracting stylish and moneyed types from all over the world to linger on its animated café terraces.

The sophisticated spectacle on the avenue evaporated in World War I, but made a brief and giddy comeback during the 1920s. This was followed by the Depression, World War II and, post-war, traffic problems, as the Champs shifted from a luxury address to a commercial one distinguished by cinemas and airline offices in the 1950s, '60s

FACT

The two fountains designed by German architect Hittorff on the left and right of the central obelisk in Place de la Concorde are modelled after those of St Peter's Square in Rome.

Place Vendôme at dusk.

The Place de la Concorde fountains are at their resplendent best at night.

and '70s. By the 1980s it was quite dowdy, with an atmosphere comparable to a tatty shopping mall.

Determined to resurrect the area, Jacques Chirac, then Mayor of Paris, budgeted the equivalent of €75 million to renovate, modernise and beautify the Champs: street parking was replaced by underground car parks; new street furniture was added, including handsome teak benches and retro Art Nouveau newspaper kiosks; dove-grey granite paving stones were laid; and the number of trees doubled. Parisians gave the avenue a second look. Today, the Champs is considered not only elegant again, but a cool place to hang out.

Browsing the Champs

The main shopping stretch of the Champs-Elysées runs from the Rond-Point to the Arc de Triomphe. Landmark stores are **Tiffany & Co** (No. 68), **Guerlain** (No. 68), with its Rococo facade and sumptuous interior; the Aladdin's cave of

beauty products, **Sephora** (No. 70); and **Louis Vuitton**, at No. 101.

In the last few years a number of swanky concept stores have opened

The Eglise de la Madeleine's bronze doors bear reliefs representing the Ten Commandments.

up as well, including one from luxury leather goods purveyor **Lancel** at No. 127, and a couple, bizarrely enough, by car manufacturers Toyota and Renault. The latter, the **Atelier Renault** at No. 53, features a swish café that serves a good choice of cocktails and light meals and has a fine view of passersby. Most of the grander designer outlets are concentrated around Avenue Montaigne and Avenue George V. This is fashion land, where prices for the majority are prohibitive, but window shopping is free. Most of the brands here are established megastars – the likes of Dior, Chanel and Prada – but in the last few years they've been joined by younger, hipper labels **Paul & Joe**, at 2 avenue Montaigne; **Jimmy Choo**, at No. 34; and upmarket children's brand **Bonpoint**, at No. 49. The Montaigne Market, at No. 57, is the avenue's sole multi-brand emporium, stocking an ever-changing selection in different price brackets.

On Rue François 1er (No. 18) is a deluxe branch of boutique **Zadig & Voltaire**, with limited-edition pieces not found in its other stores.

The Hermès flagship store on Rue du Faubourg St-Honoré, a street so chic that one of the luxury brand's fine fragrances, 24 Faubourg, is named after the exclusive address.

Galeries Nationales du Grand Palais ㉔

Address: 3 avenue du Général Eisenhower
www.grandpalais.fr
Tel: 01 44 13 17 17
Opening Hrs: Wed–Mon 10am–8pm, Wed until 10pm
Entrance Fee: charge
Transport: Champs-Elysées-Clémenceau

Between the Champs and the Seine stands the huge, glass-domed Grand Palais, built for the 1900 World Fair, but which for decades has served as central Paris's largest exhibition centre. The building's grand nave closed in 1993 after a metal rivet fell from its roof, but after more than a decade of work it reopened in 2006 as good as new: a glorious Belle Époque masterpiece of glass and iron, covering a vast open space decorated with Art Nouveau motifs. It's the venue for all manner of events and activities:

The Champs-Elysées seen from the top of the Arc de Triomphe.

FACT

Between the Champs-Elysées and Boulevard Haussmann at 2 rue Lamennais, is the Fondation Jérôme-Seydoux Pathé (Tue–Fri 1–7pm, Sat 10am–7pm; www.fondation-jerome seydoux-pathe.com), of Pathé News fame, is a must visit for fans of cinema history. It houses a collection of film-related items including posters, scripts, photographs and cameras – in the 1900s Pathé was the world's leading maker of film equipment –and is open to visitors by appointment only.

The Grand Palais, a Belle Epoque masterpiece, hosts several major art exhibitions every year.

DJs, a light installation, a Christmas funfair and fashion shows, as well as major art exhibitions.

The Grand Palais is also home to the **Palais de la Découverte**, (www.palais-decouverte.fr; tel: 01 56 43 20 20; Tue–Fri 9.30am–6pm, Sat 9:30am–7pm, Sun 10am–7pm; charge), the city's original science museum. It covers astronomy, biology, chemistry, physics and earth sciences through interactive experiments. Sadly, there's very little labelling in English.

Musée du Petit Palais

Address: avenue Winston Churchill
www.petitpalais.paris.fr
Tel: 01 53 43 40 00
Opening Hrs: Tue–Sun 10am–6pm
Entrance Fee: free
Transport: Champs-Elysées-Clémenceau

Across Avenue Winston Churchill from the Grand Palais is its smaller neighbour, inspired by the Grand Trianon at Versailles with its polychrome marble, magnificent long gallery and arcaded garden. The

The Petit Palais's ornate Belle Epoque style.

Petit Palais houses the municipal collection of fine and decorative arts, and it too reopened in 2006 after being thoroughly refurbished.

Under the Arc at dusk.

The renovation work has brought in a lot of extra natural light, which greatly benefits the eclectic collection that lives here. Its main strengths are paintings of the 19th and early 20th centuries, including works by Bonnard, Cézanne, Courbet and Sisley; but there are also Greek and Roman antiquities, icons, tapestries, ceramics and sculpture, and some fabulous Art Nouveau furniture.

Baron Haussmann.

HAUSSMANN'S LEGACY

Because they're so often described as "Haussmannian", it's frequently assumed that the buildings that went up in the French capital's mammoth restructuring between 1853 and 1870 were actually designed by Baron Georges-Eugène Haussmann (1809–91) himself. But Haussmann, then Prefect of Paris, was just the project's coordinator; he was not an architect by any means. Landscape architect Jean-Pierre Barrillet-Deschamps was responsible for designing the city's new parks while another architect, also called Deschamps, from Paris Map Services, designed the new avenues. In a curious twist of fate, his plans entailed the demolition of the building he was born in, to make way for the elegant boulevard that bears his name.

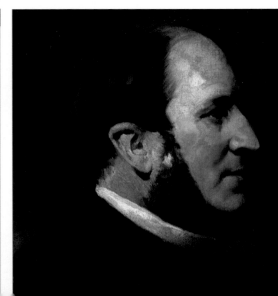

FACT

North of the Champs-Elysées at 55 rue du Faubourg Saint-Honoré is the Elysée Palace, the official home of the President of the French Republic; although President Hollande prefers to live in his own apartment in the 15th arrondissement and just has his office here. The building dates from 1722 and was designed by Armand-Claude Mollet for the Count of Evreux. Around the corner at 13 avenue de Marigny is the Hôtel de Marigny, which is used to house visiting dignitaries.

Fine art at the Musée Jacquemart André.

Arc de Triomphe ㉖

Address: place Charles-de-Gaulle
www.monuments-nationaux.fr
Tel: 01 55 37 73 77
Opening Hrs: Apr–Sept daily 10am–11pm, Oct–Mar until 10.30pm
Entrance Fee: charge
Transport: Charles de Gaulle-Etoile

Crowning the Champs-Elysées is this great memorial to megalomania. The Arc de Triomphe was commissioned by Napoleon in 1806, but the arch, ornately carved with heroic images of Revolutionary battles and the emperor's victories, was not completed until long after his death, in 1836. Napoleon's only chance to pass under it came when his body was triumphantly returned to Paris for reburial in Les Invalides in 1840. Beneath the arch is France's Tomb of the Unknown Soldier, laid to rest in 1920. Since 1923 an eternal flame has been here too, rekindled each evening at 6.30pm with a wreath-laying ceremony. The platform above the arch can be reached via a lift, and offers one of the finest Paris views.

The grand spiralling staircase of the Musée Jacquemart-André.

BELLE EPOQUE MANSIONS

Much of the old Paris that was swept away by Haussmann around his Grands Boulevards was replaced by opulent mansions typical of France's Belle Epoque, several of which now house intriguing small museums.

Musée Jacquemart-André ㉗

Address: 158 boulevard Haussmann
www.musee-jacquemart-andre.com
Tel: 01 45 62 11 59
Opening Hrs: daily 10am–6pm
Entrance Fee: charge
Transport: Miromesnil

This collection of art and furniture once belonged to wealthy collector Edouard André and his wife, erstwhile society portrait painter, Nélie Jacquemart. It includes a small Uccello masterpiece, *St George and the Dragon*, and works by Bellini,

Donatello, Rembrandt, Titian, Boucher and David. The newly renovated house and its ornate decor are also a magnificent example of Belle Epoque taste.

Parc Monceau ㉘

Opening Hrs: daily 7am–8pm, May–Aug until 10pm
Entrance Fee: free
Transport: Monceau

A 19th-century version of a theme park, with an English-style garden and lake, a fake Egyptian pyramid, Venetian bridge and Greek colonnade.

Musée Nissim de Camondo ㉙

Address: 63 rue de Monceau
www.lesartsdecoratifs.fr
Tel: 01 53 89 06 40/50
Opening Hrs: Wed–Sun 10am–5.30pm
Entrance Fee: charge
Transport: Monceau

Overlooking the park, this stately home modelled on the Petit Trianon at Versailles was built for a wealthy Jewish banking family. Its remarkable collection of 18th-century tapestries, porcelain, objets d'art, furniture and paintings was left to the state in 1935 by the passionate collector Count Moïse de Camondo in memory of his son Nissim, killed in action in 1917.

Musée Cernuschi ㉚

Address: 7 avenue Velasquez
www.cernuschi.paris.fr
Tel: 01 53 96 21 50
Opening Hrs: Tue–Sun 10am–6pm
Entrance Fee: free

This is one of the most important collections of oriental art in Europe, thanks to financier Henri Cernuschi, who amassed his holdings in China and Japan in 1871–3 and then built this residence beside Parc Monceau to house them.

Parc Monceau's Greek colonnade.

THE ARC DE TRIOMPHE

Built by Napoleon to celebrate all of his military successes, the Triumphal Arch is the focal point of French national pride and visited by millions.

It's the most recognisable Paris landmark after the Eiffel Tower and, in the words of its website, "the most illustrious symbol of French history"; victory parades flowed through it in 1919 and 1944 (a few weeks later, aviator Charles Godefroy flew his biplane through the middle); Victor Hugo lay in state beneath it in 1885. Every year since 1880, the Bastille Day Military Parade has taken place on the morning of 14 July, starting at the Arc (bar for a few years in the 1970s when President Valéry Giscard-d'Estaing varied the route) and heading down the Champs-Elysées to the Place de la Concorde. However, it is not possible to march through the arch these days as the Tomb of the Unknown Soldier has lain beneath it since Armistice Day 1920; the tomb is marked by an eternal flame. Access for visitors is via an underpass; such is the traffic chaos encircling it at all times that crossing the road would be tantamount to suicide. The roof of the Arc is reached by a narrow staircase or a small lift (so not for those with claustrophobia), and the view from the top, out over Paris in all directions, is simply glorious.

Two of the four main sculptural groups on the exterior base of the Arc, Le Triomphe de 1810 by Jean-Pierre Cortot (left) and La Marseillaise by François Rude (right).

The Essentials

Address: Place Charles-de-Gaulle; www.monuments-nationaux.fr
Tel: 01 55 37 73 77
Opening Hrs: daily 10am–10.30pm, Apr–Sept until 11pm
Entrance Fee: charge
Transport: Charles de Gaulle-Etoile

The view from the top is breathtaking; here the Eiffel Tower and Tour Montparnasse are visible in the distance.

Carved on the inside of the monument are the names of the generals who fought in the Napoleonic wars.

Viewed from the air, it's easy to appreciate why the square around the Arc de Triomphe is called L'Etoile ("Star") – no fewer than 12 avenues radiate out from it.

STANDING TALL

An eternal flame burns above the Tomb of the Unknown Soldier, buried here in 1920 and honoured every Armistice Day.

In conception, the Arc de Triomphe was a typical piece of Napoleonic self-advertisement, intended to honour the military triumphs of his armies. Although the monument was designed by Jean Chalgrin in 1806, inspired by the Arch of Titus in Rome, work didn't begin on it until 1809. It wasn't finished until 27 years later (laying the foundations alone took two years, and work was halted several times) – by which time Napoleon was dead. For all that, the names of his 128 major battles were carved on its sides, along with the names of the 660 generals who took part in them, and the entire structure is richly adorned with sculptures depicting battle scenes and allegories, of which the most famous is Rude's *Le Départ des Volontaires* (also known as *La Marseillaise*). It stands 50 metres (164ft) tall, set on the axis that runs from the Louvre, through the Arc du Carrousel and out west to the Grande Arche de la Défense.

On major national festivities, such as Bastille Day and Armistice Day, an enormous tricolour is flown underneath the main arch.

A breakdancing group entertain tourists on the steps of the Sacré-Cœur.

MONTMARTRE

One of the great birthplaces of bohemia, cabaret and modern art, Montmartre threatens to surrender to its own clichés, without ever quite doing so. The maze of steep, narrow streets around the hill still have a unique atmosphere, and even seedy Pigalle has reinvented itself with a new sense of cool.

The "village" of Montmartre occupies the highest point of Paris, nestling on a hillside in the 18th *arrondissement*, north of the city centre. Extending from sometimes seedy yet always vibrant Place Pigalle in the south to the sugar-white cupolas of Sacré-Cœur, this urban village is an alluring huddle of small steep streets and hidden steps.

In parts Montmartre resembles a country hamlet, with ivy-clad cottages and cobbled squares. Elsewhere, neon, fast food, sex shows and tourist buses set the tone. Follow the golf caps up to Place du Tertre, filled with tourist bistros, tatty gift shops and would-be artists, and Montmartre will seem brash and commercial. Enter a narrow side street, veer down a deserted flight of steps and you will be alone, wandering in one of the city's most charismatic quarters.

MONTMARTRE'S BEGINNINGS

Montmartre has always stood slightly apart from the rest of Paris. Legend has it that in AD 250 the Romans decapitated St Denis, first bishop of Paris, and two priests on the hill. St Denis picked up his head and walked off with it to where the Basilica of St-Denis now stands (see page 257).

The hill became known as *Mons Martyrium* (Martyrs' Mound). As local bar owners point out, people have been picking their heads out of the gutters of Montmartre ever since.

In the 12th century a Benedictine convent settled on the hill, and 400 years later Henri IV took shelter in it when laying siege to Paris in 1589. His only conquest of the campaign, it appears, was the 17-year-old abbess. The last Mother Superior here was guillotined during the Revolution at

Main Attractions
Moulin Rouge
Pigalle
Sacré-Cœur
Place du Tertre
Espace Salvador Dalí
Musée de Montmartre
Au Lapin Agile
Cimetière de Montmartre

Map
Page 152

Stylish Montmartre locals.

Concert venue La Cigale.

the age of 82 and the convent buildings were destroyed.

Revolution has been the district's speciality ever since. In 1871, its inhabitants seized 170 cannons to defend themselves after the fall of Paris to the Prussians. The Thiers government sent troops to recapture them, but the generals were overwhelmed, lined up on the hill and shot – so beginning the Paris Commune (see page 36).

For much of the 19th century, Montmartre was mined for gypsum, and retained a country charm with its vineyards, cornfields, flocks of sheep and 40 windmills. This charm and the hill's lofty isolation attracted artists and writers. Painters and their models frequented Place Pigalle, and people flocked to the Moulin Rouge. Impressionism, Fauvism and Cubism were conceived in the lofts, bars and dance halls of Montmartre.

When the bohemians migrated to Montparnasse, Montmartre was left to sex-shop owners, pawnbrokers and cheap hotels, and for many years afterwards it was synonymous with sleaze. Yet today, the village is fashionable once more. Dingy strip bars have been transformed into chic rock clubs and the narrow streets are lined with buzzing cafés, quirky design shops, offbeat second-hand shops and hippy-chic boutiques. A new generation of bohemians is reclaiming Montmartre.

THE CHARMS OF PIGALLE

The traditional gateway to Montmartre, at the foot of the *Butte* or hill, Pigalle is also the place where modern nightlife was invented.

Moulin Rouge ❶

Address: 82 boulevard de Clichy, www.moulinrouge.fr
Tel: 01 53 09 82 82
Opening Hrs: shows daily 9pm, 11pm
Entrance Fee: charge
Transport: Blanche

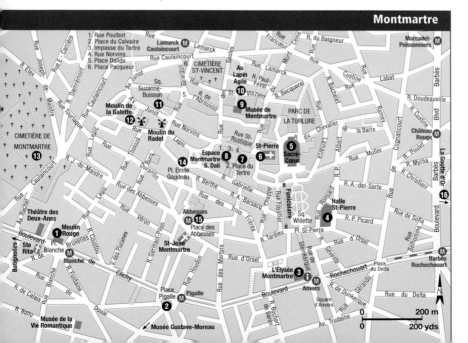

Montmartre

The kitsch Moulin Rouge with its signature neon windmill still does a roaring trade as tourists flock to see the high-kicking cabaret girls strut their stuff in feathers. Of all the glitzy Parisian floor shows it is probably the most tame and traditional (children are welcome here), but the club's history is gloriously scandalous. Toulouse-Lautrec sat here sketching the working girls' energetic cancan; in 1896, the annual Paris Art School Ball at the Moulin Rouge was the scene of the first all-the-way strip-teases, by one of the school's prettiest models. She was arrested and imprisoned, and students went to the barricades in the Quartier Latin, proclaiming "the battle for artistic nudity" – two died in subsequent scuffles with police.

Modern Pigalle

Next door to the Moulin Rouge, **La Machine du Moulin Rouge** (tel: 01 53 41 88 89; www.lamachinedumoulinrouge. com), a huge disco, has live music concerts and club nights ranging from swing to soul. A few doors away at 100 boulevard de Clichy, the **Théâtre des Deux Anes** (tel: 01 46 06 10 26; www.2anes.com) offers a dose of typical Parisian cabaret (in French, naturally).

A little further east along Boulevard de Clichy lies sprawling **Place Pigalle ②** itself. Less artistic attractions abound in Pigalle (or "Pig Alley", as it was once known to American soldiers), for this has been the core of the Paris sex trade for decades. In the surrounding streets, tasselled curtains provide glimpses of smoky interiors, signs promote live sex shows and aggressive bouncers attempt to entice tourists into "naked extravaganzas". But, Pigalle's reputation has been changing from sleaze centre to trendy nightspot. The cabarets that occupied half the houses on Rue des Martyrs in the 18th century are being taken over by hip clubs

SHOP

Some of the finest breads and most irresistible *pâtisseries* imaginable can be found just south of Pigalle at the shop of Arnaud Delmontel (www.arnaud-delmontel.com), 39 rue des Martyrs (closed Tue). Specialities include beautifully subtle cinnamon and raisin bread, and fabulous fruit tarts. He has another shop on the north side of the Butte Montmartre at 57 rue Damrémont (closed Mon).

The Moulin Rouge – you can't miss it.

The environs of the Sacré-Cœur teem with street performers.

Dancing the night away at the Bus Palladium.

– such as **Le Divan du Monde** at No. 75 – and bars.

Nothing symbolises the revival of Pigalle better than the state of the **Elysée Montmartre ❸**. Founded in 1807, rebuilt by Eiffel in 1889, frequented by Lautrec and used to host wrestling and boxing in the 1950s, this historic music and dance hall has been reborn yet again as one of the city's best live rock and club venues, hosting both big names and the up-and-coming. Following a fire in 2011 the venue is undergoing renovation and should reopen in 2016.

CLIMBING THE *BUTTE*

The wide esplanade at the foot of the Butte Montmartre, above Anvers Métro, is Square Willette.

Halle St-Pierre ❹

Address: 2 rue Ronsard, www.hallesaintpierre.org
Tel: 01 42 58 72 89
Opening Hrs: Mon–Fri 11am–6pm, Sat until 7pm, Sun noon–6pm, Aug only Mon–Fri noon–6pm
Entrance Fee: charge
Transport: Anvers

Just off the square is this former market hall designed by Victor Baltard, the original architect of Les Halles (see page 103), which is now a cultural centre housing a museum of "outsider" and Naïve art. The highly individual works are by artists from over 30 countries, many of them self-taught. Several shops in the area specialise in cheap textiles, which often attract professional designers.

PIGALLE NIGHTSPOTS

Popular venues include: **Le Divan du Monde** (75 rue des Martyrs, tel: 01 40 05 06 99; www.divandumonde.com), an old venue full of memories of the 1890s that's now a cool, relaxed nightclub and music venue with an eclectic programme; **La Cigale** (120 boulevard de Rochechouart, tel: 01 49 25 89 99; www.lacigale.fr), an old vaudeville house that now hosts big-name acts; and the **Bus Palladium** (6 rue Fontaine, tel: 01 45 26 80 35; www.lebus palladium.com), an iconic 1960s disco hall, now a refitted, fashionable venue with an all-new sound system (Serge Gainsbourg mentioned it in a song, and Dalí, Roman Polanski and the Beatles all hung out here).

Impossible to miss from Square Willette, overlooking the tide of human activity that ebbs and flows beneath it is the vast white bulk of the Sacré-Cœur. To reach it, you can either walk up through the square, laid out in terraces in 1929, or take the *funiculaire* (funicular railway – Métro tickets are valid for travel).

Sacré-Cœur ⑤

Address: 33 rue du Chevalier-de-la-Barre, www.sacre-coeur-montmartre.com
Tel: 01 53 41 89 00
Opening Hrs: basilica daily 6am–10.30pm, dome and crypt daily May-Sept: 8.30am–8pm, Oct-Apr: 9am–5pm
Entrance Fee: charge for crypt and dome
Transport: Anvers

This domed basilica was conceived by a group of Catholics in 1871, who vowed to build a church to the Sacred Heart if Paris was delivered from the Prussian siege, and to expiate the sin represented by the atheist Commune, which had begun in Montmartre. The heart of one of the men, Alexandre Legentil, is preserved in a stone urn in the crypt.

The Church took responsibility for the project in 1873, and work started two years later. Paul Abadie, the chief architect, based his design on the Romano-Byzantine cathedral of St-Front in Périgueux.

The bone-white colour of the building comes from its Château-Landon stone, which secretes calcite when it rains, bleaching the walls. Its mediocre architecture, added to its symbolic censure of a popular uprising, has made the Sacré-Cœur one of Parisians' least favourite monuments.

Completed in 1914 but not consecrated until after the war in 1919, the dome offers a stunning view over Paris, up 237 spiral steps. From the stained-glass gallery beneath there is a good view of the cavernous interior which, apart from a massive mock-Byzantine mosaic of Christ (1912–22) by Luc Olivier-Merson on the chancel ceiling, has little to offer.

Outside on the terrace, crowds gather in the early evening to drink wine, strum guitars and watch the glittering lights of Paris, overlooked by statues of Joan of Arc and St Louis on horseback.

The Sacré-Cœur was built in 1876, much later than its architectural style implies.

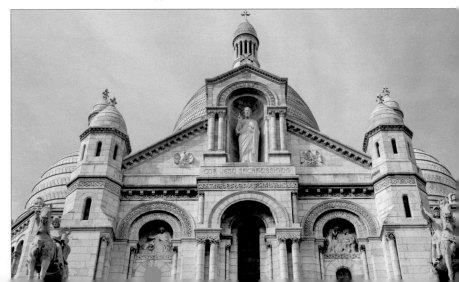

St-Pierre-de-Montmartre is Paris's second oldest church.

The Sacré-Cœur offers one of the best views of the French capital.

Around the Sacré-Cœur

Next to the Sacré-Cœur, the simple church of **St-Pierre-de-Montmartre** ❻ (daily 9am–7pm; www.saintpierrede montmartre.net) is the second-oldest in Paris (after St-Germain-des-Prés, see page 181), dating from 1133, and the only remaining vestige of the Abbey of Montmartre, where the nuns used to live. After the Revolution the church was abandoned, until it was reconsecrated in 1908. If you are here on Toussaint (All Saints' Day – 1 November), visit the small, romantic graveyard behind the church, as this is the only day of the year when it opens.

To the west, **Place du Tertre** ❼ is the tourist trap of Montmartre, laden with kitschy overpriced bistros and craft shops selling junk. The square, once the site of the village hall, now throngs with coachloads of tourists. Artists began exhibiting here in the 19th century, and now there are legions of mediocre (and sometimes aggressively pushy) painters on the square. This oppressive commercialisation makes it a place best avoided by day. It's far more appealing at night, when the square is lit up by fairy lights and retains an animated charm.

Just off the square on place du Tertre, **La Mère Catherine** (tel: 01 46 06 32 69; www.lamerecatherine.com) lays claim to being Paris's first bistro. Originally a revolutionary drinking den (where Danton pronounced the immortal words, "Eat, drink, for tomorrow we shall die"), the story goes that during the Allied occupation of 1814, the old inn greeted Russian soldiers. As they ordered their drinks (forbidden by the Russian military authorities) they shouted *"bystro"*, meaning "quickly", thereby founding a Paris institution.

Don't be put off by the masses on the square; escaping them is easy. From Place du Tertre, winding Rue Poulbot leads through Place du Calvaire – the smallest square in Paris, with a spectacular view, and a cosy magnet for lovers and drinkers – to another kitschy artistic attraction.

Espace Montmartre Salvador Dalí ❽

Address: 11 rue Poulbot, www.daliparis.com

Tel: 01 42 64 40 10
Opening Hrs: daily 10am–6pm, July–Aug until 8pm
Entrance Fee: charge
Transport: Abbesses

Over 330 sculptures and drawings by the Catalan Surrealist painter are exhibited in unusual settings, including his famous clocks, intended to represent "the fluidity of time".

A few minutes' walk to the north, **Rue des Saules** crosses **Rue St-Rustique**, a quiet, rustic street leading away from the buzz of Place du Tertre, which contains the **Auberge de la Bonne Franquette** (tel: 01 42 52 02 42; www.labonne franquette.com). It was originally called Le Billard en Bois; Vincent Van Gogh and Auguste Renoir both painted here, and the crossroads outside and other street scenes nearby were immortalised by the paintings of Maurice Utrillo. Other frequent visitors to the auberge were Cézanne, Toulouse-Lautrec, Monet, Pissarro and Sisley, and novelist Emile Zola.

Street artists conjure up quick portraits in Place du Tertre.

Selling nudes in Place du Tertre.

OLD MONTMARTRE

The further you move from the Sacré-Cœur and Place du Tertre, the easier it is to get a scent of the days when Montmartre really was just a village.

Musée de Montmartre ❾

Address: 12 rue Cortot
www.museedemontmartre.fr
Tel: 01 49 25 89 39
Opening Hrs: daily 10am–6pm
Entrance Fee: charge
Transport: Lamarck-Caulaincourt

This charming museum chronicles the life and times of Montmartre and the artists' quarter in a 17th-century manor, the oldest house on the *Butte*. It was originally the country home of Rosimund, an actor in Molière's theatre company who suffered the exact same fate as his master: in 1686 he died during a performance of *Le Malade Imaginaire*, just as Molière had done 13 years earlier (see page

Le Clos Montmartre, Paris's only remaining vineyard.

Dalí in Montmartre in 1956.

127). Many artists had studios here, including Renoir, Dufy and Utrillo; the composer Erik Satie (1866–1925) lived in the same street. The museum is an evocation of past simplicity, gaiety and bohemian living, with pictures by Kees van Dongen (1877–1968) and Dufy, Toulouse-Lautrec posters, reconstructions of Utrillo's favourite café, complete with zinc counter top and absinthe bottles, and an artist's studio, with yellowing photographs and a wonderful view over Paris.

Nearby on Rue St-Vincent is Montmartre's famous vineyard, **Le Clos Montmartre** (www.clos-montmartre.com), planted in 1933 in memory of the vines cultivated here since the Middle Ages. In early October, the grape harvest attracts hundreds of volunteers, and the streets host processions and parties. Around 300 litres of wine are sold at auction, with the proceeds going to Montmartre pensioners.

Au Lapin Agile ❿

Address: 22 rue des Saules, www.au-lapin-agile.com
Tel: 01 46 06 85 87
Opening Hrs: Tue–Sun 9pm–1am
Entrance Fee: charge
Transport: Lamarck-Caulaincourt

Opposite the vineyard is this legendary cabaret. It was the headquarters of the avant-garde around 1900, a restaurant-cabaret where Renoir and the Symbolist poet Paul Verlaine laid tables, and Guillaume Apollinaire sang with fellow poet Max Jacob. Picasso paid for a day's meals at the Lapin with one of his *Harlequin* paintings – now worth millions. Today a tourist attraction, the smoke-stained inn still has its old wooden tables, original paintings by Gill and Cubist Fernand Léger – and cabaret every evening.

TRANQUIL MONTMARTRE

Far from the helter-skelter animation of Pigalle and Place du Tertre, the west of Montmartre, on the other side of St Vincent cemetery, is a puzzle of little old streets and tumbledown houses. Take the steps from Place Constantin-Pecqueur, off Rue Caulaincourt, to **Square Suzanne-Buisson** ⓫ , a quiet, dusty square that has a children's play area. The square occupies the former garden of the Château des Brouillards, an 18th-century folly inhabited at different

SALVADOR DALÍ

A true eccentric, Catalan painter Salvador Dalí (1904–89) was desperate to go to Paris in the 1920s, for it was the world's art capital, already conquered by fellow Spaniards Picasso and Joan Miró. After studying art in Madrid, where he befriended the poet and dramatist Federico Garcia Lorca and the future film director Luis Buñuel, with whom he went on to co-write the film *Un Chien Andalou* (An Andalusian Dog, 1929), he reached Paris in 1926. With the help of introductions from the two older Spanish artists, and motivated by his "Catalan sense of fantasy", Dalí held his first Surrealist exhibition the same year. Through Miró, Dalí met other Surrealists, many of whom he was to quarrel with later. Picasso said that Dalí's imagination reminded him of "an outboard motor continually running", and the painter himself wanted to "systematise confusion". As well as painting, Dalí produced films and books, including an autobiography. "Every morning when I wake up," he stated, "I experience an exquisite joy – the joy of being Salvador Dalí – and I ask myself in rapture, 'What wonderful things is this Salvador Dalí going to accomplish today?'"

times by Renoir and the mad poet Gérard de Nerval (who hanged himself in Les Halles in 1855, leaving a note saying, "Don't wait for me, for the night will be black and white"), and which was later turned into a dance hall. During the 19th century, the "château" could only be seen when the *brouillards* (thick fogs) of Montmartre lifted, hence the name. In the middle of the square, a statue of St Denis washes the blood off his head while watching the old men playing *pétanque*.

Avenue Junot, beside the square, is one of the widest, most expensive streets in Montmartre. Constructed in 1910, the avenue cut through the ancient maquis scrubland that used to cover the hillside, where windmills turned their graceful sails and goats scampered among the trees.

The street's 1920s Art Deco elegance has attracted the cream of Montmartre society – singer Claude Nougaro lived in the big ochre house. **Le Hameau des Artistes** (No. 11) still provides artists' studios. **Maison Tristan Tzara** (No. 15) is named after the eccentric Romanian Dadaist who

The Auberge de la Bonne Franquette was frequented by all the famous Impressionists in its heyday.

once lived here, and was designed especially for him by the Austrian architect Adolf Loos.

Below, between Avenue Junot and Rue Lepic, is the last of the great windmills of Montmartre, the **Moulin de la Galette** ⑫. Built in 1604, the mill became an illustrious dance hall in the 19th century. Artists and writers living in Montmartre often hosted parties

La Maison Rose bistro on Rue de l'Abreuvoir was the subject of a lithograph by French painter Maurice Utrillo.

The Moulin de la Galette was immortalised by Renoir in his 1866 painting of the same name.

The Lapin Agile's popularity has not waned.

here, and it was on one such occasion that Auguste Renoir began sketches for his famous painting *Le Moulin de la Galette* (1866). Emile Zola held a party here to celebrate the success of his novel *L'Assommoir* (1877), set in La Goutte d'Or, just to the east. The novelist lived below the village, on Boulevard de Clichy.

Much earlier, in the 1814 siege of Paris, its owners the four Debray brothers had fought fiercely to save their windmill from the Russians. Today, the windmill is better-protected, as a notice proclaims, "Residence under electronic, radar and guard-dog surveillance".

Picturesque Rue Lepic, leading from the windmill and past the Moulin du Radet, descends to Place Blanche. This old quarry road housed Vincent Van Gogh and his brother Theo, an art dealer, at No. 54 for two years in the late 1880s. During that time Van Gogh is said to have exhibited his paintings at Le Tambourin, a seedy cabaret on Boulevard de Clichy, until the owner demanded that he remove them as they disturbed her customers.

Tranquil Square Suzanne-Buisson.

Further down the hill, Rue Lepic turns into a quaint but slightly grubby market street, lined with mouthwatering shops selling pastries and exotic produce. Grab a

A HAPPY BUNNY

The tiny Lapin Agile ("Nimble Rabbit") on Rue des Saules is the oldest surviving cabaret from Montmartre's high-kicking heyday. When it first opened in 1855 it was known as the Cabaret des Assassins, according to tradition because a gang of robbers had once broken in and killed the owner's son; but in 1875 it acquired the name it still bears today, when the painter André Gill painted a sign showing a rabbit escaping from a copper saucepan. The word "agile" described the bunny's nifty getaway, but was also a pun on the painter's name: A Gill. By the early 20th century, the cabaret was a popular spot in which painters and artists met and talked; Utrillo depicted it more than once, and Picasso's 1905 painting *Au Lapin Agile* cemented its renown; both lived and worked nearby at Le Bâteau Lavoir in Place Emile Goudeau along with other luminaries of the age, including Georges Braque, Raoul Dufy and Amedeo Modigliani (see page 161). The fame still holds good: US comedian Steve Martin wrote a successful play, *Picasso at the Lapin Agile*, in the 1990s, and visitors still flock to the Lapin to hear old-fashioned French songs from as far back as the Middle Ages.

drink at **Les Deux Moulins** (No. 15), where Amélie Poulain worked as a waitress in the eponymous movie.

Cimetière de Montmartre ⑬

Address: 20 avenue Rachel
Tel: 01 53 42 36 30
Opening Hrs: summer daily 8am–6pm, winter daily 9.30am–5pm
Entrance Fee: free
Transport: Blanche

Just west of Rue Lepic, the area's artistic bias is reflected in Montmartre's cemetery. The tombs are elegantly sculpted, and their inmates famous: here lie the 19th-century novelists Stendhal and Alexandre Dumas, poet and critic Théophile Gautier, the painter Edgar Degas, the dancer Vaslav Nijinsky, composers Hector Berlioz and Jacques Offenbach, and a bust of Emile Zola (his body was moved to the Panthéon). Film director François Truffaut was also laid to rest here, in 1984.

Heading back into Montmartre, cut left off Rue des Abbesses into Rue Ravignan, for a detour to **Place Emile-Goudeau** ⑭, a particularly attractive square. At No. 13, modern art studios have replaced the wooden ramshackle building called **Le Bateau-Lavoir**,

Bust of Parisian-born Emile Zola in the Cimetière de Montmartre.

Cimetière de Montmartre.

Café society.

*Typical Haussmannian
building in Montmartre.*

so named because it resembled a
floating laundry. This artists' den
housed Picasso and fellow Cubists
Braque and Van Dongen in its narrow, ship-like corridors. Picasso
painted *Les Demoiselles d'Avignon*
(1907) in his chaotic studio, recall-
ing the prostitutes of Barcelona,
and Apollinaire and Max Jacob
liberated verse form in the rooms
alongside. Unfortunately, the building burned down in 1970, just as it
was about to be renovated.

Turning left out of the square,
take the Passage des Abbesses, a little further on, down to pretty **Place
des Abbesses** ⓯ and its remarkable Art Nouveau Métro station,
designed by Hector Guimard. The
brownstone church is Saint-Jean-
de-Montmartre (Mon–Sat 9am–
7pm, Sun 9.30am–6pm, summer
till 7.30pm; www.saintjeandemont
martre.com), which was built from
1894 to 1904 and has a definite Art
Nouveau look about it. Rue des
Abbesses is a focus of Montmartre
life, with bustling cafés, grocery
stores, wine merchants and trendy
shops. The trio of streets east of the
station – Rue de la Vieuville, Rue
Yvonne-le-Tac, Rue des Trois Frères
– are lined with designer boutiques,
offbeat second-hand shops, little

galleries supporting local artists and boho bars that are especially lively in the evenings.

AROUND MONTMARTRE

La Goutte d'Or ⑯

To the east of Montmartre is the old working-class district of La Goutte d'Or, centred on Barbès-Rochechouart Métro station. Vividly described by Zola in *L'Assommoir*, the district may still be one of the poorest and most run-down in the city, often marked by a heavy police presence, but it's also one of the liveliest. The conglomeration of Islamic butchers, African grocers, West Indian bakers, Jewish jewellers and Arab tailors is a never-ending spectacle of sight, sound and smell. Over 30 nationalities live in the streets around Rue de la Goutte d'Or and Rue des Poissonniers. Cut-price clothes are sold at the huge flagship store of the Tati chain on Boulevard Rochechouart.

Montmartre stairways are steep.

In an attempt to develop the area, the Fédération Française du Prêt à Porter (Ready-to-Wear Association) and the Mairie de Paris have tried to make Rue des Gardes a new centre of fashion. Ten couture boutiques for emerging talents have opened in the street (Métro Château-Rouge).

Greengrocer on Rue des Abbesses.

La Nouvelle Athènes

South of Pigalle, this area has been rediscovered in the last few years. In the early 19th century writers, artists and composers, among them Chopin and George Sand, as well as actresses and courtesans came to live here, leading it to be dubbed the "New Athens". Place St-Georges and the exclusive residential streets off Rue des Martyrs give an idea of its grander past, as do two museums: the **Musée Gustave Moreau** (14 rue de La Rochefoucauld; www.musee-moreau. fr; tel: 01 48 74 38 50; Mon, Wed, Thu 10am–12.45pm, 2–5.15pm, Fri, Sat, Sun 10am–5.15pm; charge), which overflows with fantastical paintings and drawings that the symbolist painter left to the state, and the

The Métro

Wandering through white-tiled tunnels following *Correspondance* signs is as essential a part of the Parisian experience as strolling the squares and boulevards.

Deep beneath the streets of Paris is another city, with its own shops, cafés, market stalls, hairdressers, banking facilities, musicians, artists, beggars and pickpockets, even its own police force and its own microclimate. Temperatures here occasionally exceed 30°C (86°F), while wind speeds through the tunnels can reach up to 40km (25 miles) per hour.

In Luc Besson's 1985 thriller, *Subway*, audiences had a glimpse of this surreal world and the characters who make the Métro their home. In real life, every night around 1,000 people take refuge underground, most because they have nowhere else to go.

A growing network

Construction of the Paris Métro began in 1898. The first line, 10.3km (6.4 miles)

Art Nouveau Abbesses station.

long, between Porte de Vincennes and Porte Maillot, opened on 19 July 1900. Since then the Métro has extended in every direction, and is hailed as one of the world's cheapest and most efficient underground rail systems, carrying 3.5 million passengers daily on over 200km (124 miles) of track to 372 stations on 14 Métro, five RER and two railway lines. Two new stations – Mairie de Montrouge on Ligne 4 and Front Populaire on Ligne 12 – are due to open in 2013 and three more are due to open by 2019.

The massive station at Châtelet-Les Halles is the hub of the network. Five Métro lines and three RER lines meet here, disgorging millions daily into its labyrinth of corridors. As you search this nightmarish warren for an exit, you may wonder if you'll ever come up for air. Trudging the Métro's 75km (47 miles) of corridors, it seems unsurprising that the Parisian's average body weight is among the lowest in the industrialised world.

The architecture

At no point in the city are you further than 500 metres (550yds) from a Métro station. Some station entrances retain their elegant Art Nouveau features, designed by architect Hector Guimard, characterised by soft flowing lines and motifs evoking the growth of plants. Two that are still covered by his beautiful iron-and-glass pavilions are at Porte Dauphine and Abbesses.

Underground, walls are mostly covered in white tiles, apart from a few stations such as St-Michel, with a mosaic ceiling, and Bastille, with scenes from the Revolution.

In an attempt to make commuting slightly more bearable, the RATP (which runs the Métro and city buses) organises a variety of cultural events, from photography exhibitions to fashion shows, classical concerts to puppet theatre. Less organised but equally ubiquitous are the train-hopping buskers and beggars, hoping to profit from a captive audience – it's calculated that the average Parisian spends a year and four months of his or her life below ground.

Musée de la Vie Romantique (16 rue Chaptal; www.parismusees.paris.fr; tel: 01 55 31 95 67; Tue–Sun 10am–6pm; charge).

Rue Clauzel is an enclave of retro clothing outlets, bric-a-brac and boho clothes shops, while the lower half of Rue des Martyrs has several good bakeries and delis.

Batignolles

West of Place de Clichy, this area developed in the 19th century with a very different atmosphere from that of the grand mansions and apartment blocks in the western half of the 17th *arrondissement*, around Parc Monceau. Sliced through by huge railway depots, it still retains its authentic urban fabric, with old workers' cafés, budget hotels, craft workshops and picturesque alleys and courtyards, but is also being colonised by quirky boutiques and arty bistros.

Square des Batignolles was once an empty space, where the Fêtes des Batignolles were held. Transformed in 1862 into Napoleon III's idea of a London park, it still has its 19th-century chalets, kiosks, glass-enclosed lookout and miniature river and waterfall. Black swans cruise its little lake. Towards the *Périphérique*, a great swathe of former railway land is being made into an all-new park, the **Parc Clichy-Batignolles**.

TIP

Tucked away among the atmospheric streets of La Nouvelle Athènes is a hidden gem. The Musée de la Vie Romantique is a lovely, evocative museum, dedicated to the novelist George Sand and her intellectual circle of friends – Flaubert, Delacroix, Liszt and, of course, her lover Chopin. The museum has a pretty garden, open to the public for tea among the roses and wisteria.

Cutting-edge fashion on Rue Montmartre.

The reliable Parisian Métro.

CABARET LIFE

Cabaret used to be high kicks, frou-frou and unbridled revelry; today, it's high kicks, sequins, tasteful nudity and good behaviour.

The iconic Mistinguett performed her risqué routines at the Folies Bergère, the Moulin Rouge and Eldorado.

It wasn't until the Revolution that costumed masquerades and dancing became a democratic phenomenon; previously they'd been confined to the powdered world of the aristocracy. But by the 19th century, every stratum of Paris society had its *bals, café-concerts* and cabarets, though the different classes stuck to separate parts of the city: the chic crowd frequented establishments on the Grands Boulevards and Champs-Elysées, while the bohemians and lower classes whooped it up in Montparnasse. Another popular hotspot, especially in the 1890s, was the hill of Montmartre, with iconic cabarets. Le Moulin Rouge was immortalised by Henri de Toulouse-Lautrec and was where dancer "La Goulue" aka Louise Weber invented the cancan. Le Chat Noir is considered to be the first modern cabaret and its iconic poster by Théophile-Alexandre Steinlen is still a striking image around the city. Au Lapin Agile was another hotspot. (see page 158). Cabaret's heyday didn't last beyond the 1920s, and today's surviving examples are too expensive to qualify as populist entertainment, their tightly choreographed routines only occasionally catching the atmosphere of yesteryear. Still, they're good fun: the best being Le Lido and Le Moulin Rouge, (see page 152) while French speakers might enjoy the ultra-camp Cabaret Michou (80 rue des Martyrs; tel: 01 46 0616 04; www.michou.com). Some of the original 19th-century cabaret premises have now been turned into hip nightclubs.

The Moulin Rouge still trades on the image of Toulouse-Lautrec.

The short-lived Montmartre cabaret Le Divan Japonais is still remembered today thanks to this poster by Toulouse-Lautrec.

The Crazy Horse cabaret (12 avenue Georges V, 8th) elevates striptease to an art form.

The Belle Epoque cabarets of Montmartre were especially popular with the writers and artists of the day – figures such as Pierre-Auguste Renoir, who painted this famous view of revellers at the Moulin de la Galette.

ICONIC CABARET STARS

Aristide Bruant, shown on this advertisement by Toulouse-Lautrec, was an entertainer who flourished in the Montmartre cabarets: his act was largely song, with some comedy thrown in. He later became a cabaret owner.

Cabaret wouldn't be cabaret without its dancers – female dancers, that is. The first can-can performers were often part-time courtesans, but the leading lights of cabaret's Belle Epoque heyday – figures such as La Goulue and Jane Avril – were purely entertainers. Avril and La Goulue were huge stars and made a lot of money, though La Goulue lost hers in unlucky business ventures. Another hugely popular dancer in later years was Josephine Baker, a Missouri dancer who made her Paris premiere in 1925 and wowed the capital with her frenetic dancing and skimpy costumes: a skirt made of bananas and little else. Soon she was a fixture at the Folies Bergère and one of the most popular entertainers in France; Hemingway described her as "the most sensational woman anyone ever saw". Baker recorded the iconic Paris song "J'ai deux amours" in 1931.

Joséphine Baker.

The tree-lined Canal St-Martin is a delightful place to amble.

BASTILLE AND EAST PARIS

St-Germain and Montmartre may have the fame,
but the tree-lined avenues, grungy alleyways,
canalside walks and bohemian-chic streets east
from the Bastille form one of the most vibrant
parts of the modern, multicultural city.

Traditionally, Paris has been divided into the Right and Left Banks (north and south), but these days the division between the east and west is more marked. The eastern side of Paris has long been associated with the workers and – unsurprisingly – social rebellion, beginning with that most famous revolutionary act of them all, the storming of the Bastille. This was the heartland of the Paris Commune, and today trade unions still begin their May Day marches and other big demonstrations at Place de la Bastille.

Architecturally, the east of the city suffered under the reforming drive of the 1960s and 1970s. However, it is the tantalising whiff of a less salubrious past, of a grittier, less conventional Paris, that makes the most appealing areas in the east – namely Bastille, Oberkampf and, to a lesser extent, République – intriguing alternatives to the bourgeois conservatism prevailing in the western *arrondissements*. The east is certainly very run down in parts, but however much sophistication and glamour may be lacking, creativity and youthful energy abound.

QUARTIER DE LA BASTILLE

Once a fearsome symbol of royal strength, the Bastille and its surroundings fell into disrepair after the prison was destroyed during the Revolution. On 14 July 1789, when crowds stormed the prison, freeing the inmates – all seven of them – Louis XVI was unimpressed, recording in his diary, "Today – nothing." Following the dismantling of the Bastille, an enterprising workman made sculptures of the prison from the rubble and sold them to local councils, who were denounced as anti-Republican if they refused the price demanded.

Main Attractions

Place de la Bastille
Opéra Bastille
Oberkampf
Canal St-Martin
Cimetière du Père-Lachaise
Bercy Village
Parc de Bercy
Cinémathèque Française

Map

Page 171

Watching the world go by at Chez Prune.

Faubourg St-Antoine played an important role in the French Revolution.

Medieval Bastille covered present-day **Place de la Bastille** ❶ and the Arsenal to the south, at the junction of the Seine and Canal St-Martin. The modern square is a wide, busy traffic hub, with the Colonne de Juillet in the middle. The tall column was erected to commemorate the victims of the 1830 and 1848 revolutions, who are buried underneath it.

Opéra National de Paris – Bastille ❷

Address: Place de la Bastille; box office, 130 rue de Lyon
www.operadeparis.fr
Tel: 08 92 89 90 90 (within France)/ 01 71 25 27 25 (outside France)
Opening Hrs: box office Mon–Sat 11.30am–6.30pm; guided tours, days and times vary, tel: 01 40 01 19 70
Entrance Fee: charge for tours
Transport: Bastille

Dominating the square, this giant structure is now Paris's primary venue for opera and ballet, having taken over pride of place from its opulent predecessor the Palais Garnier (see page 137). Ever since it

Busy Place de la Bastille.

was opened by Mitterrand in 1989,

the "new" opera house has been the subject of much vitriol from politicians, critics, musicians and public alike. Aside from its appearance, the opera house was actually crumbling, with nets in place to keep the limestone plaques on its outer walls from falling on people's heads. The problem was resolved in 2010 with composite plaques and the façade is finally without nets.

The district to the east has changed enormously over the past 20 years. Shabby streets have been gentrified and their down at heel inhabitants displaced. Some of the rebellious charm remains in streets but the influx of the upwardly mobile has led to an epidemic of dimly lit bistro-bars. Designer boutiques and trendy cafés have sprouted up, particularly on Rue Keller, Rue Charonne, Rue de la Roquette and Rue de Lappe. Clothes shops have replaced some of the artisanal furniture workshops and shops on historic Rue Faubourg-St-Antoine.

Le Balajo (www.balajo.fr) and **La Chapelle des Lombards** (www.la-chapelle-des-lombards.com) are two Salsa clubs on Rue de Lappe that attract a mix of local Latinos and tourists. For a change of scene, **Théâtre de la Bastille** (76 rue de la Roquette; www.theatre-bastille.com) offers contemporary theatre and dance.

At 17 rue de la Roquette, **La Rotonde** (www.rotondebastille.com) is a chic bar, restaurant and nightclub. Off Rue du Faubourg-St-Antoine, you can wander through passages with workshops producing furniture, rugs and jewellery, as they have for

centuries. **Passage du Cheval Blanc** leads off from the Bastille, with courtyards named after the months of the year. **Passage de la Main d'Or**, further east, is equally intriguing.

OBERKAMPF AND RÉPUBLIQUE

As a rule, Paris is a city that doesn't change that quickly, but recent history has proved Oberkampf the exception. This area just north of Bastille has come a long way from the slums of Edith Piaf's childhood. Even ten years ago this was just another run-down district,

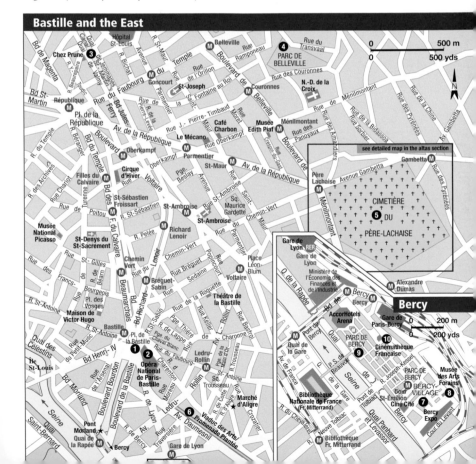

Bastille and the East

Canal views.

but these days it is one of the hippest neighbourhoods in town. Remember, though, this is the east, so we're talking urban edge rather than glamour. The vanguard may have moved on, but the bars, restaurants and clubs that make it so vibrant still remain.

The Canal St-Martin is still used by a surprising amount of boat traffic today.

Rue Oberkampf is the coolest part of the 11th *arrondissement*, especially at the upper end, east of Avenue de la République, where there's a high concentration of cafés, bars and unusual shops. Look out for trendy bars **Le Mécano** (http://lemecanobar.fr; tel: 01 40 21 35 28) and **Café Charbon** (tel: 01 43 57 55 13), with its club venue alongside, the **Nouveau Casino** (www.nouveaucasino.fr; tel: 01 43 57 57 40)

If you're looking for some of the old flavour of the area, wander down the side streets off Rue Oberkampf. Rue St-Maur, which crosses Rue Oberkampf and Rue Jean-Pierre Timbaud are lined with tiny Middle Eastern food stores and cafés.

Canal St-Martin ❸

The Canal St-Martin begins at Pont Morland by the Seine, disappears underground at Bastille (supposedly to allow troops faster access to subdue potential uprisings), then re-emerges in the 10th *arrondissement*

near Place de la République and leads up to Place Stalingrad, before continuing eastwards as the Canal de l'Ourcq through the Parc de la Villette (see page 237). The canal was dug in 1821 as a transport link for the area's factories and warehouses, many of which now house art galleries and small shops.

The canal is shielded by trees, dotted with small squares and crossed by iron bridges. It is a popular strolling and busking ground, particularly on balmy summer evenings. The bend in the canal is where you'll find the trendy **Chez Prune** café and a row of pastel-coloured shop fronts belonging to **Antoine et Lili** (www.antoine etlili.com). On the opposite bank is the **Hôtel du Nord** (www.hoteldunord. org; tel: 01 40 40 78 78), subject and title of a 1930s French film classic and now a stylish bar and restaurant. With its nine locks, the canal also makes for an attractive boat trip (Paris Canal; tel: 01 42 40 96 97; www. pariscanal.com).

BELLEVILLE AND MÉNILMONTANT

More than 60 nationalities make Belleville the melting pot of Paris. It is gradually becoming gentrified, which adds yet another layer of complexity. There are no major

The canal is just as atmospheric at night.

The canal was completed in 1825 to improve the supply of drinking water to the city.

The Marché d'Aligre (rue d'Aligre; Tue–Fri 7.30am–1.30pm; Sat–Sun 9am–2.30pm; http://marchedaligre.free.fr) is one of Paris's best and cheapest open-air food markets. Sharing the same square at the end of the street, the covered market hall the Marché Beauvau (place d'Aligre; Tue–Fri 9am–1pm; 4–7.30pm; Sat 9am–1pm; 3.30pm–7.30pm; Sun 9am–1pm), reopened after a fire in 2015, sells a wealth of oysters, foie gras, cheeses and, in season, wild boar and venison.

Reminiscing in the Parc de Belleville.

tourist attractions, five-star hotels or three-star restaurants, but it is a fascinating neighbourhood for an off-the-beaten-path excursion. In the 19th century, Belleville was a fertile country village whose springs were tapped to channel water into Paris. There are still a few old stone *regards* left – control stations for the aqueducts, particularly in the little lanes that wind around **Parc de Belleville** ④.

The park is a terraced crescent of green atop a hill with a panoramic view of Paris. The **Maison de l'Air** (currently closed) occupies one of the terraces with amazing views over the city.

Legend has it that Edith Piaf was born under a lamp-post in the Rue de Belleville, outside No. 72. There is now a plaque over the doorway that claims: "On the steps of this house, on 19 December 1915, was born, in the greatest poverty, Edith Piaf, whose voice would later take the world by storm."

The tiny **Musée Edith Piaf** (5 rue Crespin-du-Gast; tel: 01 43 55 52

Statue of a praying girl in Père Lachaise.

72, Mon–Wed 1–6pm by appointment only; donations requested), run by some of her true fans, is a

touching tribute to the diminutive queen of French *chanson*.

Incorporating part of Rue Oberkampf, the eastern district of **Ménilmontant** is another hotbed of alternative culture. The area is home to a large number of the city's immigrants, forming a melting pot of cultures. It's not unusual to find a kosher butcher, a Chinese DVD store and a Turkish snack kiosk on the same corner.

Cimetière du Père-Lachaise ❺

Address: boulevard Ménilmontant
www.pere-lachaise.com
Tel: 01 55 25 82 10
Opening Hrs: mid-Mar–Oct Mon–Fri 8am–6pm, Sat 8.30am–6pm, Sun 9am–6pm, Nov–mid-Mar closes daily at 5.15pm
Entrance Fee: free
Transport: Père Lachaise

The great tourist draw in the east is this giant cemetery, an oasis of peace in Paris. The list of famous people buried here reads like a who's who of the

city's history – Abélard and Héloïse, Apollinaire, Balzac, Edith Piaf, Oscar Wilde, Molière, Proust, Gertrude Stein, Sarah Bernhardt, Chopin and, of course, Jim Morrison, the cemetery's most visited grave, manned by a stony-faced attendant. You can get a free map at the entrance, or purchase a better one from shops that border the cemetery or sellers by its gates.

Oscar Wilde's tomb in Père Lachaise was designed by Modernist sculptor Jacob Epstein.

View over Paris from the Parc de Belleville.

Edith Piaf is buried in Père Lachaise, under a simple polished marble slab next to her last husband Theophanis Lamboukas.

The cemetery was the site of the last battle of the Paris Commune (see page 36) against the troops of the right-wing Versailles government on 27 May 1871. At dawn the next day, the remaining 147 Communards were lined up against a wall and shot. They were buried in a ditch where they fell, and the **Mur des Fédérés** (Communards' Wall) has become a socialist shrine. Nearby are monuments to both world wars.

SOUTH OF THE BASTILLE

The area south of Place de la Bastille has become a potent symbol of urban regeneration in the 21st century. A disused railway viaduct and dilapidated wine-warehouse district have been brought back to life, and are now thriving commercial and recreational centres.

Viaduc des Arts ❻

Address: 15–121 avenue Daumesnil
www.leviaducdesarts.fr

Tel: 01 71 18 75 68
Transport: Gare de Lyon
Built in 1859, during the golden age of the railways, the Viaduc de Paris supported a railway that ran from Bastille to the Bois de Vincennes, at

The winding cobbled lanes of Père Lachaise.

the viaduct have been converted into glass-fronted *ateliers* (workshops) and craft boutiques.

After exploring the shops under the viaduct you can take one of the city's most unusual walks along the former tracks on top, all the way across the south of the Bastille quarter. The railway tracks have been replaced by the **Promenade Plantée**, a leafy walkway planted with herbs and roses that provides a welcome green breathing space amongst the urban regeneration. Stretching for some 4km (2.5 miles) along the viaduct, and continuing at ground level through the Jardin de Reuilly and eastwards to the Bois de Vincennes, the promenade is accessible via staircases from the street.

It makes a very pleasant walk and an excellent way to see the city from a completely different angle.

Artist painting on fine porcelain at Le Tallec workshop in the Viaduc des Arts.

BERCY

For centuries, wine was brought to Paris by boat from Burgundy to the river port of Bercy. Today, it's Paris's newest neighbourhood. The city is busy reclaiming the old river port, while creating a "new" Left Bank across the river, around the glass towers of the National Library (see page

The Cimetière de Picpus, where the victims of the French Revolution are buried.

a time when the area between Gare de Lyon and Bastille was a thriving den of artisan workshops. But, as the railways declined in the 20th century, the viaduct fell into disrepair. Thankfully, it was saved from demolition, and reopened in 1998 as the Viaduc des Arts. The arches beneath

RELICS OF REVOLUTION

Père Lachaise is atmospheric, tranquil, and packed with the mortal remains of the great and good. But a little to the south is another graveyard that's much less known, yet just (in its way) as interesting: the **Cimetière de Picpus** (35 rue de Picpus, 12th; tel: 01 43 44 18 54; Mon–Sat 2–6pm; Métro Picpus). It's part of a still functioning convent, so privately owned, and houses the bones of thousands guillotined in the Revolutionary years: 1,298 of 1,306 people executed in nearby Place du Trône (now Place de l'Ile-de-la-Réunion) in July 1794 are here; the plots still belong to the families of the original victims. Family plots belonging to the Chateaubriands, La Fayettes (the tomb of the general is draped with an American flag due to his involvement with the American Revolutionary War), Montalamberts, Crillons, La Rochefoucaulds and more. There are also two mass graves, discovered in 1929, in one of which are the bones of the poet André Chénier. As you walk around, or sit in the little chapel, you may encounter nuns in white lace bonnets – and feel as if Paris is very far away.

FACT

Cruises along the Canal de l'Ourcq to La Villette leave from the Quai de la Loire, parallel to the Bassin de La Villette, and are organised by Canauxrama (13 quai de la Loire; tel: 01 42 39 15 00; www.canauxrama.com) and Paris Canal (see page 173).

207). A fully automated, driverless "Meteor" Métro line was opened in 1998 (line 14, the first new Métro line since 1935), linking both areas to central Paris (stops at Bercy and Cour St-Emilion for the park and village, and Bibliothèque François Mitterrand for the New Left Bank; line 6 also goes to Bercy and Quai de la Gare on the Left Bank). The two areas were linked in 2006 by a new footbridge, the elegant **Passerelle Simone de Beauvoir**.

Old stone-walled warehouses and cobbled streets have been given a new lease of life in the shape of **Bercy Village** ❼ (www.bercyvillage. com). The car-free village, centred on the cobbled Cour St-Emilion, is full of boutiques, restaurants and cafés. Parisians visit its Club Med complex to enjoy a themed meal or drink designed to inspire them to book a holiday. The futuristic UGC Ciné Cité is Paris's biggest multiplex cinema, with 18 screens showing both mainstream and arthouse films, usually in their original language with French subtitles.

Musée des Arts Forains ❽

Address: 53 avenue des Terroirs de France
www.arts-forains.com
Tel: 01 43 40 16 22
Opening Hrs: by appointment
Entrance Fee: charge
Transport: Cour St-Emilion

Another less obvious attraction is this delightful collection of antique fairground attractions. It's officially only open to groups, but individuals can call ahead to join a group tour. The beautifully crafted carousels, amusement stalls, organs and mechanical figures are displayed in the Pavillons de Bercy (www. pavillons-de-bercy.com), a former wine depot.

Parc de Bercy ❾

The busy road running down Quai de Bercy is backed by this vast park, graced by centuries-old chestnuts and plane trees. This charming green belt has nine themed sections, among them Le Jardin Romantique and Le Jardin du Philosophe. The Maison du

Students in Parc de Bercy.

Jardinage (House of Gardening) is an 18th-century building where green-fingered people share their secrets. The park has a lake filled with water from the Seine, neo-classical ruins and a trio of ornate bridges.

On the north side of the park, the former American Centre juts out among the houses and offices around the park. According to architect Frank Gehry, it expresses the spirit of a "younger country with fewer laws and fewer constraints" than Europe. It's now the magnificent and long-awaited new home for the **Cinémathèque Française** ❿ (51 rue de Bercy; museum Wed–Mon noon–7pm; www.cinematheque.fr).

The reclaimed area is also the site of the vast new Ministry of Finance, whose edifice extends out over the Seine as if it were intended to be a bridge. Its architects, Paul Chemetov and Borja Huidobro, claim it is "the monumental entrance which the east of Paris had always lacked".

The neighbouring structure, the **AccorHotels Arena**, originally known as Palais Omnisports

de Paris-Bercy, was refurbished and enlarged in 2015. Now it's a state-of-the-art sports hall, seating 20,300 spectators, which offers a varied menu of concerts and sporting events from Thai boxing to opera recitals and reggae festivals. For the current programme, see www.accorhotelsarena.com or tel: 01 40 02 60 60.

The pyramid-shape AccorHotels Arena, formerly known as Palais Omnisports de Paris-Bercy.

Frank Gehry's Cubist building now houses the iconic Cinémathèque Française.

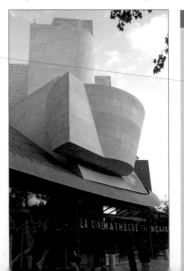

SCREENS ON THE GREEN

Paris loves cinema and cherishes its cinemas: you'll find some of the best in the world, with some of the best programming. Paris's most prestigious picture house, the **Cinémathèque Française**, reopened in 2006 in Bercy, its fifth home in 70 years. Frank Gehry's Cubist building was originally designed, in 1992, for the American Centre but was cleverly re-purposed to give a more streamlined, more ambitious edifice. There are guided tours detailing the building's architecture.

Film buffs will head straight to one of the four screens, which screen retrospectives of contemporary, vintage, undervalued and forgotten film-makers, themed seasons, B-movies, kids' screenings, avant-garde cinema, shorts, even dance films. Keep an eye out for the lively programme of conferences, talks and classes. Don't miss the museum, guarded by the robot from Fritz Lang's *Metropolis*, a treasure trove of cinematic history. Find time to explore the library, picture library, exhibition spaces, bookshop, restaurant and outdoor terrace. The feel is light, airy and inviting, and the parkside location is lovely. A truly inspiring place.

The legendary Left Bank Café de Flore.

THE LATIN QUARTER AND ST-GERMAIN-DES-PRÉS

Writers, artists and thinkers have made these districts their home since Roman times. Nowadays, fashion rules as much as philosophy on the Left Bank, but the literary legacy lives on in its historic colleges, cafés, theatres, book stalls and street markets.

The Latin Quarter and St-Germain-des-Prés, side by side, make up the heart of the Left Bank. Once the home of artists and intellectuals, they have changed over the past few decades, with high fashion replacing high art. Nevertheless, the *Rive Gauche* maintains its charm in its elegant tree-lined boulevards, narrow streets, neatly manicured parks and imposing monuments. This is the place to stroll, imbibe and look cool. Sit in the shaded parks and on café terraces by day, and scan the menus in the fairy-lit streets by night.

THE DIVIDING BOULEVARD

What is generally referred to as the Latin Quarter lies east of Boulevard St-Michel, which runs from Place St-Michel on the banks of the Seine, to cross Boulevard St-Germain in front of the ancient Roman baths of Cluny – a reminder that this was once part of the Roman city of Lutetia. This maze of ancient streets and squares has been the stamping ground of students for nearly eight centuries, and Latin was virtually its mother tongue until the French Revolution.

To the west of the Boulevard St-Michel is St-Germain-des-Prés, the historical centre of literary Paris

and Existentialism, with the oldest church in Paris at its heart, but now brimming over with designer boutiques. If St-Germain's literary credentials remain intact it is thanks to Flammarion, Gallimard, Grasset and smaller publishers, who have refused to be tempted by luxury groups' lucrative offers for their premises. As for the three monuments to the district's literary heyday – the Café des Deux Magots, Café de Flore and Brasserie Lipp – they are certainly thriving, even if their current clients

Main Attractions

Musée National du Moyen
   Age
La Sorbonne
Le Panthéon
Mosquée de Paris
Jardin des Plantes
Institut du Monde Arabe
Jardin et Palais du
   Luxembourg
St-Sulpice
Eglise St-Germain-des-Prés

Map

Page 182

Metro sign in the Latin Quarter.

Latin Quarter, St-Germain-des-Prés and Montparnasse

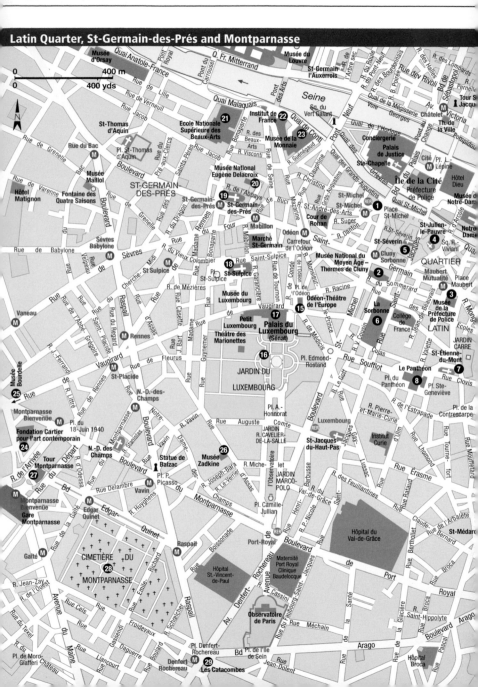

are more likely to have Cartier than Camus on their minds.

THE LATIN QUARTER

Settled by the Romans in 53 BC and a cradle of philosophy and art since the Middle Ages, the Quartier Latin conjures up contradictions and delights in paradox, epitomised by the words of student and poet François Villon in 1456, as he declared "I laugh in tears." Villon debated with professors at the Sorbonne by day, and drank with thieves in the brothels of St-Michel by night.

Villon's legacy of rebellion survived him. In 1871, Place St-Michel was the headquarters of the Commune. Then in May 1968 – a turning point in the history of post-war France – demonstrations at conditions in the Nanterre faculty led to students tearing up the old cobblestones of Boulevard St-Michel to hurl at riot police. Hundreds of students were arrested, but a year later General de Gaulle relinquished power.

The Latin Quarter had been the centre of academic life in France since the 13th century, and the university had enjoyed immense privileges (included that of obliging all who entered it to speak Latin). After 1968, however, the University of Paris was decentralised to the suburbs, and the ancient cobblestones were buried under concrete. Protests, albeit far more subdued, still take place these days, and roads are sometimes blocked by squatting students, but the academic-hothouse atmosphere of the old Quartier has gone.

Nevertheless, the Latin Quarter remains a place of happy incongruity, where numerous Greek kebab shops stand amid traditional French cafés spilling over onto the pavements, and arthouse cinemas occupy buildings with ancient academic facades.

*Cheap eateries abound
near the Boulevard
St-Michel.*

St-Michel locals.

ALONG THE BOUL' MICH

Place St-Michel ❶ revels in reck-
lessness, across the river from the
palaces of justice and salvation (the
Préfecture de Police and Notre-
Dame). Its fountain depicting St
Michael and a surprised dragon often
seems buried under scooters, lovers
and *clochards* (tramps), sitting philo-
sophically amid the youthful chaos.
Extending south from the square,
the grand Boulevard St-Michel (Boul'
Mich to the locals) will nourish the
senses, the mind as well as the stomach, with an eclectic assortment of
stalls, bookshops, alternative cinemas
and fast-food joints.

Musée National du Moyen Age – Thermes de Cluny ❷

Address: 6 place Paul-Painlevé,
www.musee-moyenage.fr
Tel: 01 53 73 78 16
Opening Hrs: Wed–Mon
9.15am–5.45pm
Entrance Fee: charge
Transport: Cluny-La Sorbonne
At the crossroads of Boul' Mich
and Boulevard St-Germain stands
the fine Hôtel de Cluny, built in
1485–98 and a rare example of a

late-medieval urban mansion. Once
the residence of the Abbots of Cluny,
these Flamboyant Gothic walls
house one of the world's finest collections of medieval artefacts. Many
of its treasures reflect life in religious
communities, such as illuminated
manuscripts, embroideries, stained

glass, liturgical vestments and various church furnishings.

Among the numerous tapestries is the exquisite 15th-century *La Dame à la Licorne* (The Lady and the Unicorn) on the first floor of the rotunda. The six panels are beautifully worked in the millefleurs style of design, using rich, harmonious colours to create a delicate allegory on the worth of the five senses. The museum also holds 21 of the original heads of the Gallery of Kings, sculpted in 1220 for the facade of Notre-Dame but vandalised during the Revolution.

The Hôtel de Cluny was constructed on the remains of a huge Gallo-Roman bathhouse complex, believed to have been built in 200 AD by the guild of *nautae* (boatmen) – ships' prows are carved on the arch supports of the *frigidarium* (cold bathhouse). As elsewhere in their empire, the Romans living in Lutetia regarded bathing as the essence of civilisation.

Cluny's medieval garden is not a reproduction of a medieval garden but an imaginative modern evocation of the Middle Ages, taking its inspiration from objects in the collection and evoking the two spheres of the spiritual and the profane that governed the medieval world.

Romanesque columns in the Musée de Cluny.

A section of the six-panel, 15th-century tapestry La Dame à la Licorne, in the Musée de Cluny.

English bookshop Shakespeare and Company.

Latin lanes

Heading east along Boulevard St-Germain you'll reach Place Maubert, a bustling market square at the centre of a network of small, medieval streets lined with a jumble of boutiques revealing their shadowy interiors to the curious. The **Musée de la Préfecture de Police ❸** (4 rue de la Montagne-Ste-Geneviève; tel: 01 44 41 52 50; Mon–Fri 9.30am–5.00pm, third Sat of each month 10.30am–5.30pm; www.prefecturedepolice.interieur.gouv.fr; free), on the second floor of a pretty bleak police station, houses an intriguing collection of macabre objects, weapons and documents, including many relics of Napoleon's much-feared police chief Joseph Fouché.

St-Julien-le-Pauvre ❹

Address: 1 rue St-Julien-le-Pauvre; www.sjlpmelkites.fr
Tel: 01 43 54 52 16
Opening Hours: daily 9:30am–1pm, 3–6.30pm

Entrance Fee: free
Transport: Cluny-La Sorbonne

Back on the banks of the Seine, quiet repose is to be found in this tiny 12th-century church, in the shadow of Notre-Dame and now a Greek Orthodox church. The Italian poet Dante is said to have prayed here in 1304. In the adjoining Square René-Viviani is one of Paris' oldest trees, a 300-year-old false acacia. Behind it is Rue du Fouarre, named after the bales of hay on which students used to perch during open-air lectures in the Middle Ages.

La Huchette

The streets around St-Julien and across Rue St-Jacques make up the Quartier de la Huchette, remarkably missed by Haussmann's 19th-century boulevard-building and today one of the most engaging and liveliest parts of the Left Bank.

Shakespeare and Company (37 rue de la Bûcherie, www.shakespeareandcompany.com) follows in the

shop was founded in 1956 by the late George Whitman, an American, who passed it on to his daughter Sylvia. It stocks a wide range of literature, from the Bard to the Beatniks, and famous expatriate writers such as William Burroughs and James Baldwin were frequent visitors. Today, it still stays open until midnight.

Le Petit Pont close by is a perfect spot from which to see the lights of the Seine shimmer at night. Here, the Quais St-Michel and Montebello offer picture-book views of the Ile de la Cité. By day, ancient bookstalls line the river banks, offering expensive antique volumes.

Trial by Revolutionary council has been replaced with jazz at the **Caveau de la Huchette** (5 rue de la Huchette). Danton and Robespierre selected guillotine victims in the cellars where musicians now jam. At No. 10, a young Napoleon dreamed of power.

St-Séverin ⑤

Address: 3 rue des Prêtres-St-Séverin; www.saint-severin.com
Tel: 01 42 34 93 50
Opening Hrs: Mon – Sat

footsteps of Paris's most famous English bookshop founded in 1921 by Sylvia Beach in Rue de l'Odéon, which published the first edition of Joyce's *Ulysses*. It closed down during World War II, and the present

> **FACT**
>
> Most of the striking stained-glass windows in the side chapels of church St-Séverin are by 19th-century Chartres master Emile Hersch.

Fresh sardines for sale on Rue Mouffetard.

The daily market on Rue Mouffetard.

TIP

The bowling alley (tel: 01 43 31 09 35; www.bowling mouffetard.fr) on 73 rue Mouffetard offers a pleasant alternative to the cheap bistros and souvenir shops.

11am–7.30pm, Sun 9am–8.30pm
Entrance Fee: free
Transport: Cluny-La Sorbonne
This beautiful flamboyant Gothic church is famous for its palm-tree vaulting and twisting spiral columns, fine stained glass, mighty organ loft and the oldest bell in Paris in its bell tower, dating from 1412.

La Sorbonne ⑥

Address: 17 rue de la Sorbonne, www.sorbonne.fr
Tel: 01 40 46 22 11
Opening Hrs: tours by appointment, tel: 01 40 46 23 48, visites.sorbonne@ ac-paris.fr
Entrance Fee: free
Transport: Cluny-La Sorbonne
Continue south along Rue St-Jacques and you'll come to the vast complex of the Sorbonne. Established in 1253 by King Louis IX (St Louis) and his confessor Robert de Sorbon, France's oldest university has been rebuilt many times since its inception as a dormitory for 16 theology students, when it began to attract thinkers from all over Europe.

In 1469, France's first print-ing press was set up here by three

Mouffetard bowling alley.

Germans summoned by Louis XI, which encouraged the growth of intellectual life. Sorbonne alum-nus Cardinal Richelieu rebuilt the university in the 1630s, but it was closed down during the Revolution, and allowed to become dilapidated. Napoleon then reopened, revitalised and expanded it to become, once more, the most important univer-sity in France. Since decentralisa-tion in 1970, though, there are now

Léon Foucault's pendulum inside the Panthéon.

THE PANTHÉON

Panthéon is one of the world's most exclusive clubs. To take up residence, you need to be a high achiever, French – and dead. It also helps if you're a man, as all but four of those interred are men. Marie Curie was the second woman to be interred but the first to be honoured in her own right. In 2015, Geneviève de Gaulle-Anthonioz and Germaine Tillion, heroines of the French resistance who were captured and deported, were honoured in a moving ceremony. One of the world's most famous artworks – *The Thinker* by Rodin – stood outside the Pantheon from 1906–22.

Here are some of France's greatest writers, Rousseau, Voltaire, Hugo and Zola; scientists, like the Curies; and politicians, including a president, Sadi Carnot, who was assassinated in 1894.

Others took longer to get to the Panthéon, as if their membership took a while to be ratified: André Malraux was reinterred here in 1996, 20 years after his death; and Alexandre Dumas *père* only joined the illustri-ous throng in 2002 – in a coffin draped in blue velvet with the motto of the Three Musketeers, "One for all, all for one". A lapse between death and national consecration was also the lot of the man who designed the Panthéon, J. G. Soufflot: he had to wait 59 years.

The mosque's tranquil main courtyard.

13 universities in Paris, and the Sorbonne has lost its omnipotence, if not its reputation.

The 17th-century chapel, commissioned by Richelieu and containing his marble tomb, overlooks the university's main courtyard. Above the tomb, beautifully carved by François Girardon, hangs a hat believed to be the cardinal's. Legend has it that the hat will fall when Richelieu's soul is released from hell.

Across Rue St-Jacques is the **Collège de France** (11 place Marcelin Berthelot; www.college-de-france.fr Oct–June Mon–Fri and Sat am; free), set up by François I in 1530 on the inspiration of the great humanist Guillaume Budé, to offer a more liberal education unfettered by the intolerance and dogmatism of the Sorbonne.

Today the college still has its academic independence, even though financially dependent on the state; lectures are open to the public without charge. Next door, the Lycée Louis-le-Grand is the school from which the 19th-century poet Charles Baudelaire was expelled, and in which Jean-Paul Sartre taught.

Montagne Ste-Geneviève

Further along Rue St-Jacques the ground rises to the top of Montagne Ste-Geneviève, site of the hermitage of the devout woman credited with saving the city from destruction by Attila the Hun in AD 451 (see page 30). She became the city's patron saint and the hilltop her shrine.

St-Etienne-du-Mont ⑦

Address: place Ste-Geneviève
www.saintetiennedumont.fr
Tel: 01 43 54 11 79
Opening Hrs: Tue–Fri 8.45am–7.45pm, Sat 8.45am–noon, 2–7.45pm, Sun 8.45am–12.15pm, 2.30pm–7.45pm
Entrance Fee: free
Transport: Cardinal Lemoine

Built in a mixture of late Gothic and Renaissance styles in the 16th century, this beautiful church was part of the abbey of Ste-Geneviève, closed by the Revolution. Inside, the remains of the saint are buried in an ornate shrine. Playwright Jean Racine (1639–99) and the scientist and philosopher Blaise Pascal (1623–62) are also buried here, and a marble slab

TIP

The Latin Quarter boasts many arthouse cinemas; film buffs will enjoy these three cinemas: Grand Action, Le Desperado (5 and 23 rue des Ecoles, 5th) and Christine 21 (4 rue Christine, 6th): all screen a rich variety of international arthouse fare, classic and modern.

near the entrance marks the spot where the Archbishop of Paris was stabbed to death by a priest in 1857.

Le Panthéon ❽

Address: place du Panthéon
www.monuments-nationaux.fr
Tel: 01 44 32 18 00
Opening Hrs: daily Apr–Sept 10am–6.30pm, Oct–Mar 10am–6pm (last admission 45 minutes before closing)
Entrance Fee: charge
Transport: Cardinal Lemoine

St-Etienne shares its commanding hilltop site with this monumental edifice. It was intended to be a new church to Ste-Geneviève, rashly promised by Louis XV when he recovered from a serious illness in 1744. Money was short, however, so public lotteries were organised to raise funds. Designed by neoclassical architect Jacques-Germain Soufflot (1713–80), who drew inspiration from Rome's Pantheon, the building was only finished just in time for the Revolution. The Revolutionaries had no use for a vast new church, however, so in 1791 it was designated a pantheon or resting-place for the "Founders of Liberty",

a monument to rival the royal mausoleum at St-Denis (see page 257). Thus Voltaire, who was transferred from the country, and Jean-Jacques Rousseau came to lie in the crypt, to be joined later by Victor Hugo, Emile Zola and Louis Braille. Nobel Prize-winning scientists Pierre and Marie Curie joined them in 1995, and the remains of World War II Resistance hero Jean Moulin were reburied here in 1964; the man who read his eulogy at the ceremony, André Malraux, did not join him until 1996.

After the Revolution, the use of the Panthéon yo-yoed from church to mausoleum to church to headquarters of the Commune, until it finally became a secular temple and mausoleum in 1885. The interior is in the shape of a Greek cross, with the iron-framed dome towering above the centre. Frescoes by Puvis de Chavannes on the life of St Geneviève line the south wall; her glorification is portrayed on the upper section of the dome. Foucault's 67-metre (220ft) pendulum hangs from the centre of the dome, returned here from the Musée des Arts et Métiers in 1995; the one hanging there today is a replica.

Playing boules in the Arènes de Lutèce.

Rue Mouffetard

Rue Mouffetard, originally the road to Rome, is one of the oldest streets in Paris; narrow, crowded, and full of cheap and cheerful places to eat. Hidden beneath it, now flows the River Bièvre, whose stench in medieval times, known as *moffettes*, gave the street its name. In its lower half is a street market (Tue–Sat, Sun am; www.rue-mouffetard.com) around the Gothic church of **St-Médard**. Walk there via the picturesque **Place de la Contrescarpe** (a few minutes from Place du Panthéon eastwards), a lively place to sit and people-watch with students skipping class, amid a maze of surrounding streets.

In the corner house (No. 1) Rabelais (1494–1553) composed his risqué rhymes, as had François Villon a century earlier. At No. 122, towards the bottom of the hill, the well carved onto the facade dates from Henri IV's reign.

THE JARDIN DES PLANTES

East of Rue Mouffetard is a quieter section of the Left Bank, the site of one of Paris's oldest parks, a distinguished mosque and intriguing museums and other attractions.

Mosquée de Paris

Address: 2 place du Puits-de-l'Ermite, www.mosqueedeparis.net
Tel: 01 45 35 97 33
Opening Hrs: Sat–Thu 9am–12am / 2pm–6pm.
Entrance Fee: charge
Transport: Monge

This green-and-white mosque was built in Hispano-Moorish style in 1922 by French architects

Literary St-Germain.

Skeletons inside the Grande Galerie de l'Evolution, Muséum d'Histoire Naturelle.

Beautiful flower display in the Jardin des Plantes.

Moving some plants around in the Jardin des Plantes.

to commemorate North African participation in World War I. Incorporating the Institut Musulman, the complex of buildings includes a museum of Muslim art, a patio inspired by the Alhambra in Granada, and an impressive selection of carvings and tiles. There is also a library, a restaurant, a delightful Moroccan tearoom and the ever popular Hammam with steam baths.

EXOTIC IMPORTS

When the Jardin des Plantes was expanding in the early 18th century, the royal doctor, Fagon, and botanists such as Tournefort and the three Jussieu brothers travelled far and wide bringing back seeds from around the world. The wild and wonderful collection of flora that resulted includes a 2,000-year-old American sequoia, a Ginkgo biloba and a Persian iron tree. A laricio pine was grown from a seed brought back from Corsica in 1774, and the pistachio tree is almost 300 years old. The oldest Lebanese cedar in France, planted in 1734, was brought from Kew Gardens in England by the Jussieu brothers' nephew, Bernard de Jussieu. The story goes that after dropping and breaking the pot containing the young plants, he nurtured the seedlings in his hat. The oldest tree in Paris, a false acacia or Robinia brought from America in 1635, is also here. The most attractive features for children are the zoo (founded by botanist Bernardin de Saint-Pierre with animals from the royal menagerie at Versailles in 1795), the 18th-century maze, the model of a stegosaurus in his garden of ancient plants and the Grande Galerie de l'Evolution, part of the Muséum National d'Histoire Naturelle.

Arènes de Lutèce ⑩

Address: rue Monge
Opening Hrs: daily summer
9am–9.30pm, winter 8am–5.30pm
Entrance Fee: free
Transport: Cardinal Lemoine

Behind a nondescript wooden doorway is the ancient gladiatorial arena of Roman Lutetia. The 15,000-seat arena – destroyed by barbarians in AD 280 – was unearthed during the construction of Rue Monge in 1869; Victor Hugo led the campaign to preserve it. Today, the arena where gladiators fought serves as a children's playground, and on a fine day echoes with the clink of *pétanque* balls.

Jardin des Plantes ⑪

Address: rue Geoffroy-St-Hilaire
www.jardindesplantes.net
Tel: 01 40 79 56 01
Opening Hrs: daily summer
7.30am–8pm, winter 8am–5.30pm
Entrance Fee: free
Transport: Gare d'Austerlitz

Paris's botanical garden was inaugurated in 1640 as a medicinal herb farm for Louis XIII. The oldest tree in Paris, a false acacia planted in 1635, is here. The garden expanded in the 1700s, with the addition of a maze, amphitheatre and exhibition galleries. In 1889, the Galerie de Zoologie opened in the grounds, to display and study the millions of specimens brought back by globe-trotting naturalists and explorers.

Opened in 1794, the **Ménagerie** or zoo (www.parczoologiquedeparis.fr, daily Sep–Jun: 10am–5pm, Jul–Aug: Mon–Fri: 10am–6pm, Sat–Sun 9.30am–7.30pm; charge) is popular with children, with its panthers, monkeys, orangutans, flamingos, reptile house and petting zoo.

Muséum National d'Histoire Naturelle ⑫

Address: 36 rue Geoffroy-St-Hilaire, www.mnhn.fr
Tel: 01 40 79 54 79
Opening Hrs: Wed–Mon 10am–6pm
Admission Fee: charge
Transport: Gare d'Austerlitz

France's official natural history museum – one of many institutions created just after the Revolution, in 1793 – has galleries on palaeontology, mineralogy, geology and even a micro-zoo, but its great attraction is the lavishly restored **Grande Galerie de l'Evolution**. Its objective is to illustrate principles of evolution

The new futuristic pavilion in the courtyard of the Institut du Monde Arabe.

Musée de la Sculpture en Plein Air ⓭

Address: quai St-Bernard - Square Tino Rossi
Opening Hrs: Daily, 24 hours a day.
Entrance Fee: free
Transport: Gare d'Austerlitz

For a riverside stroll, leave the Jardin des Plantes at Place Valhubert and head west to this park-cum-modern sculpture exhibit. It's not the prettiest space, and noisy by day, but it takes on a whole new character on summer evenings, when it's a venue for free salsa and tango sessions.

Institut du Monde Arabe ⓮

Address: 1 rue des Fossés-St-Bernard,
www.imarabe.org
Tel: 01 40 51 38 38
Opening Hrs: Tue–Thu 10am–6pm, Fri 10am–9.30pm, Sat–Sun 10am–7pm.
Entrance Fee: charge
Transport: Jussieu

One of the most striking buildings on the Seine is this high-tech blend of modern and traditional

The shuttered windows inspired by the screens of Moorish palaces at the Institut de Monde Arabe.

Basketball game in the Jardin du Luxembourg.

and dramatise the impact of human behaviour on the natural environment. The hall has retained elements of a 19th-century museum – parquet floors, iron columns, display cases – but has been completely modernised and equipped with the latest audiovisual techniques and interactive displays (mostly in French). The museum's *pièce de résistance* is the great herd of stuffed African animals that sweeps through the atrium.

panoramic terrace (free) and Le Zyriab restaurant, are breathtaking.

ODÉON AND LUXEMBOURG

The Odéon district acts as a buffer between the boisterous Latin Quarter (5th *arrondissement*) and the more refined St-Germain-des-Prés (6th *arrondissement*). From St-Michel Métro, walk along Rue St-André-des-Arts to the **Cour de Rohan**. It's worth popping in to admire the picturesque courtyards with Renaissance facades. Turn left into **Rue de l'Ancienne-Comédie**, the next street along, where **Le Procope** (www.procope.com), the first-ever café in Paris and credited with introducing coffee to the city in 1686, is still doing good business.

At Carrefour de l'Odéon, a statue of the Revolutionary leader Georges Danton marks the spot where his old house once stood. Fellow Revolutionary Camille Desmoulins lived at No. 2 before storming the Bastille in 1789. Others plotted in neighbouring streets, which now shelter some of the most bourgeois boutiques and apartments in Paris.

Arab styles, symbolic of the Institute's *raison d'être* – to deepen cultural understanding between the Western and Islamic worlds. A cultural centre and museum of Arab-Islamic art and civilisation, the nine-storey palace of glass, aluminium and concrete was designed by Jean Nouvel: its southern facade is a flat patterned wall of gleaming symmetry that recalls traditional Arab latticework. Its light-sensitive camera-like irises are supposed to open and close according to the movement of the sun, but have been plagued with problems, and most stay fixed at one setting. Fully redesigned and renovated, the museum reopened to the public in early 2012 after three years' work. In 2011, a futuristic pavilion designed by Iraqi-born architect Zaha Hadid 'landed' in the museum's main courtyard, bringing some curves to the very linear main museum. Views from the 9th floor

Stained-glass window, St-Sulpice.

Inside St-Sulpice.

The aptly-named Pont des Arts.

From here, Rue de l'Odéon – first street in Paris to have gutters and pavements – leads to Place de l'Odéon and the neoclassical **Odéon-Théâtre de l'Europe** ⓫ (www.theatre-odeon.fr; tel: 01 44 85 40 40), founded by the Comédiens Ordinaires du Roi in 1782. This is one of France's leading public theatres, and as the "Theatre of Europe" hosts many international productions – albeit mostly performed in French.

Jardin du Luxembourg ⓰

Address: rue de Vaugirard
www.senat.fr/visite/jardin
Opening Hrs: daily 8am–dusk
Entrance Fee: free
Transport: Odéon/RER Luxembourg
Beautifully landscaped, this is the quintessential Parisian park, a haven of manicured greenery where young couples rendezvous under plane trees by the romantic Baroque Fontaine de Médicis, while children push toy boats across the carp-filled pond. Statues of queens of France gaze down from the terrace, while

the thwack of tennis balls disturbs the quiet reverie of sunbathers and smartly clad nannies push babies in expensive prams.

On Wednesdays and weekends, the famous Guignol puppet show is performed in the **Théâtre des Marionnettes** (tel: 01 43 29 50 97; www.marionnettesduluxembourg.fr). More serious entertainment is found by the corner with Rue de Vaugirard, where chess is played under the fragrant orange trees. There are 200 varieties of apple and pear trees in the orchard, and an apiary that produces hundreds of kilos of honey a year. The **Musée du Luxembourg** (19 rue de Vaugirard, www. museeduluxembourg.fr; tel: 01 40 13 62 00; daily 10am–7pm, till 9.30pm Fri and Mon) puts on crowd-pulling major exhibitions.

Palais du Luxembourg ⓱

Address: www.senat.fr
Tel: 01 44 54 19 49
Opening Hrs: guided tours by appointment

Entrance Fee: free
Transport: Odéon/RER Luxembourg

The palace that presides over the gardens was built for Marie de Médicis after the murder of her husband Henri IV, on the site of a mansion that had belonged to Duke François of Luxembourg. Its Italianate style, modelled on the Pitti Palace in Florence, was intended to remind her of home. The widowed queen moved into the palace in 1625, but was forced into exile by Richelieu before its completion. During the Revolution it was used as a prison, and in World War II it was the German headquarters. Today it is the seat of the French Senate, and the adjacent Petit Luxembourg is the residence of its president.

St-Sulpice ⓲

Addess: place St-Sulpice
www.pss75.fr
Tel: 01 42 34 59 98
Opening Hrs: daily 7.30am – 7.30pm
Entrance Fee: free
Transport: St-Sulpice

From the Petit Luxembourg, Rue Garancière leads to this imposing church. Apart from one of the finest organs in Europe (used for many recitals) and Delacroix's *Jacob Wrestling with the Angel fresco*, inspired by the painter's own struggle with art, the great cavern of a church has little to offer, but attracted worldwide attention after featuring in the 2003 book *The Da Vinci Code*.

In front of the huge colonnaded facade, with mismatching towers, is a square with a magnificent fountain by Joachim Visconti, dating from 1844.

ST-GERMAIN-DES-PRÉS

Historic heart of literary Paris, St-Germain-des-Prés covers an area roughly from St-Sulpice to the Seine. Its elegant streets now house chic boutiques, yet it retains a sense of animation, with cafés spilling out onto the pavements. In the 1940s the area became a breeding ground for literature and ideas. Existentialists, inspired by Jean-Paul Sartre, Simone de Beauvoir and Albert Camus, gathered in local cafés such as Les Deux Magots and Café de Flore.

The days of black polo necks and beret-clad Existentialists locked in debate are well and truly over; the area has been colonised by designers and antique dealers. The **Marché St-Germain** shows how things have changed. Tastefully restored, the old stone market hall now contains fashion shops, a swimming pool and a concert hall, as well as a local market.

The hub of St-Germain is the junction of Boulevard St-Germain and Rue Bonaparte, with, opposite each other, **Café de Flore** and **Les Deux Magots**, which serve some of the best hot chocolate in Paris – and some of the most expensive. Once favourite haunts of the literati, these cafés are now packed with tourists.

Street art depicting Van Gogh.

Waiter at Les Deux Magots.

Eglise St-Germain-des-Prés

Address: 3 place St-Germain-des-Prés
www.eglise-sgp.org
Tel: 01 55 42 81 18
Opening Hrs: daily 8am – 7.45pm
Entrance Fee: free
Transport: St-Germain-des-Prés

Overlooking the crossroads is the oldest church in Paris, begun in AD 543, when it was built as a basilica for holy relics. It is named after St Germain, cardinal of Paris, who is buried here. Ransacked and rebuilt over centuries, the heavily restored 11th-century building blends Romanesque, Early Gothic, Baroque tombs and 19th-century frescoes. In the small square outside stands a Picasso sculpture, a tribute to his friend, the poet Apollinaire.

Musée National Eugène Delacroix ⑳

Address: 6 place Furstenberg,
www.musee-delacroix.fr
Tel: 01 44 41 86 50
Opening Hrs: Wed – Mon

Café de Flore was a favourite haunt of writer Jean-Paul Sartre.

Bouquiniste along the Quai des Grands-Augustins.

9.30am – 5.30pm
Entrance Fee: charge
Transport: St-Germain-des-Prés

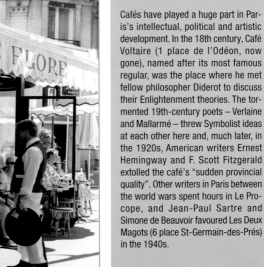

LEFT BANK RENDEZVOUS

Cafés have played a huge part in Paris's intellectual, political and artistic development. In the 18th century, Café Voltaire (1 place de l'Odéon, now gone), named after its most famous regular, was the place where he met fellow philosopher Diderot to discuss their Enlightenment theories. The tormented 19th-century poets – Verlaine and Mallarmé – threw Symbolist ideas at each other here and, much later, in the 1920s, American writers Ernest Hemingway and F. Scott Fitzgerald extolled the café's "sudden provincial quality". Other writers in Paris between the world wars spent hours in Le Procope, and Jean-Paul Sartre and Simone de Beauvoir favoured Les Deux Magots (6 place St-Germain-des-Prés) in the 1940s.

Heading east down Rue Jacob, filled with fascinating antiques and design shops, you pass Place Furstenburg, with the studio where Romantic painter Eugène Delacroix (1798–1863) lived from 1857 to his death, while he painted the frescoes in St-Sulpice. Now a museum, it has engaging sketches and memorabilia.

Ecole Nationale Supérieure des Beaux-Arts ㉑

Address: 14 rue Bonaparte, www.beauxartsparis.com
Tel: 01 47 03 50 00
Opening Hrs: exhibitions Tue–Sun 1–7pm
Admission Fee: charge
Transport: St-Germain-des-Prés

Paris's finest art school fills two *hôtels* fronting the Quai Malaquais. Begun in 1608, the main building was a monastery until the Revolution; the School of Fine Arts moved here in 1816, and today holds exhibitions of students' work and works from its extensive collection, notably of French and Italian Old Master drawings.

Close by is the imposing **Institut de France ㉒**, seat of the Académie Française, established in 1635. The select members of the illustrious institution are guardians of the French language, protecting it from the insidious onslaught of English.

Musée de la Monnaie ㉓

Address: 11 quai de Conti, www.monnaiedeparis.fr
Tel: 01 40 46 56 66
Opening Hrs: Daily 11am–7pm (till 10pm on Thu)
Entrance Fee: charge
Transport: Pont Neuf

Next door is the neoclassical **Hôtel des Monnaies**, designed by Jacques Antoine for Louis XV to replace an earlier royal mint, and completed in 1775. The *hôtel* now houses a comprehensive museum of France's money and medals.

Quai des Grands-Augustins is the oldest quay on the Seine, and is lined with antiquarian bookshops and antique dealers. Picasso lived for 20 years on Rue des Grands-Augustins, which branches off the quay.

FACT

One of the most popular bridges in Paris is the cast-iron Pont des Arts – an appropriate name for a footbridge that spans the river between the Institut de France and the Louvre. It was built in 1804, but by the 1970s had been severely damaged by three boat collisions and was closed to the public. It was rebuilt from the original plans and reopened in 1984; today it's a popular spot for picture-taking and picnics.

The Pont des Arts leads to the imposing Institut de France.

JARDIN DU LUXEMBOURG

The quintessential Paris park has leafy pathways, statues, boules, a bandstand, a boating pond and a lovely, civilised atmosphere.

The Jardin du Luxembourg is one of the largest parks in Paris: 25 hectares (63 acres). It's also one of the loveliest, with its atmosphere of quiet panache and relaxed bonhomie. Its regulars, a mongrel crowd of smart locals, students, artists, joggers, and nuns from the nearby convents, refer to it by the affectionate nickname "Luco", a shortening of the Roman name for the area, Lucotitius. As well as an art museum (the Musée du Luxembourg, see page 196), the park contains an apiary, an orangery, a bandstand, both tennis and basketball courts, *boules* pitches, a puppet theatre, tables for chess, as well as a small café. The grand Palais du Luxembourg, located on its northern edge, was constructed in 1615 for Queen Marie de Médicis, the widow of Henri IV of France, who ordered a building in Florentine style to remind her of the Pitti Palace of her childhood; she also commissioned Florentine engineer Tomasso Francini in 1630 to design her a fountain, which looks like a grotto and is a popular place to head on a warm day thanks to its shady trees. Since 1958, the palace has been home to the French parliament's upper house, the Senate.

Many people come to the tranquil gardens simply to read. Chess players meet regularly in the park.

The Essentials

Address: rue de Vaugirard
www.senat.fr/visite/jardin/index.html
Opening Hrs- daily 8am–dusk
Entrance Fee: free
Transport: Odéon/RER Luxembourg

The Palais du Luxembourg, centrepiece of the park.

The park is dotted with sculptures of varying size and theme.

Colourful toy sailing boats are available for hire on the ornamental pond directly in front of the Palais.

ART AND LITERATURE IN THE PARK

The park is studded with nearly 100 sculptures, of varying styles, eras and subject matters. Famous artists are a dominant group: Baudelaire, Flaubert, Verlaine and George Sand to name but a few. *Le Marchand de masques* features a young boy holding the face of Victor Hugo and the sculpture also features the faces of Balzac and Berlioz. Historical figures, including French queens and saints, are also present: Blanche de Castille, St Geneviève and Marie de Médicis, among others; and allegorical subjects include a scaled-down version of the Statue of Liberty (although the original scale model was cleaned up and moved to the Musée d'Orsay in 2012). The park has also featured in some famous works of literature: the two lovers, Cosette and Marius Pontmercy, first meet here in Victor Hugo's *Les Misérables* while Lambert Strether, the main protagonist in *The Ambassadors* by Henry James, has a pivotal moment in the gardens; the place also provide the backdrop to the final chapter in William Faulkner's controversial 1931 novel *Sanctuary*.

The gilded Salle du Livre d'Or inside the Senate.

MONTPARNASSE AND BEYOND

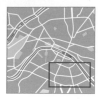

Once a backwater, Montparnasse has a unique place in modern culture – at some point between 1910 and 1939, Picasso and Matisse, Lenin and Stravinsky, Hemingway and Joyce could all be found here. Their legacy lives on amid tower blocks and redevelopment schemes, in a thriving café and nightlife scene.

The once-rural area southwest of the Jardin du Luxembourg was christened Mount Parnassus – after the classical home of Apollo and his Muses – by a local poetry society in the 17th century, when they gathered on quarry mounds to recite verses. In the early years of the 20th century, the area became a magnet for artists, composers and revolutionaries, including Chagall, Léger, Soutine, Picasso, Modigliani, Lenin and Stravinsky. Some decamped from Montmartre because of the inflated rents; others were émigrés in search of refuge or a new beginning, drawn to a place that embraced freethinkers and the avant-garde. They rented studios in the newly built-up area, and gathered in cafés and brasseries such as Le Select, Le Dôme, La Rotonde and La Coupole. Their bohemian lifestyle is as much a part of the Paris myth as the era's legacy of artworks (see page 208).

After World War II, writers and philosophers such as Jean-Paul Sartre, Simone de Beauvoir, Henry Miller and Louis Aragon moved in, patronising the same cafés clustered around the lively **Carrefour Vavin**, where the district's inescapable artery, the **Boulevard Montparnasse**, crosses Boulevard Raspail. Now relabelled Place Pablo Picasso, the Carrefour still throbs with life well into the early hours. Further east, the Closerie des Lilas was another favourite artistic haunt.

AROUND MONTPARNASSE

Above the Carrefour on Boulevard Raspail stands Rodin's dramatic **Statue de Balzac**. This sculpture so shocked the Société des Beaux-Arts when unveiled at the 1898 Salon

The Tour Montparnasse looming behind the Edgar Quinet Métro station.

– by showing the great writer in a dressing gown – that it was turned down, and only finally cast and installed here in 1939.

Fondation Cartier pour l'art contemporain ㉔

Address: 261 boulevard Raspail
www.fondation.cartier.com
Tel: 01 42 18 56 50
Opening Hrs: Tue–Sun 11am–8pm; Tue till 10pm
Entrance Fee: charge
Transport: Raspail
Jean Nouvel's impressive glass and steel building holds major contemporary art exhibitions across design, photography, fashion, performance art, video installation and painting. These are accompanied by live events called Nuits Nomades (Nomadic Nights). There are also workshops for children and the amazing gardens designed by the artist Lothar Baumgarten.

Musée Bourdelle ㉕

Address: 18 rue Bourdelle
www.bourdelle.paris.fr
Tel: 01 49 54 73 73

Opening Hrs: Tue–Sun 10am–6pm
Entrance Fee: free
Transport: Montparnasse-Bienvenüe
A showcase for the work of Modernist sculptor Antoine Bourdelle spread over his former apartment and studio. A pupil of Rodin, Bourdelle is best known for his friezes on the Théâtre des Champs-Elysées.

Musée Zadkine ㉖

Address: 100bis rue d'Assas
www.zadkine.paris.fr
Tel: 01 55 42 77 20
Opening Hrs: Tue–Sun 10am–6pm
Entrance Fee: free
Transport: Vavin
Among the influx of émigrés from Russia was Cubist sculptor Ossip Zadkine, who moved into this tiny house and studio in 1928. His sculptures are displayed around the house and garden, along with his drawings and engravings, and paintings by his wife Valentine Prax.

Tour Montparnasse ㉗

Address: 33 avenue du Maine
www.tourmontparnasse56.com

Musée Zadkine sculpture garden.

The fabulous view from the top of Tour Montparnasse.

Street art.

Tel: 01 45 38 53 16
Opening Hrs: Apr–Sep daily 9.30am–11.30pm, Oct–Mar 9.30am–10.30pm, till 11pm Fri–Sat
Entrance Fee: charge

Transport: Montparnasse-Bienvenüe Monparnasse – and the whole southern skyline – is dominated by this lumbering 59-storey tower, built in 1974 and the only skyscraper in central Paris (as no more have been allowed since then). If you've a head for heights and the stomach for a lightning-fast lift, the roof terrace offers superb views of Paris. At the foot of the tower, by an ugly shopping centre, is **Place du 18 Juin 1940**, commemorating the day when General de Gaulle sent his famous BBC radio message urging the French to carry on resisting German occupation: "We have lost a battle, but not the war."

Behind the tower is the **Gare Montparnasse**, which serves northwestern France. In the mid-19th century, thousands of Bretons emerged from this station, fleeing rural poverty and famine in Brittany, hence the many crêperies in the area.

La-Butte-aux-Cailles has a village atmosphere.

Cimetière du Montparnasse ㉘

Address: boulevard Edgar-Quinet
Tel: 01 44 10 86 50

Opening Hrs: Mar–Nov daily 8am–6pm (8.30am on Sat, 9am on Sun), Nov–Mar daily 8am–5.30pm (8.30am on Sat, 9am on Sun).
Entrance Fee: free
Transport: Raspail
Boulevard Edgar-Quinet, as well as some nice cafés and a lively morning market on Wednesdays and Saturdays, contains the third of Paris's giant cemeteries, with Père Lachaise and Montmartre. Among those buried here are artists Antoine Bourdelle and Man Ray, composer Saint-Saëns and writers Charles Baudelaire, Guy de Maupassant, Jean-Paul Sartre and Irish writer and long-term local resident Samuel Beckett.

Les Catacombes ㉙

Address: 1 avenue Colonel Henri Rol-Tanguy
www.catacombes.paris.fr
Tel: 01 43 22 47 63
Opening Hrs: Tue–Sun 10am–8pm (last entry at 7pm)
Entrance Fee: charge
Transport: Denfert-Rochereau
If you're still in macabre mood after the Cimetière, visit this labyrinth beneath Place Denfert-Rochereau,

FACT

Baudelaire, one of the star residents of Montparnasse cemetery, has two memorial stones: the first is his grave, in the sixth division; the second is the cenotaph on avenue Transversale, an eerily lifelike recumbent sculpture of the poet watched over by a brooding figure representing Ennui.

The floating Piscine Joséphine-Baker.

SHOP

Chinatown's shops are a treasure trove of gaudy decorations, trinkets and figurines, alongside elegant rice bowls, fine teas and tea sets, and good-quality Chinese dresses. Tang Frères (48 avenue d'Ivry, 13th) is a sprawling Chinese supermarket with aisle upon aisle of exotic goods, including fruit, herbs and teas, all at reasonable prices.

where the neatly stacked skulls, femurs and tibias of some 6 million departed souls line long passageways. The former Roman quarries were converted into ossuaries in 1785, when cartloads of skeletons were removed from the overflowing cemeteries at Place des Innocents and other areas. Take a torch, and someone to hold your hand, as the inscription on the door reads: "Stop. You are entering the empire of the dead."

AROUND PLACE D'ITALIE

Place d'Italie ㉚ is the traffic hub of the 13th *arrondissement*, where old districts alternate with soulless 1960s tower blocks. The square is dominated by the modern Centre Commercial Italie, but more down to earth is the food market on Boulevard Auguste-Blanqui (Tue, Fri, Sun am).

Les Gobelins is the oldest part of the neighbourhood. Traces of a Gallo-Roman necropolis were discovered here, and the tomb of the first Archbishop of Paris, St-Marcel. The district's name stems from the **Manufacture Nationale des Gobelins** (42 avenue des Gobelins; tel: 01 44 08 53 49; www.mobilier

La-Butte-aux-Cailles graffiti.

national.culture.gouv.fr; daily 11am–6pm; charge) the tapestry factory founded in 1662. Visitors can watch weavers at work.

Paris-Plage in full swing.

OFF THE WATERFRONT

The "New" Left Bank is one of the locations for Paris-Plage, which brings the beach to the city in July and August (see page 107). Since 2006 the fun on the Left Bank has revolved around a new floating swimming pool, Piscine Joséphine-Baker, that's moored up by the Bibliothèque Nationale. It's a purpose-built barge that also features a huge sun deck, cafeteria and children's play area. Water is pumped from the river before being treated to crystalline cleanliness. A huge, sliding glass roof covers the pool, and when the sunshine's hot enough, it's pulled back to let in the open air. There's even a packed programme of exercise classes.

Hidden just south of Place d'Italie is the tranquil, village-like *quartier* of **La Butte-aux-Cailles**. In the 1900s the hill was still covered with working windmills and water mills. Its narrow, cobbled streets offer some of Paris's friendliest, cheapest bars. The hub of activity is around the Rue de la Butte-aux-Cailles and Rue des Cinq-Diamants. A few trendy restaurants have opened here, but it's still an unassuming, delightful area to visit.

Chinatown is a close neighbour, roughly bordered by Avenue d'Italie and Avenue d'Ivry – a mini-city of skyscrapers where streets are lined with kitsch gift shops, Thai grocery shops, Vietnamese pho noodle bars and Chinese *pâtisseries* and tearooms.

THE "NEW" LEFT BANK

The "new" *Rive Gauche* is Paris's biggest urban renewal project since the 1860s, when Baron Haussmann

sliced up the city's medieval heart to carve out his tree-lined boulevards. New streets and buildings are going up in a zone of rusty factories and disused railway tracks extending south for 130 hectares (320 acres) from Gare d'Austerlitz. With the new national library as its centrepiece, the area is gradually taking shape as new offices, apartments and schools go up, and the **MK2-Bibliothèque** multiplex cinema draws in the public at weekends. A new parked has been constructed, the Jardin des Grands-Moulins Abbé-Pierre, which is split into three areas: a sports section, a green space and a children's playground. Art galleries, upmarket cafés, restaurants and boutiques have cropped up, and the **Rue Louise-Weiss** is the focus of a small gallery scene.

Bibliothèque Nationale François-Mitterrand ③

Address: quai François-Mauriac

Restaurant in La Butte-aux-Cailles.

Paris Schooling

"Paris was where the 20th century was," said Gertrude Stein, and for a time all the fads and fashions, the art and ideas of modernity came together in Montparnasse.

Today the name "Ecole de Paris" still conjures up the incredible artistic momentum of Paris between the wars, the mood of intellectual ferment, of artistic and literary debate, and the arrival of cocktails, jazz and the tango. It was neither a school nor a movement, nor an organised group – rather it is a label that has come to designate those mostly foreign-born artists who congregated around Montmartre in the first years of the 20th century and, after World War I, in the cafés and studios of Montparnasse.

A magnet for artists

Paris was an intellectual and cultural magnet; a bold city, where academic tradition had been challenged by the Impressionists,

Multi-talented Kiki de Montparnasse.

Cézanne and the Fauves; a city open to avant-garde currents like Cubism, Expressionism and Dadaism. Paris was a magnet also for foreign artists, in search of refuge or a new beginning, be they Jews escaping the ghetto, Russians fleeing the Revolution or Americans after adventure escaping from Prohibition.

Though not a style, the Ecole de Paris is associated with figuration, not abstraction, a form of expressionism and a certain relationship to the contemporary world, not Surrealism. At its centre were Chagall, Soutine, Modigliani, Foujita, Pascin, Kisling and Van Dongen. More peripheral figures include Picasso, Chana Orloff, Marie Vassilieff and Maurice Utrillo.

Life imitates art

The Ecole de Paris, though, was as much to do with lifestyle as artistic style. Artists rented studios at La Ruche, Cité Falguière, Villa Seurat and countless other studio courtyards around Montparnasse. Exchanges also took place in the area's cafés and brasseries, such as Le Dôme, La Rotonde and the glamorous La Coupole.

The artists painted each other, but also writers, critics and poets like Apollinaire, Max Jacob, Gertrude Stein and Henry Miller. Their paintings captured drinkers, dancers and prostitutes, Parisian icons like the Eiffel Tower, and themes like clowns and the circus.

The queen of Montparnasse

Curiously, though, the figure that best epitomised the spirit of artistic Montparnasse was not an artist, but model and muse Kiki de Montparnasse. Born Alice Prin in 1901, she arrived in Paris during World War I and became part of the artistic circle who met at La Rotonde. Painted by Soutine, Van Dongen, Kisling and Foujita with her characteristic black fringe, she also entered the Surrealist pantheon, as mistress and model of Man Ray; she starred in several of his experimental films and in his photo *Le Violon d'Ingres*. Beautiful, charming, outrageous, Kiki painted, danced, sang lewd songs at Le Jockey and published her memoirs at the age of 28.

www.bnf.fr
Tel: 01 53 79 59 59
Opening Hrs: Mon 2–8pm,
Tue–Sat 9am–8pm, Sun
1–7pm
Entrance Fee: charge
Transport: Bibliothèque François
Mitterrand

Designed by Dominique Perrault and opened in 1997, the library cost over €1 billion to build. Its 90-metre (300ft) glass towers are meant to evoke open books on end, set on top of a plank-covered plinth 305 metres (1,000ft) long. Like it or not, the library is undeniably impressive.

Nightlife on the Seine

The new Left Bank is to have its own "Latin Quarter", with 30,000 students on a new campus around a giant rehabilitated grain store. Streets have been extended to the Seine and the river banks landscaped, and this is Paris's hottest new nightlife area, with boats and barges where you can eat, drink and dance: the **Batofar**, **La Dame de** **Canton**, and **El Alamein**, to name but a few, are all moored by Quai de la Gare near the Bibliothèque.

The imposing Bibliothèque Nationale François-Mitterrand.

The barges along the Seine have become a nightlife hotspot.

The Eiffel Tower, world symbol of the French capital.

THE EIFFEL TOWER AND LES INVALIDES

Enjoy the views from the top of Paris's great iron tower and in the dark depths of its sewers. At ground level, there are elegant boulevards, imperial splendour and art galore: Impressionists at Musée d'Orsay, exotic artefacts at Quai Branly and new creativity at Palais de Tokyo.

The Eiffel Tower looms up above the Seine like a giant playing hide-and-seek among the grand apartment blocks of the 7th *arrondissement*. At its foot is the **Champ de Mars**. This stretch of parkland, once a military exercise ground, now teems with tourists all year-round. Facing the tower at the southern end of the Champ de Mars is the **Ecole Militaire**, the military academy where Napoleon learned his trade. Glimpses through the shuttered security are rare, but occasional open doorways reveal fountains, statues and soaring stairways. To the east, the **Esplanade des Invalides** is another splendid carpet of green that rolls from the gleaming gilt-domed church of the **Hôtel des Invalides** to the Seine and the Pont Alexandre III.

Drift away from the crowd-filled Champ de Mars and savour the gracious tree-lined streets bordered by *hôtels* (mansions), whose sumptuous apartments are occupied by senior civil servants, captains of industry and rich, retired Americans.

THE TROCADÉRO

Across the river lies the 16th *arrondissement*. This takes up a sizeable slice of western Paris and, like the 7th, it is full of smart residences occupied by wealthy inhabitants. Not for those in search of the arcane or the avant-garde, this is the bastion of BCBG (*bon chic, bon genre*), a never-never land of big hair, Burberry plaid, diamond rings, pedigree dogs and Berthillon ice cream. The reason most tourists and Parisians venture here is to visit one of the museums around Place du Trocadéro, or to gaze at the magical views across the Seine to the Eiffel Tower.

Main Attractions

Trocadéro
Musée d'Art Moderne de la Ville de Paris
Palais de Tokyo
Eiffel Tower
Musée du Quai Branly
Les Egouts (the Sewers)
Les Invalides
Musée Rodin
Musée d'Orsay

Map

Page 212

The Musée Rodin's beautifully landscaped garden.

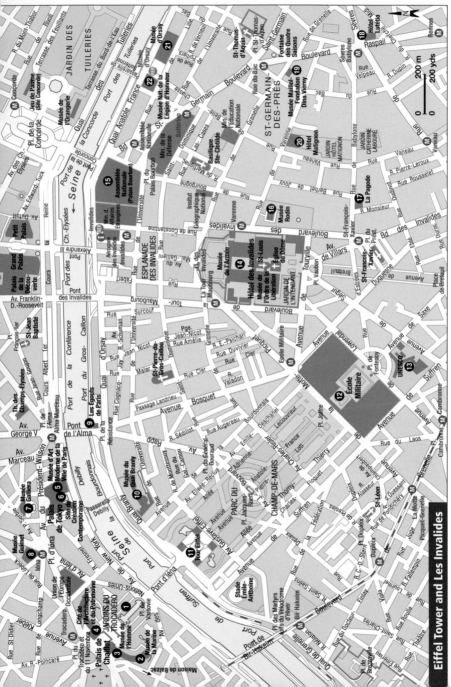

Eiffel Tower and Les Invalides

Begin by crossing the Pont d'Iéna to the Trocadéro. From here, framed by the cascading fountains and gold statues of the **Jardins du Trocadéro** **①**, the Eiffel Tower can be seen at its most magnificent. Dominating the Place du Trocadéro is the **Palais de Chaillot**, built for the Paris International Exhibition of 1937. The imposing pseudo-classical palace was designed in the shape of an amphitheatre, with its wings following the original outline of the old Trocadéro, built for Paris's 1878 Exhibition. The building holds three museums and the Théâtre National de Chaillot.

Musée de la Marine **②**

Address: www.musee-marine.fr
Tel: 01 53 65 69 69
Opening Hrs: Wed–Mon 10am–6pm
Entrance Fee: charge
Transport: Trocadéro
In the west wing, this museum charts the history of France as a seafaring nation. Hundreds of models, often of extraordinary craftsmanship, cover everything from historic battleships and three-masted schooners to langoustine fishing boats and primitive canoes. A fine painting collection includes Vernet's series of the ports of France, but the centrepiece of the museum is the carved and gilded imperial barge built for Napoleon. Other displays include navigational instruments, sections on shipbuilding and rope-making, carved whale teeth and giant lighthouse lenses.

Musée de l'Homme **③**

Address: www.museedelhomme.fr
Tel: 01 44 05 72 72
Opening Hrs: Wed–Mon 10am–6pm, till 9pm on Wed
Entrance Fee: charge
In the same wing, the renovated "Museum of Mankind" presents the evolution of humanity and society in a biological, social and cultural context. It is also a research and educational centre with workshops, lectures dedicated to the past as well as to the future of humankind.

Cité de l'Architecture et du Patrimoine **④**

Address: www.citechaillot.fr
Tel: 01 53 58 51 52 00

Gilded statue on the terrace of the Place des Droits de l'Homme, in front of the imposing Palais de Chaillot.

View from the Eiffel Tower.

DRINK

The Musée du Vin (rue des Eaux, 16th; tel: 01 45 25 63 26, www.musee duvinparis.com), with its inappropriate address, is a sweet little museum devoted to all things related to the vine: tools, bottles, corkscrews and more. Visits conclude, naturally, with a glass of wine.

Young skaters enjoy the vast, smooth open spaces of the Trocadéro.

Striking an Eiffel Tower pose for the camera.

Opening Hrs: Wed–Mon 11am–7pm, till 9 pm on Thu
Entrance Fee: charge
Transport: Trocadéro
Located in the east wing, this museum and research centre hosts large-scale exhibitions on related topics. A state-of-the-art audiovisual centre is open to the public.

AROUND THE TROCADÉRO

Against the backdrop of the Palais de Chaillot, the terraces and grassy banks of the garden play host to flamboyant skateboarders and rollerbladers. At night, when the ornamental pool's huge fountains are lit up, the sight is spectacular.

West of Chaillot, villagey **Passy** is an upmarket residential area around busy shopping streets, on Rue de Passy and Rue de l'Assomption.

Maison de Balzac

Address: 47 rue Raynouard
Tel: 01 55 74 41 80
Opening Hrs: Tue–Sun 10am–6pm
Entrance Fee: free
Transport: Passy

Wealthy Passy also hides the atmospheric house where the great writer Honoré de Balzac penned much of his massive *Comédie Humaine*,

furnished as at the time and with a rich collection of Balzacian manuscripts and memorabilia, including the coffee pot that sustained his legendary 15-hour writing sessions.

PLACE D'IÉNA

Between the Trocadéro and the Champs-Elysées, this busy boulevard-hub is the site of an unusual mix of museums and culture centres.

Musée d'Art Moderne de la Ville de Paris ❺

Address: 11 avenue du Président-Wilson
www.mam.paris.fr
Tel: 01 53 67 40 00
Opening Hrs: Tue–Sun 10am–6pm
Entrance Fee: free, charge for special exhibitions
Transport: Iéna

To the east, another of the 1937 Exhibition buildings, the Palais de Tokyo, contains the city of Paris's own, underrated modern art collection. It gives a coherent survey of 20th-century art, especially relating to Paris, with strong holdings of the Fauvists, the *Ecole de Paris* (see page 208) and conceptual art from the 1970s. Its masterpieces include works by Picasso, Matisse (among them *La Danse*, 1932), Modigliani, Van Dongen and Soutine, and Raoul Dufy's gigantic mural *La Fée Electricité* (Electricity Fairy), a celebration of light and energy commissioned for the 1937 Exhibition; displayed in an oval room, it serves as a reminder of the building's original purpose as the Electricity Pavilion.

Palais de Tokyo – Site de Création Contemporaine ❻

Address: 13 avenue du Président-Wilson
www.palaisdetokyo.com
Tel: 01 81 97 35 88
Opening Hrs: Wed–Mon noon–midnight
Entrance Fee: charge
Transport: Iéna

In the east wing of the Palais, this state-funded contemporary arts centre, opened in 2002, is intended

The Musée d'Art Moderne de la Ville de Paris.

Wall relief at the Musée d'Art Moderne de la Ville de Paris.

Tribal art at the Musée du Quai Branly.

to serve as a laboratory for current art production. In 2012 it reopened after increasing its size from 8,000 sq metres (86,111 sq ft) to 22,000 sq metres (236,806 sq ft), making it one of Europe's largest contemporary art centres. An adventurous, multi-disciplinary programme focuses on young artists through a dynamic mix of exhibitions, performances and workshops, and its fresh atmosphere, the hip "Tokyo Eat" restaurant-café, a stylish souvenir shop and the unique late-night opening hours have made it hugely popular.

Musée Galliera – Musée de la Mode de la Ville de Paris ❼

Address: 10 avenue Pierre 1er de Serbie
www.palaisgalliera.paris.fr
Tel: 01 56 52 86 00
Opening Hrs: during exhibitions Tue–Sun 10am–6pm, till 9 pm on Thu
Entrance Fee: charge
Transport: Iéna

The imposing Italianate Palais Galliera is hard to miss. It houses the municipal collection of some 12,000 outfits and 60,000 accessories dating from the 18th century to the present day. To rotate these rich holdings, only a fraction of which can be displayed at a time, two exhibitions are held each year focusing on a historic period, a theme or a designer.

Musée Guimet ❽

Address: 6 place d'Iéna
www.guimet.fr
Tel: 01 56 52 54 33
Opening Hrs: Wed–Mon 10am–6pm
Entrance Fee: charge
Transport: Iéna

One of the world's finest museums of Asian art, the Guimet begun as the private collection of industrialist Emile Guimet but later taken over by the French state, the once-dusty museum has been enlarged and rejuvenated with spacious daylit galleries that give its collections new visibility. The superb collection includes oriental art, statuary and textiles from China, Japan, India, Tibet, Nepal, Pakistan, Afghanistan, Korea and Vietnam – a reflection of France's colonial past. The prize exhibits are the Cambodian Buddhist sculptures from the temples of Angkor.

ACROSS THE PONT DE L'ALMA

Cross the Pont de l'Alma to discover two very different but equally fascinating museums.

Les Egouts de Paris – The Paris Sewers ❾

Address: entrance by 93 quai d'Orsay
www.egouts.tenebres.eu
Tel: 01 53 68 27 81
Opening Hrs: Sat–Wed May–Sept
11am–5pm, Oct–Apr 11am–4pm
Entrance Fee: charge
Transport: RER Pont de l'Alma

For a surprisingly entertaining experience, descend into the bowels of Paris for an excursion into the sewer system, and a museum full of interesting facts about waste and water. Described by Hugo in *Les Misérables* as the "other Paris", this network of tunnels follows the well-known streets above ground. Accompanied by a film and, unsurprisingly, a strong odour, this is the alternative tour of Paris.

Musée du Quai Branly ❿

Address: 37 quai Branly
www.quaibranly.fr
Tel: 01 56 61 70 00
Opening Hrs: Tue, Wed, Sun
11am–7pm, till 9pm Thu, Fri, Sat
Entrance Fee: charge
Transport: RER Pont d'Alma

FACT

The branches of the city's sewers, which follow the road network almost exactly, are signposted with the same names (and the same blue-and-white plaques) as the streets above them. There are 2,050km (1,274 miles) of sewers inside the Paris ringroad; the first public tours took place in 1867, during that year's Paris Exhibition.

The Musée du Quai Branly was designed by French architect Jean Nouvel.

View of the Musée du Quai Branly from the Eiffel Tower.

Taking in the spectacular view from the top of the tower.

Unlike his predecessor François Mitterrand, President Jacques Chirac was not known for his *grands projets*, but in his last years in office he sponsored this new museum of world cultures, in a multicoloured building by architect Jean Nouvel. It houses a fabulous collection of tribal art, including African, Aztec and Mayan artefacts, many formerly in the Musée de l'Homme or other museums but which can now be seen in a whole new light.

THE EIFFEL TOWER

It's a short walk from the Musée du Quai Branly to Paris's trademark.

Tour Eiffel ⑪

Address: www.toureiffel.paris
Tel: 08 92 70 12 39
Opening Hrs: daily mid–June–early Sept 9am–midnight, early Sept–mid–June 9.30am–11pm
Entrance Fee: charge
Transport: RER Champ de Mars-Tour Eiffel

The view up from the tower's second floor.

When Gustave Eiffel's icon of iron girders was chosen as the centrepiece to the Exhibition of 1889, he was delighted. But his designs were met with a barrage of opposition. Opéra architect Charles Garnier

No less than 12kg (26 lb) of gold were needed when the Eglise du Dôme was regilded in 1989.

and novelist Guy de Maupassant were the most vocal opponents; Maupassant organised a protest picnic under the tower's four legs

EIFFEL STATISTICS

At 321 metres (1,054ft) high, including the masts, the Eiffel Tower was the tallest structure in the world until the Chrysler Building was constructed in New York in 1930. On hot days, the ironwork expands, enabling it to grow as much as an incredible 15cm (6ins).

A masterpiece of engineering, Gustave Eiffel's tower, world symbol of Paris, is held together with 2.5 million rivets, and the 10,100 tonnes of iron exert a pressure of 4kg per sq cm (57lb per sq inch), equivalent to the weight of a man sitting on a chair. Even in the strongest winds, the tower has never swayed more than 12cm (4ins). Up to 40 tonnes of paint are used when it is painted, every seven years. There are 360 steps to the first level, where there's an audiovisual presentation of the tower's history, and another 700 to the second. There's always a queue for the lifts, which travel 100,000km (62,137 miles) a year. On the third level is Gustave Eiffel's sitting room. On a clear day panoramas of over 65km (40 miles) can be seen; enjoy a tipple in the champagne bar while taking in the view

Strolling in the Parc du Champ de Mars.

– "the only place out of sight of the wretched construction".

However, the Parisian public loved their new tower, and only a few years later it was being lauded by writers and artists such as Apollinaire, Jean Cocteau, Dufy and Utrillo. Surviving a proposal for it to be dismantled in 1909, when the placing of a radio transmitter at the top saved the day, the tower is now swarmed over by some 6 million visitors a year.

The first two floors are negotiated on foot or by lift, and then another lift goes up to the top which, as well as a weather station and air navigation point, is an observation platform with space for up to 800 people at a time. With the recently fitted new transparent floor and glass balustrades, the 1st floor of the tower situated 57m from the ground offers a brand new experience, if somewhat vertiginous. But the views are awesome. At night, the tower is transformed into a giant piece of diamond-studded jewellery, as 20,000 flashbulbs start flashing on the hour to create a stunning five-minute display.

Along the Champ de Mars

Stretching beneath the Eiffel Tower are the ever-crowded gardens of the Champ de Mars. For centuries this was a market garden supplying vegetables to Parisians, but after the Ecole

Napoleon's tomb inside the Eglise du Dôme.

The interior of the dome was painted by Charles de la Fosse.

Militaire was built in 1752 it became a parade ground, with capacity for 10,000 men. The first balloon filled with hydrogen rather than hot air was launched from here in 1783, and it was the venue for the first-anniversary celebration of the storming of the Bastille – a miserable Louis XVI was forced to attend.

At the far end of the gardens is the imposing **Ecole Militaire ⑫** (closed to the public). Louis XV commissioned the military college to help men of little means learn the art of soldiering, and a young Napoleon studied here for a year in 1784. The splendid 18th-century academy, designed by Jacques-Ange Gabriel, is still the foundation stone of French military expertise. With its Cour d'Honneur enclosed by colonnades, the main façade borders Avenue de Lowendal.

UNESCO ⑬

Address: 7 place Fontenoy
www.unesco.org
Tel: 01 45 68 10 00
Opening Hrs: visits by reservation

Entrance Fee: free
Transport: Ségur

Behind the Ecole Militaire is the foundation for reconciliation and understanding, the headquarters of the United Nations cultural

Statue of Napoleon in his coronation robes.

Bronze casts of Rodin's work are displayed in the lovely rose garden.

organisation. The graceful, Y-shaped building was designed by an alliance of American, French and Italian architects, and engineers led by Bauhaus member Marcel Breuer. Inside, 195 countries cooperate on educational, scientific and cultural projects. A temple of modern art, its decoration is equally cosmopolitan: Joan Miró ceramics, Henry Moore sculptures, an Alexander Calder mobile as well as a huge Picasso mural. The Japanese garden displays a spine-chilling relic: a stone angel found after the atomic bomb blast at Nagasaki in 1945.

LES INVALIDES – MUSÉE DE L'ARMÉE ⑭

Address: www.musee-armee.fr
Tel: 08 25 05 44 05
Opening Hrs: daily Apr–Oct
10am–6pm, Nov–Mar 10am–5pm
Entrance Fee: charge, includes Dôme and museums
Transport: Invalides

The gleaming dome of the **Hôtel des Invalides** is a masterpiece of French Baroque architecture and one of Paris's most prominent landmarks. Behind it is a remarkable set of 17th-century buildings commissioned by Louis XIV to house and care for retired and wounded soldiers. It also served as the royal arsenal, and it was from here, in 1789, that revolutionaries comandeered 30,000 rifles for the storming of the Bastille. Napoleon, whose wars kept the hospital full, restored the institution to its former glory, making the church a necropolis and regilding its dome. The **Eglise du Dôme**, built as a royal chapel for Louis XIV, now contains Bonaparte's tomb. The emperor's body was returned to the city from St Helena in 1840, with much pomp and ceremony, and eventually laid to rest in the church crypt.

Spread across either side of the Cour d'Honneur, the large **Musée de l'Armée** offers an extensive view of man's inhumanity to man and skill at warfare from the Stone Age to Hiroshima, with a terrifying selection of weapons and armour, and

The 7th arrondissement is a smart, residential neighbourhood.

Open tour bus on its way to Les Invalides.

Rodin's The Thinker.

dog-walkers and rollerbladers. On its west side is a series of *pétanque* courts, and nearby is a small airport coach terminal, by the Métro-RER station.

Around Les Invalides

Heading east along the Seine towards the Musée d'Orsay, you immediately pass the august colonnades of France's parliament, the **Assemblée Nationale (Palais Bourbon)** ⓕ (www.assemblee-nationale.fr). The extravagant neo-Grecian columns facing the river were grafted onto the earlier 18th-century palace by Napoleon, to complement his Madeleine across the river, and they now shelter an armed guard in charge of protecting the 577 *députés* (Members of Parliament).

Musée Rodin ⓖ

Address: Hôtel Biron, 79 rue de Varenne
www.musee-rodin.fr
Tel: 01 44 18 61 10
Opening Hrs: Tue–Sun 10am–5.45pm, till 8.45pm Wed
Entrance Fee: charge
Transport: Varenne

poignant displays on the two world wars. In a separate wing, the **Musée de l'Ordre de la Libération** (www.ordredelaliberation.fr) commemorates the Resistance fighters who received the Order of Liberation, created by De Gaulle in 1940.

Stretching to the Seine, the grassy **Esplanade des Invalides** is much loved by strollers, joggers,

Just next to Les Invalides stands the **Hôtel Biron**, a charming

SOLID GENIUS

François-Auguste-René Rodin was born in the Quartier Latin in 1840 to a working-class family, and grew up wandering the markets of Rue Mouffetard. Trained at the Petite Ecole from age 14, but rejected by the Ecole des Beaux-Arts, he worked as an assistant for ornamental artists and the sculptor Carrier-Belleuse, training himself while visiting the Jardin des Plantes and horse markets on Boulevard St-Michel for inspiration. A trip to Italy in 1876, where he discovered Michelangelo, transformed his career. Further stimulus came from his incessant love affairs, notably with the now internationally acclaimed fellow artists Camille Claudel and Gwen John, interrupted only for a while when he took holy orders as a reaction to the death of his sister in a convent, after she had been rejected in love by one of his own close friends. Chastity did not suit him, though, and he soon returned to his mistresses and his art. Among his masterpieces are *The Kiss, The Thinker, The Burghers of Calais* and the unfinished *Gates of Hell*, on which he worked from the 1880s until his death from influenza in 1917. Many of his sculptures were criticised during his lifetime.

18th-century *hôtel particulier* that's now forever linked to its most famous occupant. Auguste Rodin's first critically acclaimed sculpture was *The Age of Bronze* (1877), depicting a naked youth caressing his hair, modelled by a Belgian soldier. The establishment was shocked, maintaining that the statue was too lifelike to be regarded as art. Eventually, the French government bought the statue, and Rodin's reputation was confirmed.

Rodin came to live in the Hôtel Biron in 1908, and stayed here until his death in 1917. He paid his rent with his best works, which form the basis of the museum's exquisite collection. Here you can admire *The Kiss* (removed from the Chicago World Fair of 1893 for being too shocking), *The Thinker* (reputedly Dante contemplating the Inferno), *The Burghers of Calais*, *The Hand of God* and many other works.

Restored to their white marble finish, the statues ripple with life. Bronze casts of many of Rodin's major works are displayed outside in the beautiful rose garden, amid the lawns, hedged enclosures, pools, mature trees and topiaried yews, providing a context for the studies and smaller works around the house. Also in the garden is one of Paris's most atmospheric museum cafés.

Faubourg St-Germain

The area lying east of Les Invalides is well worth exploring, an elegant, aristocratic extension of St-Germain-des-Prés built up in the 18th century. Begin with Paris's most interesting cinema and teahouse, **La Pagode** (www.etoile-cinemas.com/pagode/) **17** in Rue de Babylone. The tea is strong, the gardens tropical and the films up to date, and the building itself is simply stunning, a 19th-century replica of a Far Eastern pagoda whose main auditorium is lined with golden dragon motifs.

When the nobility moved out of the Marais in the 18th century, the rich and famous built new town houses across the river from the Tuileries. Beautifully preserved, they are now mostly shut away behind heavily secured gates, since only French ministries and foreign governments can afford the rent. On Boulevard Raspail (at No. 45) stands

The Musée d'Orsay's architecture is as impressive as the collections inside.

FACT

The smart 16th arrondissement is the domain of the wealthy. Passy and Auteuil, in its southern half, were spa towns in the 17th century; Passy still has a villagey air, but has a few busy shopping streets; Auteuil, less commercial, has many grand residences.

the **Hôtel Lutétia** ⑱ (http://lutetia-hotel.parishotelinn.com), its extravagant statued facade fronting a deluxe four-star hotel where Charles de Gaulle enjoyed his first night of married life. When the hotel was requisitioned by the Gestapo in 1940, the owner bricked up the vintage wine cellar and, even though the hotel staff were interrogated to reveal the whereabouts of the *cave*, no one talked.

Continue walking along Boulevard Raspail towards the Seine until you come to Rue de Grenelle on the left, a narrow street stacked with beautiful buildings, including the Swiss and Dutch embassies, the Ministry of Education and the National Geographic Institute.

Musée Maillol – Fondation Dina Vierny ⑲

Address: 61 rue de Grenelle
www.museemaillol.com
Tel: 01 42 22 59 58
Opening Hrs: daily 10.30am–7pm, till 9.30pm Fri
Entrance Fee: charge
Transport: Rue du Bac

The Hôtel Bouchardon is a distinguished 18th-century residence

The clocks are vestiges from the museum's past as a railway station.

where the poet Alfred de Musset lived between 1824 and 1839, before going on an oriental voyage of discovery with George Sand. Since 1995 it has housed this museum displaying the works of sculptor Aristide Maillol, along with art by contemporaries Cézanne and Degas, drawings by Matisse, multiples by Duchamp, and works by Russian and Naïve artists. Dina Vierny, its founder and owner, was an art dealer and model for Maillol, whose sculptures adorn the Tuileries.

Rue de Varenne, one street over, has a collection of fine old houses, the most famous being the Paris residence of the French Prime Minister, **Hôtel Matignon** ⑳, which has the biggest private garden in the city.

MUSÉE D'ORSAY ㉑

Address: 62 rue de Lille
www.musee-orsay.fr
Tel: 01 40 49 48 14
Opening Hrs: Tue–Sun 9.30am–6pm, till 9.45pm Thu
Entrance Fee: charge
Transport: RER Musée d'Orsay

No visit to Paris is complete without a pilgrimage to this spectacular former railway station, crammed

FAIR'S FAIR

Paris owes many famous buildings and monuments – even its most famous, the Eiffel Tower – to the series of World Fairs, *Expositions universelles*, it staged in the 19th and 20th centuries. The first Trocadéro was built for the Exhibition of 1878, and demolished to make way for the Palais de Chaillot, centrepiece of the city's last big fair in 1937, an event that also produced the Palais de Tokyo. Other durable constructions are the Grand and Petit Palais, built for the *Exposition* of 1900 – as was the Gare d'Orsay, now the Musée d'Orsay.

World Fairs were grand jamborees of national pride, a chance to show the world a catalogue of French triumphs in technology and the arts. The idea came from London, but Paris took to it with verve, staging its first fair in 1855; the second, in 1867, gave its patron Napoleon III great popular prestige. The 1937 fair was very different, a symbolic face-off between Nazi Germany and Soviet Russia, whose grandiose pavilions were opposite each other. Notably, the Spanish pavilion featured Picasso's famous *Guernica* – while the Exhibition jury awarded a Grand Prix to Hitler's architect Albert Speer, for his design for the Nazi rally grounds at Nuremberg.

The Palais de Chaillot, built for the Paris International Exhibition of 1937.

full of the finest art spanning the period from 1848 to World War I. Built in two years in 1898–1900, it was almost torn down to make way for a hotel in 1970. Prompted by public outcry, the government fulfilled the prophecy of painter Edouard Détaille, who said at the opening ceremony in 1900 that the station would make a better museum. Its glass-and-iron construction was a triumph of modernity, rivalling Eiffel's tower, while the facade reflected the Louvre across the river. Redesigned as a museum by Italian architect Gae Aulenti, it opened in 1986.

The museum is arranged on five levels around a vast central aisle, a grand setting for sculpture by artists such as Rudé, Cavalier and Guillaume. The best pieces are by Carpeaux, the Second Empire's foremost sculptor, including his controversial *La Danse* for the Opéra Garnier.

Other artworks are displayed in chronological order; starting on the ground floor, there are famous works by Ingres (notably *La Source*), Romantic painting by Delacroix, like the colourful *La Chasse aux Lions (Lion Hunt)*, and Manet's nude *Olympia* (1863), pronounced pornographic at the 1865 Paris salon and considered the first "modern" painting.

The museum's biggest draw, its Impressionist paintings, hang on the crowded top floor, bathed in soft light from the glass-vaulted roof. The galleries are full of paintings by Monet, Manet, Renoir, Pissarro, Degas and Cézanne. At the end is a small café with great views of Paris.

On the mezzanine is the gallery of neo and Post-Impressionists which includes the work of Van Gogh, Gauguin, Seurat and Signac. There is also a fine collection of Art Nouveau decorative arts here.

Next door, the **Musée National de la Légion d'Honneur** 22 (www.legiondhonneur.fr; tel: 01 40 62 84 25; Wed–Sun 1–6pm; Tue groups only), with a pleasant courtyard, tells the story of France's most celebrated award.

THE EIFFEL TOWER

It's the thing that, more than any other, says "Paris" – a true icon that was originally intended to stand for a mere 20 years.

It's the most famous monument in the world – or at least, a member of a very select club: only the Pyramids and the Statue of Liberty (whose framework was also designed by Eiffel) enjoy similar renown. Built for the 1889 Exposition Universelle, it took over two years to build; it remained the world's tallest building until 1930, when it was overtaken by the Chrysler Building in New York (though the tower gained another 20 metres (65ft) in 1957, with the addition of television aerials). Not everyone liked it at first, but today the tower is the most visited attraction in Paris. It has three platforms open to the public, at 57, 115 and 276 metres from the ground as well as three lifts (although not all are in operation concurrently). There are two restaurants: Le 58 Tour Eiffel (www.restaurants-toureiffel.com) on the first level, and the haute cuisine Jules Verne on the second plus a champagne bar at the top. Highlights of any visit include an exhibition on the history of the tower on the first level and the view from the terrace on the second level. Whatever you do, don't leave without buying an Eiffel Tower clock, keyring or snowdome.

The tower took two years to build. The first man to climb it was the Prince of Wales (later Edward VII).

View over the Champ de Mars from the tower.

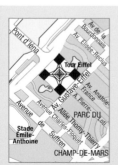

The Essentials

Address: www.toureiffel.paris
Tel: 08 92 70 12 39
Opening Hrs: daily mid-June–early-Sept 9am–midnight, early-Sept–mid-June 9.30am–11pm
Entrance Fee: charge
Transport: RER Champ de Mars-Tour Eiffel

The Trocadéro esplanade and gardens, built for the 1937 World Fair, offer a splendid view of the Eiffel Tower.

This stamp dates from 1939 and commemorates the 50th anniversary of the Eiffel Tower.

Braving the 360 steps up to the first level.

MAN OF IRON

Gustave Eiffel.

"Gustave Eiffel epitomises all that is best of 19th-century architecture, heralding the Modern movement: inventiveness, lightness, structural expression, movement… The [Eiffel Tower] still inspires us today." So says Richard Rogers, and he's not alone. Born in Dijon in 1832, Eiffel was a prolific engineer who made a lasting mark: his bridge designs, for instance, were exported all over the world, including to Portugal where his viaduct still crosses the river Douro. He was also responsible for designing a bridge over the river Truyère in the Massif Central region of France, Pest railway station in Hungary and the dome of the observatory in Nice. When his most famous creation was finished, he drew some heavy fire for its design, but always argued that the structure's curves had been chosen more for their structural benefits than for their looks. Like his works, the man was an enduring figure: he died in 1923, aged 91.

Even after nightfall, the tower is an unmissable landmark: thousands of flashbulbs fire in a dazzling diamond-like frenzy every hour.

MUSÉE D'ORSAY

The national museum of 19th-century art is best-known for its French Impressionist paintings, but its collection also contains key pieces from other artistic movements.

Reminders of the museum's former life as a railway station.

When the Gare d'Orsay was built to coincide with the Exposition Universelle of 1900, painter Edouard Détaille said it looked like a palace of fine art – and that, just over eight decades later, is exactly what it became. For all that, the Musée d'Orsay is the museum that very nearly didn't happen. It was no longer a railway station by 1950 (its platforms were too short for modern trains) and was lined up for demolition. However, after a short spell as a theatre, President Giscard d'Estaing had it turned into a museum devoted to art – painting, sculpture and decorative works – from the period between 1848 and 1914, and since then it has been one of the city's three most important museums. The building itself is an impressive sight.

The Essentials

Address: www.musee-orsay.fr
Tel: 01 40 49 48 14
Opening Hrs: Tue–Sun 9.30am–6pm, till 9.45pm Thu
Entrance Fee: charge
Transport: RER Musée d'Orsay

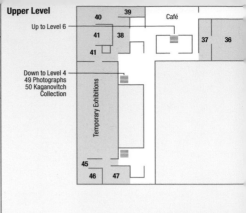

Upper Level

Up to Level 6

40 · 39 · Café
41 · 38 · 37 · 36
41

Down to Level 4
49 Photographs
50 Kaganovitch Collection

Temporary Exhibitions

45
46 · 47

Middle Level

54 · 52 · 53 · 56
51 · 55

Restaurant

72

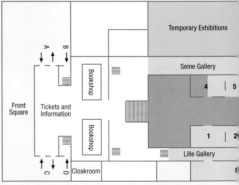

Ground Floor

Temporary Exhibitions

Seine Gallery

A · B

Front Square

Tickets and Information

Bookshop

4 · 5

Bookshop

1 · 2

C · D

Cloakroom

Lille Gallery

8

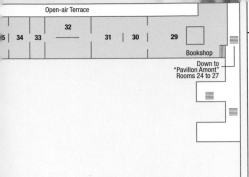

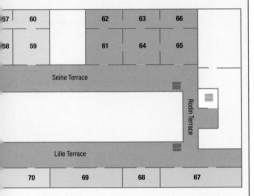

Admiring the smaller works.

THE HIGHLIGHTS

The Musée d'Orsay follows a chronological route, from the ground floor to the upper level and then to the mezzanine, thereby showing links between the Impressionist painters and their forerunners.

Ground Floor

In the central sculpture aisle, there are several works by Carpeaux including the charming *The Crown Prince and his dog Nero*; lifelike busts of proud citizens of the African colonies by Cordier; and a sensuous, naturalistic *Eve after the fall* by Delaplanche. To the rear of the aisle is a superb model of the Opéra Garnier. The decorative arts galleries on the ground floor and mezzanine parallel developments in fine art: on the lowest level, don't miss the wardrobe by Diehl and Brandoly. The ground floor also has a number of paintings: the scandalous *Origin of the World* by Courbet; Daumier's expressive *Scène de Comédie* and his 24 painted clay heads, *Célébrités du Juste Milieu*, and Ingres's *La Source*, are also worth looking out for on this floor.

Middle Level

The Rue de Lille side houses a gallery of neo and Post-Impressionists including the major works by Van Gogh and also a terrace with sculptures by Rodin, Bourdelle and Maillol.

Edouard Manet's Le Déjeuner sur l'Herbe caused a scandal when it was first exhibited in 1863.

Renoir's The Bathers (1818–19). The theme of the bathers dominates the final season of the painter's work.

Claude Monet's wife Camille is the Woman with a Parasol (1886).

The Gare d'Orsay was converted into a museum between 1977 and 1986. From the museum's upper level, visitors get a strong sense of the original railway station layout: the platforms ran either side of what is now the central sculpture aisle. The vast, curved glass-and-iron roof is also shown to advantage, as is the elaborate decoration over the side arches. The glorious gilded clock at the far end is original.

Hippolyte Moulin's Secret from on High (1879) depicts a life-size nude Mercury (Hermes) whispering a secret to a herm, knowing that it will never repeat what he tells it.

UPPER LEVEL

Take a break from all the art at the museum's Café Campana.

Most visitors come to see the Impressionist paintings in the Galerie des Hauteurs. In the first room (29) is Manet's master-piece *Le Déjeuner sur l'Herbe*; his pastels are exhibited in rooms 39 and 40. Room 30 mainly has works by Sisley but also contains Monet's *The Poppies*, an image that went on to sell thousands of greetings cards. Next along (rooms 31 and 33) are Degas's elegant bronze dancers, which were originally created in wax then cast in bronze after his death, and also his beautifully lit paintings of dance classes and performances; interestingly, although one of the founders of the movement, Degas considered himself to be a "realist" and not an "impressionist". Monet and Renoir (rooms 32, 34,36) stuck closest to the Impressionist ideal of pure colour and modelling through light, while the 3D, still lifes of Cézanne (room 35), who originally exhibited with the Impressionists but differed from them in his search for underlying structure, pave the way for Cubism and modern art. The Impressionists would have been proud of Café Campana, the eaterie here named after the Brazilians who designed it; the shimmering walls and lights transport diners to a watery, dreamlike environment that Monet himself could have conjured up. Before leaving, step out onto the terrace and take in the view over the Seine.

Snapping the masters.

L'Absinthe by Edgar Degas (detail). In its first showing in 1876, the picture was panned by critics, who called it ugly and disgusting.

Achieving almost perfect symmetry in the Jardin du Luxembourg.

PARIS PARKS

Paris may often have seen itself as the quintessential city, but even born-and-bred Parisians feel a yearning for open spaces – and in the past few decades highly inventive, all-new parks have been added alongside the city's charming gardens and historic woodland.

I
n 1759 Voltaire wound up his famous novel *Candide* with the line "We must cultivate our garden", but it was not until the 19th century that Paris began to make parks and gardens a touchstone for the health of the capital. While the 1980s may be remembered as the decade of the *grands projets* and monumental building, the 1990s and the new millennium have seen the city's parks and gardens flourish. Politicians have realised that improving the urban environment is a vote-winner, and thus derelict industrial sites are flowering and blossoming into suburban parks with a fervour not seen since Haussmann's day. More than ever, Parisians are looking to their green spaces as an escape from the increasing congestion and stress of urban living.

BOIS DE BOULOGNE ❶

Transport: Porte Maillot, Porte Dauphine, Porte d'Auteuil, Les Sablons
Past the *Périphérique* ringroad to the west of Paris, the Bois de Boulogne is one of the reasons why the 16th *arrondissement* alongside it is preferred by the wealthy as a place to live – Avenue Foch, perhaps the most expensive residential street in the capital, leads straight to its park gates. Cradled by an elbow of the Seine,

this 860-hectare (2,125-acre) expanse of woods and gardens has been the Sunday afternoon playground for generations of Parisian families. Historically, it has also had a reputation for love, as successive kings used to house their mistresses here, and after Louis XIV opened the woods to the public in the 17th century, it was noted that "marriages from the Bois de Boulogne do not get brought before the Right Reverend".

In 1852, Napoleon III had the surrounding wall of the royal hunting

Main Attractions
Bois de Boulogne
Parc de la Villette
Parc Floral de Paris
Jardins Albert Kahn

Map
Page 237

Boating in the Bois.

TIP

Every June and July, the lovely Orangerie de Bagatelle, in the Bois de Boulogne, hosts candlelit recitals of the music of Chopin. For information, tel: 01 45 00 22 19 or see www.frederic-chopin.com

ground, built by Henri II, demolished and the park remodelled following the example of Hyde Park in London. Today it offers gardens, wild woods, horse racing at two of France's most famous racecourses, Longchamp and Auteuil, a sports stadium, boating, museums, restaurants and theatre.

Discovering the Bois

The best way to explore the Bois is by bicycle, which can be rented (May–Sept daily, Oct–Apr Sat–Sun) opposite the Porte des Sablons entrance. A network of cycle paths and nature trails criss-crosses the woods, giving easy access to the vast park and its lakes and waterfall. Note that walking around the park at night is a risky undertaking. It is also possible to fish and rent a boat in the Bois. For details visit www.paris.fr/jardins.

Near the Porte des Sablons is the **Jardin d'Acclimatation**: (www.jardin-dacclimatation.fr; tel: 01 40 67 90 85; daily 10am–7pm), an amusement park for children, with a hall of mirrors, zoo, go-kart racing, a wooden fort, theatre and puppet show (Wed, Sat, Sun at 3pm and 4pm, daily during school

holidays). However, the main attraction of the Bois is the **Fondation Louis Vuitton** complex (www.fondationlouis vuitton.fr; tel: 01 40 69 96 00; Mon, Wed–Fri noon–7pm, till 11pm Fri, Sat–Sun 11am–8pm) designed by world famous architect Frank Gehry who called it a "cloud of glass" (although locals prefer to call it the "iceberg"). Opened in late 2014, it houses 11 art galleries including the fabulous collection of France's richest man – Bernard Arnault, and is the biggest contemporary art museum in the capital.

Further west, the **Parc de Bagatelle** (charge) surrounds a small château built by the Count of Artois, later Charles X, who bet Marie-Antoinette he could build a house in three months. The bet was won at great cost, hence the ironic name *bagatelle* (meaning "paltry sum"). The gardens are magnificent, with 8,000 roses blooming from June to October, a walled iris garden flowering in May and a display of water lilies in August. Art exhibitions and classical concerts are held in the Trianon and Orangerie during the summer season.

The vast Bois de Boulogne seen from the Eiffel Tower.

In the centre of the Bois is the **Pré Catalan**, the most romantic spot in western Paris. In spring, narcissi, tulips and daffodils carpet the manicured lawns, bathing the foot of the colossal copper beech, over 200 years old, whose branches span over 500 metres/yds. **Le Pré Catalan** (http://restaurant.leprecatelan.com; tel: 01 44 14 41 14) restaurant offers sumptuous fare in elegant Belle Epoque surroundings.

Nearby, the **Jardin Shakespeare** (tel: 06 12 39 30 69; www.jardinshakespeare.com;) is planted with flowers, trees and shrubs that feature in Shakespeare's plays: there's *Macbeth's* heather, Mediterranean herbs from *The Tempest* and Ophelia's stream. In summer, open-air productions of the Bard's plays (usually in French) are presented in the leafy theatre.

Musée Marmottan ❷

Address: 2 rue Louis Boilly, www.marmottan.fr
Tel: 01 44 96 50 83

Opening Hrs: Tue–Sun 10am–6pm, till 9pm Thu
Entrance Fee: charge
Transport: La Muette

Just inside Passy by the eastern border of the park is this dazzling little museum, with 65 paintings by Monet that were donated by his son Michel in 1971, among them his celebrated *Impression Soleil Levant* (1872), which gave its name to the Impressionist movement. Once home to avid art collector Paul Marmottan, this beautiful 19th-century mansion also exhibits its works by Pissarro, Renoir, Gauguin and Berthe Morisot, as well as a superb collection of First Empire furniture.

PARC DE LA VILLETTE ❸

Address: www.lavillette.com
Transport: Porte de Pantin, Porte de la Villette

In northeast Paris, nestling against the *Périphérique*, this multi-purpose park and leisure area was one of the most spectacular 1980s *grands projets*.

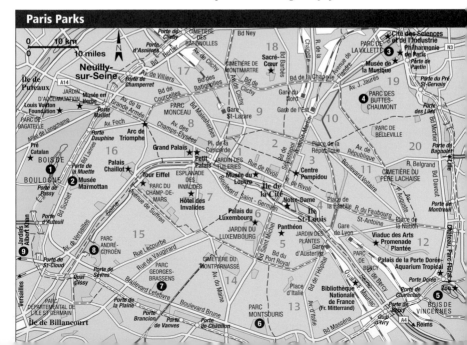

Paris Parks

Philharmonie 2 exhibit.

Model boat on one of the lakes within the Bois de Boulogne.

Built on the site of a huge abattoir, rendered obsolete by improved refrigeration techniques and poor design (the cows could not even get up the steps), its 55 hectares (136 acres) of futuristic gardens surround a colossal science museum, the **Cité des Sciences et de l'Industrie** (www.cite-sciences.fr; tel: 01 40 05 80 00; Tue–Sat 10am–6pm, 10am–7pm). It's not a museum for academics: exhibits are interactive, with buttons, levers, keyboards and screens to keep mind and body alert. There's even a Mirage jet fighter to inspire budding aviators.

Begin at *L'Univers*, with a spectacular planetarium and explanation of the inexplicable Big Bang. *La Vie* is an eclectic mix of medicine, agriculture and economics. *La Matière* reproduces a nuclear explosion and lets you land an Airbus 320, and *La Communication* has displays of artificial intelligence, three-dimensional graphics and virtual reality.

La Géode (www.lageode.fr; tel: 01 40 0579 99; Tue–Sun 10.30am–8.30pm) is a giant silver ball housing an IMAX cinema; there is also L'Argonaute (charge), a decommissioned submarine, and Cinaxe (charge), a flight simulator-cum-cinema, which is definitely not for the queasy. The refurbished Planétarium (charge) boasts digital projectors that bring new visual panache to its virtual journeys through space.

Music and *Folies*

Further south is the ultra-modern **Philharmonie de Paris 1** (http://philharmoniedeparis.fr; tel. 01 44 84 44 84; Tue–Fri noon–6pm, Sat–Sun 10am–6pm, evening of day of events) designed by Jean Nouvel, who accused Philharmonic management of sabotaging his project but eventually lost his case. Opened days after the 2015 Charlie Hebdo terrorist attacks, it boasts a multi-level concert hall, rehearsal rooms, an educational centre, exhibition spaces and conference hall. The adjacent building is the **Philharmonie 2**, formerly known as the Cité de la Musique, designed by Christian de Portzamparc. It houses an amphitheatre, a concert hall, learning spaces, a media library and the **Musée de la Musique** (Tue–Fri noon–6pm, Sat–Sun 10am-6pm). The museum charts the development of classical, jazz and folk music, with a collection of over 4,500 rare musical instruments from the 17th century

onwards. Some of the highlights include a Stradivarius violin and a Pleyel piano that belonged to Chopin.

Portzamparc also designed the 34,000 m2 **Conservatoire national supérieur de musique et de danse de Paris** (www.conservatoiredeparis.fr; tel. 01 40 40 45 45; Mon–Sat 8am– 10pm, Sun 9am–8pm). One of the world's greatest training grounds for music and dance, students put on 300 free shows throughout the year, to reserve a place tel. 01 40 40 48 47. Also in La Villette is the **Zénith de Paris** (www.zenith-paris.com), a multi-purpose, indoor arena. Seating 6,293 people, this is one of the largest venues in Paris and attracts all the big name acts.

The gardens of La Villette are the biggest built in Paris since Haussmann's time. Designed by Bernard Tschumi and opened in 1993, they comprise several thematic areas, such as the **Jardin des Frayeurs Enfantines** (Garden of Childhood Fears), with a huge dragon slide, and the **Jardin des Vents** (Garden of Winds), home to multicoloured

bamboo plants. Abstraction continues in the form of Tschumi's *folies*: red, angular tree houses – minus the trees – that are scattered throughout the park, each with a special function, such as play area, workshop, day-care centre or café. After dark, blue strip lighting gives the gardens a strange, other-worldly aspect.

PARC DES BUTTES-CHAUMONT ❹

Opening Hrs: daily 7am–dusk
Transport: Botzaris, Buttes-Chaumont

South of La Villette towards Belleville, this charmingly eccentric park was built by Haussmann in the 1860s on the site of a rubbish dump and gypsum quarry. The uneven ground provided a perfect setting for some wooded, rocky landscaping, and a lake was created around an artificial 50-metre (165ft) "mountain", capped by a Roman-style temple, with a waterfall and a cave containing artificial stalactites. It's a little like a picturesque fantasy, and children love to explore here. Ice-skating, boating and donkey rides are also on offer

Blue skies reflected in La Géode in the Parc de la Villette.

TIP

From mid-July to the end of August every year, the Parc de la Villette stages a popular free film season, Le Cinéma en Plein Air; seating is on one of the park's big lawns, and the huge screen is inflatable. The park also holds a 10-day jazz festival each September. For information about both events, tel: 01 40 03 75 75 or log on to www.villette.com.

Fun and games at the Cité des Sciences.

Musée de la Musique posters.

down below, and the puppet show or "Guignol" in the open-air theatre has been a popular attraction for over 150 years.

BOIS DE VINCENNES ⑤

Transport: Château de Vincennes, Porte de Charenton, Porte Dorée

On the southeast edge of Paris lies this expanse of wood and parkland, another former royal hunting ground, which Philippe-Auguste enclosed in the 12th century with a 12km (7-mile) wall to protect its forests from poachers. Renowned for its château, racecourse and zoo, the Bois de Vincennes has other modern attractions such as **La Cartoucherie** (http://cartoucherie.fr), which was once an ancient arsenal, but is now a complex of theatres where plays are staged by some of France's most avant-garde companies.

Château de Vincennes

Address: www.chateau-vincennes.fr
Tel: 01 48 08 31 20
Opening Hrs: 21 May–22 Sept 10am–6pm, 23 Sept–20 May 10am–5pm
Entrance Fee: charge

King Charles V built much of this medieval fortress in the 1360s, and Henry V of England died here in 1422. Over the centuries it has had many uses: it has served as a prison – incarcerating among others the philosopher Diderot and Revolutionary Mirabeau – a porcelain factory and, under Napoleon I, an arsenal. Napoleon III began a restoration programme, but the château was severely damaged by the Germans in 1944. Restoration is now complete, and there is a museum in the 14th-century keep.

Parc Floral de Paris

Address: www.parcfloraldeparis.com
Tel: 01 49 57 24 84
Opening Hrs: daily 9.30am–dusk
Entrance Fee: charge

Just south of the château, this park within the Bois is a favourite with families, who wander the Vallée des Fleurs, in bloom all year-round, the pine wood and the water garden, and take advantage of the adventure playground. At weekends in summer it puts on an excellent season of jazz and classical concerts by the lake, which are free for visitors already inside the park.

Parc Zoologique de Paris

Address: www.parczoologiquedeparis.fr
Tel: 01 44 75 20 00
Opening Hrs: July–Aug daily
9.30am–7.30pm; Sept–mid Oct
Mon–Fri 10am–6pm, Sat–Sun
9.30am–7.30pm; mid-Oct–Jun daily
10.am–5pm.
Entrance Fee: charge

On the western side of the Bois is Paris's main zoo. It was all the rage when it opened in 1934, because its animals roamed free. Each enclosure is different, inspired by the animals' natural environment, and a giant artificial mound is home to 60 species of animals, including monkeys, gazelles and goats.

Palais de la Porte Dorée – Aquarium Tropical

Address: www.aquarium-portedoree.fr
Tel: 01 53 59 58 60
Opening Hrs: Tue–Fri 10am–5.30pm,
Sat–Sun 10am–7pm
Entrance Fee: charge

A few minutes' walk from the zoo is the city's aquarium, which has tropical fish and also a crocodile pit, in the basement. The Palais is a masterpiece of Art Deco design, built as a "Museum of the Colonies" at the height of the colonial era; its sculpted facade celebrates the *"Gloire"* of the French Empire in Africa, Asia and the South Pacific. It was formerly also home to a museum of tribal art, but this collection has been absorbed by the **Musée du Quai Branly** (see page 217). The Palais also houses the Cité Nationale de l'Histoire de l'Immigration dedicated to the history of immigration in France (www.histoire-immigration.fr; same opening hours as above).

NEW-AGE EXPERIMENTS AND ORIENTAL GARDENS

Parc Montsouris ❻

Transport: Porte d'Orléans, RER Cité Universitaire

In the south of Paris, this 19th-century park is made up of 16 hectares (40 acres) of gently undulating grass and trees. It was much loved by Cubist Georges Braque and the exiled Lenin, who both used to live close by. On the day the park opened in 1878, the lake suddenly and inexplicably drained dry, and its engineer committed suicide.

Roman-style temple at les Buttes.

High spirits in the Parc des Buttes-Chaumont.

Playing boules.

Parc des Buttes-Chaumont.

Parc Georges-Brassens ❼

Transport: Porte de Vanves

The far-flung southwest of Paris is the capital's most populated district and home to two of its newest parks. Parc Georges-Brassens was opened in 1982 on the site of another old abattoir, and is now a child's playground paradise, with playhouses, rock piles, rivers and mini-lakes. It includes a garden designed for the blind: close your eyes and follow the trickling of fountains and smell the fragrant foliage. Braille signs give relevant information on herbs and shrubs. Along Rue des Morillons there are also 700 vines, which produce a few hundred bottles each year of the red Clos des Morillons (full-bodied, fine bouquet). It is sold at the wine shop **Le Repaire de Bacchus** (www.lerepairede bacchus.com) at 75 rue des Morillons, and proceeds go to charity. At weekends, the ancient market halls host a giant antiquarian book market.

Parc André-Citroën ❽

Transport: Balard, Javel-André Citroën, RER Boulevard Victor

Further west on the banks of the Seine, the once-derelict site of the Citroën

car factory has been turned into this stunning modern park, designed by Gilles Clément and Alain Prévost, where futuristic formal gardens mix with spacious lawns and a wild garden; two huge glasshouses glisten next to the esplanade, and children leap in and out of spurting fountains.

Beyond the glass greenhouses lie two themed gardens – one "black"

GREEN-FINGERED EMPEROR

It was Napoleon III who gave Paris its first public gardens; before that, the only landscaped green spaces in the city were owned by noblemen, who sometimes let ordinary citizens have the use of them, and sometimes didn't. Napoleon's motives had as much to do with a desire to improve the city's hygiene as with philanthropy. The Parcs et Plantations department, set up by Haussmann to turn the emperor's gardening zeal into reality, created most of the parks and gardens visible in the city today: some 1,834 hectares (4,532 acres) in all. The gardens were actually designed by Jean-Pierre Barillet-Deschamps, who was inspired by the "English garden" style, and built by the engineers Jean-Charles Alphand and Eugène Belgrand (the latter's other major achievement was to improve the Parisian sewerage system). Napoleon took a close interest in the work; he had acquired a taste for English landscape gardening styles during his years of exile in London, and he oversaw the laying out of the Bois de Boulogne personally. Other notable green spaces landscaped during his rule included the Bois de Vincennes, the Parc de Montsouris and, one of the greatest triumphs of the Parcs et Plantations designers, the Parc des Buttes-Chaumont.

and one "white" – and on the park's northeast side a series of six more colourful gardens have been planted to a different colour scheme – gold, silver, red, orange, green and blue. Each garden is linked to a metal, a planet, a day of the week, and a sense: thus gold is linked to the sun, Sunday and the intangible sixth sense. The tethered **Ballon de Paris** hot-air balloon (www.ballondeparis. com; charge) lifts 135 metres (440ft) into the air at weekends to give visitors a stunning panoramic aerial view over the capital.

Jardins Albert Kahn ❾

Address: 14 rue du Port, Boulogne-Billancourt
http://albert-kahn.hauts-de-seine.fr
Tel: 01 55 19 28 00
Opening Hrs: Oct–Apr Tue–Sun 11am–6pm, May–Sept Tue–Sun 11am–7pm.
Entrance Fee: charge
Transport: Boulogne-Pont St-Cloud

More traditional horticulture is found beyond the city limits in the suburb of Boulogne-Billancourt, where the legacy of financier Albert Kahn (1860–1940) takes the form of an

extraordinary park, created between 1895 and 1910. Japanese, English and French gardens lie alongside an Alpine forest and North American prairie. The grass is cut at different levels, from "beatnik" style to "sailor boy". Kahn called the gardens "the plant expression of my thoughts concerning a reconciled world", an idea complemented by 72,000 photographs of world landscapes taken between 1910 and 1931, and exhibited on permanent rotation.

The Japanese garden in the Jardins Albert Kahn.

Amongst the ferns and flowers at the Parc Floral.

LA DÉFENSE

West of the capital, just outside the city ringroad, is a brave new world of glass-faced skyscrapers and architectural daring.

Named after a 19th-century statue called *La Défense de Paris*, which commemorated the French soldiers who defended Paris during the Franco-Prussian war, La Défense was a business district from the outset, and its visitor attractions are understandably few: mainly a shopping mall and a multiplex cinema. That said, it's worth visiting for the buildings themselves: from the 1950s, when the first landmark edifice went up (the vast, parachute-shaped CNIT), La Défense has been an architectural playground. The most iconic sight is La Grande Arche a 110-metre (360ft) rectangular arch that once housed a couple of techy museums and a gourmet restaurant as well as offices. However, following problems with the lifts, the Arche is now closed to the public. Throughout La Defence, monumental modern art such as Calder's The Red Spider and Miro's Two Fantastic Characters jostle for space with the skyscrapers. Plans are afoot for two major new edifices to be completed by 2020: Tours Soeurs (200 metres/984ft), conceived by Christian de Portzamparc, and the Norman Foster-designed Hermitage Plaza, two skyscrapers that will reach 320 metres/1050ft and will be the tallest buildings in the European Union.

The Essentials

Address: www.la defense.fr
Tel: 01 49 07 27 27
Opening Hrs: daily Apr–Aug 10am–8pm, Sept–Mar 10am–7pm
Entrance fee: charge
Transport: La Défense

Office workers running on their lunch break near the Quatre-Temps shopping centre.

The glass-clad sphere of the IMAX theatre.

The Arche was designed as a 20th-century version of the Arc de Triomphe, with which it aligns along the Axe Historique that runs through Paris.

La Défense isn't only concrete and glass – there are fountains, gardens and sculptures like Red Spider (1976), by Alexander Calder.

SKYSCRAPERS, CAMERA, ACTION!

Jacques Tati in Playtime.

With such a striking alternative to the classic Paris topography right on their doorstep, it's surprising that relatively few French film-makers have brought their cameras to La Défense: this is, after all, the nearest thing France has to Manhattan. When it does come to the screen, the districts' emphatically 21st-century urban scenery is used either for sheer dramatic impact, or as visual shorthand for the soullessness of modern life, as in Bertrand Blier's social satire *Buffet Froid*. With similar intentions, Jacques Tati set his 1967 comedy *Play Time* in a concrete jungle clearly intended to represent La Défense – although it was all built on a studio back lot in Joinville, some distance from Paris. In the British film *Mr Bean's Holiday*, the hapless protagonist ends up by accident at La Grande Arche instead of the Gare de Lyon. The area has also appeared in several French music videos, notably the song *Ding Dang Dong* by Les Rita Mitsouko where the band drives through the streets of Paris.

The extensive use of glass on many of the buildings at La Défense fosters a certain futuristic feel – and the multiple reflections make for some interesting photo opportunities.

DISNEYLAND PARIS

A fairy tale castle, classic Disney fantasy and eye-popping rides, plus a full-scale hands-on movie studio, crashing cars and state-of-the-art special effects – Walt's vast dream world promises fast fun for the entire family.

Main Attractions
Big Thunder Mountain
Pirates of the Caribbean
It's A Small World
Space Mountain

Map
Page 257

With twice as many visitors a year as the Eiffel Tower or the Louvre, Disneyland Paris (www.disneylandparis.com; tel: 01 60 30 60 53; for more details, see box) is the most popular tourist attraction in Europe. Located at Marne-la-Vallée, 32km (20 miles) east of Paris, on an 83-hectare (205-acre) site, this is, as Disney put it, the land "where dreams come true".

According to the Disney marketing machine, Disneyland Paris was something of a homecoming – Walt's family originally came from Isigny-sur-Mer in Normandy, and their name d'Isigny (from Isigny) became Disney in America. But generous financial incentives from the French government rather than family history were behind the final decision to bring Disneyland to Europe.

This complex is in fact properly named **Disneyland® Resort Paris**, and it has three parts: the main park, the hotels and shops of **Disney Village** and **Walt Disney Studios**, a self-contained park that offers a behind-the-scenes look at the history of animation, film and television. But it doesn't end there. If present plans are maintained, the whole site will not be fully developed until 2017, by which time there will be another new golf course and 13,000 more hotel rooms.

GETTING YOUR BEARINGS

Disneyland Paris theme park is divided into five main areas, or "lands", each with attractions, restaurants and shops on a particular theme – the same floor plan as other Disneylands in California, Florida and Tokyo. Designed by "Imagineers", the artistic and mechanical wizards who spend their lives thinking up weird and wonderful attractions, this is Disney's

Sleeping Beauty's castle.

most technologically advanced park, benefiting from state-of-the-art robotics and audio-animatronics, so that life-size, lifelike figures speak, sing and dance with gusto.

Decide what you want to do in order of priority, and get there early, as queues at popular rides soon get pretty long – up to 45 minutes. The circular train chugs clockwise so heading round the park in an anticlockwise direction cuts down crowds.

Main Street USA

Once through the Victorian turnstiles you enter this trademark Disney souvenir and shopping area, replicating one idea of 19th-century, small-town America. **City Hall**, on the left, is the central information centre and contact point for lost children and property. Here, too, is **Main Street Station**, from where the Disneyland train circles the park. The Disney Train leaves the Central Plaza at 1.30pm, 2.30pm and 3.30pm each day. The station is often quite crowded, so it's a good idea to board the train at one of the other stations en route, such as Frontierland.

The bandstand in Main Street square is the best place to view the parades that traverse the park at least once every day, passing around the bandstand and out through the large green gates. The Disney Magic Parade takes place at 7pm while Disney Dreams is a dinner-show (charge), which takes place at the end of the day in the Central Plaza. Winnie the Pooh and Duffy the Disney Bear are around here throughout the day.

Frontierland

To the left of Main Street, Frontierland evokes dreams of the Wild West (at least that's the idea). Its centrepiece, **Big Thunder Mountain**, is a towering triumph of red rock reminiscent of a Western movie. The small town of Thunder Mesa surrounding the mountain represents a pioneer settlement, including Cavalry Fort and Lucky Nugget Saloon, where Miss Lil entertains on a vaudeville stage. **Phantom Manor**, home to some spectacular animatronics, provides a high-tech rollicking ride through a haunted house. The house itself was copied from Norman Bates's abode in Hitchcock's *Psycho*.

TIP

Don't miss this 4D experience - embark on a thrilling adventure with heroes of the *Ratatouille* film. The angry Chef Skinner will chase you "through the sights, sounds and smells of Gusteau's famous Parisian restaurant".

Take a trip down the Rivers of the Far West on this paddle steamer.

TICKET INFORMATION

Disneyland Paris is open every day of the year. Times vary slightly, but in general from Sept–mid-July the main park is open 10am–7pm, Walt Disney Studios 10am–6pm, often with later hours at weekends; mid-July–Aug, the main park opens daily 10am–11pm, the Studios 10am–7pm. For all details, including bookings, current prices and places where you can buy tickets, tel: 01 60 30 60 53or visit www.disneyland paris.com.

A standard Disney ticket is valid for one day's entry to either the main park or Walt Disney Studios; there are several ticket types available to save money. Staying in one of the Resort hotels can also cut costs.

TIP

Disneyland is easy to reach from central Paris, via RER line A to Marne-la-Vallée-Chessy (from Châtelet-Les Halles). The trip takes about 35 minutes. A combined RER and single Disney ticket is available from many RER stations and tourist offices. Disneyland Paris also has its own train station, with direct Eurostar services from London and fast TGV connections from Roissy airport and many other destinations. It's also possible to take a bus, the Disneyland Express (www.disneylandparis-express.com), from Paris.

The Mad Hatter's Tea Cups ride.

Inside are singing cowboy skeletons and holographic ghosts.

The **Rivers of the Far West**, an artificial lake in the middle of Frontierland, can be enjoyed by Mississippi paddle steamer, keelboat or Indian canoe. The Indian canoe station, verdant and full of birdsong (taped, but it fools the real birds) is a tranquil contrast to the roller-coaster ride. Also in Frontierland you'll find the Pocahontas Indian Village, inspired by the Disney film of the same name. An hour-long show, The Tarzan Encounter, takes place in The Chaparral Theatre several times each afternoon

Adventureland

Paths lead on to Adventureland: sparse scrub gives way to bamboo and flowers, and the twang of guitar fades into the beat of African drums. Here is another unforgettable attraction, **Pirates of the Caribbean**. As you descend, the air cools, water drips and the darkness is punctuated only by flickering firelight. The water ride, through tropical swamp to the open sea, is orchestrated by jovially barbaric Disney workers. For

The Hollywood Tower Hotel attraction will spook you out.

the six-minute journey you are spellbound by animated pirates invading a treasure-rich port – here, a singing donkey, there, an inebriated pig

DISNEY VILLAGE

Open every day, for several hours after the main park and Walt Disney Studios have closed – so that visitors needn't fear having nothing to do once they've left their last ride – the "Village" between the park and the hotels buzzes with shops, restaurants, nightclubs and a huge cinema complex. Family entertainment takes the form of **Buffalo Bill's Legend**, a 90-minute Wild West show with Indian chiefs, buffaloes and carousing cowboys.

For places to eat, **Planet Hollywood** offers burgers, salads and pasta while surrounded by movie memorabilia; **King Ludwig's Castle** is a fairy tale Bavarian castle, the kind that inspired the Disney castle, where diners can enjoy Bavarian and European food in a beamed dining hall. With tropical forests, giant aquariums and life-size model animals, the **Rainforest Café** has a more exotic menu. Slightly more low-key, **Annette's Diner** is well priced and entertaining, and fills up early with young families; taking the theme of an American 1950s diner, it serves burgers, fries and beer, brought by roller-skating waiters. Across the strip, **Billy Bob's** presents simple chicken dishes with a background of country tunes. The area around the lake is more sedate and more expensive, and appeals to couples on a romantic night out.

that taps its trotters in time to the music. Jack Sparrow can usually be found lurking near the Blue Lagoon Restaurant in the afternoons.

Rival to Big Thunder Mountain, the first-ever 360-degree looping roller-coaster created by Disney is **Indiana Jones and the Temple of Peril**, near Explorers' Club Restaurant. Hold on to your stomach as the ore-carts plunge through rainforest and turn upside down above a mock archaeological dig inspired by the Indiana Jones saga. As with other top rides, get here early.

Elsewhere, Adventureland offers the ultimate treehouse, **La Cabane des Robinson**, home of the Swiss Family Robinson; an **Adventure Isle** based on *Treasure Island*, with a rope bridge and Ben Gunn's cave; and **Captain Hook's Pirate Ship** that, with Skull Rock, acts as a playground.

Fantasyland

The most popular land for younger children, with Disney's emblem **Le Château de la Belle au Bois Dormant** (Sleeping Beauty's Castle), centrepiece of the park, where Sleeping Beauty's tale is told through rich tapestries and stained-glass windows. Underneath lies **La Tanière du Dragon** (The Lair of the Dragon), hiding a 27-metre (88ft) creature that roars, curls its claws and hisses smoke. Next door, **Blanche-Neige et les Sept Nains** (Snow White and the Seven Dwarfs) leads children through the classic fairy tale in cars from the dwarfs' mine, and terrifies them with a holographic floating witch's head.

Peter Pan's Flight is another one to visit early in the day, before the tour buses arrive; here you can take a pirate galleon into the skies above London, as far as Never-Never Land. More sedate amusement is found in **It's a Small World**, a cheerful puppet kingdom of singing children, a real Disney classic. Mickey Mouse and Princess Daisy are around and about here throughout the day.

Discoveryland

The futuristic high-tech experiences in Discoveryland are great for older kids. **Space Mountain** is a roller-coaster ride into outer space inspired by Jules Verne's *From the*

Indiana Jones and the Temple of Peril, the first ever 360-degree roller-coaster.

Fans of the Cars movies will enjoy Cars Race Rally.

When you get to the park (as early as possible!) go straight to the Fastpass desks by the most popular rides, such as Space Mountain or Buzz Lightyear Laser Blast. For no extra charge, Fastpass allows you to book a time for the ride later in the day; so when you go back at the right time, you don't have to queue. Resort hotel guests also cut queues, as they can enter the parks an hour early.

Walt Disney Studios look back at the story of animation film.

Earth to the Moon, and **Star Tours** offers a trip with George Lucas's *Star Wars* characters. To get there, you walk past hard-working robots complaining about the trials of life. On the ride itself, the five minutes spent in the flight simulator are riveting as the spaceship crashes through meteors and engages in a laser battle. Captain EO is a futuristic film starring, and with the music of, Michael Jackson.

Discoveryland also has **Buzz Lightyear Laser Blast**, based on the *Toy Story* films. Allow plenty of time for queuing: it's rather like a giant video game, in which participants use their laser pistols to shoot down baddies, all under the guidance of Buzz. A photo is taken of players as they end the ride, with their score printed in the corner.

WALT DISNEY STUDIOS PARK

Walt Disney Studios, built alongside the main park, is a park of rides and attractions inspired by the world of cinema. The park is supposedly arranged around a working film

studio, and guests learn about the movie-making process and can step into the action themselves. Instead of "Lands", this park is made up of four zones.

Front Lot

As you walk through the majestic Studio Gates, the first thing you see are palm trees, a Mickey Mouse "Sorcerer's Apprentice" water fountain and a 33-metre (110ft) water tower, the traditional symbol of a Hollywood film studio. Strolling down the 1940s Hollywood Boulevard and watching starlets in veiled hats pose for the cameras, you soon realise this is all an elaborate set, complete with hundreds of movie props. Don't be surprised when "producers" try to recruit you as an actor.

Toon Studio

This is Disney's homage to the art of film animation – from its origins in Europe to the greatest animated pictures of the 21st century. A film highlighting moments from Disney's cartoon classics is followed by a cartooning demonstration, and guests can try out their own animation skills at interactive play stations.

Animagique is a colourful show in the tradition of Czech "black light" theatre, bringing to life scenes from pictures like *The Lion King* and *Pinocchio*. The genie from *Aladdin* invites kids of all ages onto a film set called **Flying Carpets over Agrabah** – the mayhem begins when the actor-turned-director tries to organise a film shoot, with guest actors whizzing round a giant lamp on magic carpets. For the resort's 15th anniversary this was expanded with two high-excitement new attractions: **Crush's Coaster**, a spinning rollercoaster based on the film *Finding Nemo*, and **Cars Race Rally**, an interactive ride based on the film *Cars*.

Production Courtyard

This is the heartbeat of the studio production facilities, with productions and shows almost every day. The **Walt Disney Television Studios** is the European home of Disney Channel. You get a glimpse of a busy production facility, and there's even a chance guests may be chosen to appear in one of the shows. Combining live performers and special effects, **CinéMagique** is a magical journey through 100 years of the moving image.

The **Studio Tram Tour** takes you on a tour of the studios, offering a peek behind the scenes at sets, movie props, special effects, decor and costumes. When the tram visits **Catastrophe Canyon**, a dam bursts, releasing a deluge of recycled water.

The Twilight Zone **Tower of Terror** takes you on a gravity-defying 13-storey drop and will delight all thrill seekers. Kids will enjoy a live encounter with **Stitch**.

Back Lot

This is home to some of the biggest thrills – the special effects facility, recording stages and the stunt workshops. The **Rock 'n' Roller Coaster**, starring Aerosmith, gives you the chance to "ride the music" in a sight-and-sound spectacular, featuring hairpin turns, loops and heart-stopping drops (it is too scary for small children). **Armageddon** takes guests on a voyage through the history of special effects, and into a full-sized set of a Mir Russian space station (from the Bruce Willis sci-fi hit *Armageddon*). Wind tunnels howl, meteors crash and guests dodge fireballs until an explosion in the heart of the ship brings the action to a climax.

The highlight of the Back Lot is **Stunt Show Spectacular**. This live-action show trashes cars, motorcycles and jet-skis in a crescendo of movie stunts performed in a Mediterranean village seaside set.

WHERE TO STAY

The wider resort – **Disney Village** and the hotels – is a celebration of "Americana". **Hotel Cheyenne** is the most imaginative: a film-set Western hotel, with saloon, sheriff's jail and wooden-planked stores. At the other "moderately priced" hotel, **Santa Fe**, Clint Eastwood grimaces down from a mock drive-in movie screen above the reception. The hotel style recalls Mexican villages.

The more expensive **Sequoia Lodge** and **Newport Bay Club** hotels overlook Lake Disney. One recalls Hitchcock's *North by Northwest* in its pine surroundings, and the other is a New England mansion. Across the lake, **Hotel New York** offers luxury rooms in a Manhattan-style skyscape designed by Michael Graves.

The jewel of the resort's hotels is naturally the four-star **Disneyland Hotel**, its Victorian style whispering 19th-century elegance. In a forest 5km (3 miles) from the main park is **Davy Crockett Ranch**, with 97 camping and caravan places, 498 fully equipped cabins in "pioneer village" style and sports facilities.

There is a shop, World of Disney, at the entrance to Disney Village whose Art Deco design mirrors the elegant department stores of Paris. Five minutes away from the park is the designer shopping outlet La Vallée Village (daily 10am–7pm; www.lavalleevillage.com), which has more than 95 boutiques for men, women, children and the home.

There's no shortage of places to eat at Disneyland Paris.

Monet's lily pond at Giverny.

TRIPS OUT OF TOWN

Within easy reach of Paris can be found the grand palaces beloved of Louis XIV and Napoleon, medieval gems such as Chartres or St-Denis, and the natural world that has inspired so many artists, at Barbizon and Monet's fabulous garden at Giverny.

Many of the fascinating places beyond the city limits are just a train ride away. Alternatively, you can hire a car (see page 275) to venture off the beaten track – your meanderings may lead to quaint old *auberges* serving hearty evening meals by the fire or lunch on a riverside terrace. If time is limited, then a trip to Versailles or **Disneyland Paris** ❶ (see page 246) is an obvious choice, but you could take a day or two to visit towns such as Rouen or Chartres further away, stopping at sights along the way. The forests of the Ile-de-France and surrounding regions are dotted with châteaux and monuments.

SNCF trains are generally fast and efficient, and, on arrival at your destination, you'll find the needs of visitors well catered for, with a plentiful supply of maps and information on tourist sights, hotels, restaurants and taxis. Some places, such as St-Denis, St-Germain-en-Laye and Versailles itself, are stops on Paris's speedy RER suburban train network (see page 273). Tours to all the main destinations are also available from hotels and many agencies in Paris.

Ornate lampstands inside the Château de Versailles.

THE SHORTEST HOPS

Château de Versailles ❷

Address: www.chateauversailles.fr
Tel: 01 30 83 78 00
Opening Hrs: Tue–Sun Apr–Oct 9am–6.30pm, Nov–Mar until 5.30pm; other parts of the estate have separate opening times
Entrance Fee: charge
Transport: RER C5 to Versailles-Rive Gauche, bus 171
The RER line C5 from St-Michel-Notre-Dame will drop you very near

Main Attractions
Château de Versailles
Château de Malmaison
Château de St-Germain-en-Laye
Basilique de St-Denis
Chantilly
Vaux-le-Vicomte
Château de Fontainebleau
Chartres
Rouen
Fondation Monet, Giverny

Map
Page 257

Boating at Versailles.

Empress Joséphine's bed in the Château de Malmaison.

the Sun King's magnificent château and gardens. You will have to pick and choose what you most want to see, as you need much more than a day to take in everything.

Apart from the main palace there is the **Grand Trianon** in the north of the park, the **Petit Trianon** and the nearby **Hameau de la Reine**, Marie-Antoinette's fantasy farmhouse, where she played at being a shepherdess. In the vast gardens (open daily dawn until dusk), the fountains dance to music every Saturday and Sunday afternoon from April to September (extra charge), while on most Saturdays in July and August the gardens stay open at night for a superbly lit repeat performance, the dazzling *Grandes Eaux Nocturnes*.

Musée National de Céramique – Sèvres ❸

Address: www.sevresciteceramique.fr
Tel: 01 46 29 22 00
Opening Hrs: Wed–Mon 10am–5pm
Entrance Fee: charge
Transport: Pont de Sèvres

Half a day will suffice for a visit to Sèvres, set on the edge of the lovely wooded Parc de St-Cloud, laid out by Le Nôtre around a château that no longer exists. The suburb has been famous for its porcelain for more than 200 years, and the ceramics workshops, set in a wooded park, contain this beautiful museum.

Château de Malmaison ❹

Address: www.chateau-malmaison.fr
Tel: 01 41 29 05 55
Opening Hrs: Apr–Sept Mon–Fri 10am–12.30pm, 1.30–5.45pm, Sat–Sun 10am–12.30pm, 1.30–6.15pm, Oct–Mar Mon–Fri 10am–12.30pm,

1.30–5.15pm, Sat–Sun
10am–12.30pm, 1.30–5.45pm
Entrance Fee: charge
Transport: RER A to La Défense, bus
258

Further west in Rueil-Malmaison,
this château was the favourite home
of Napoleon Bonaparte's first wife,
Empress Joséphine, and he allowed her
to live on here after their divorce; she
died here in 1814. Before the break-up,
Napoleon used to retreat here between
battles. Along with the neighbouring little **Château de Bois-Préau**, it
forms an important museum of the
First Empire, with period interiors
that include Joséphine's bedroom and
other Napoleonic memorabilia. The
magnificent rose garden looks much
as it did in Joséphine's day.

Château de St-Germain-en-Laye – Musée des Antiquités Nationales ❺

Address: http://musee-
archeologienationale.fr

Tel: 01 39 10 13 00
Opening Hrs: Wed–Mon 10am–5pm
Entrance Fee: charge
Transport: RER A1 to St-Germain-en-
Laye, bus 258

The wealthy suburb of St-Germain-
en-Laye has perched above Paris
since the 12th century, and was once
a royal retreat. Its château, which has
a lovely Gothic chapel, was rebuilt
for François I (his royal salamander
and "F" can be seen in the courtyard).
Inside, you won't find period furnishings or portraits, but a museum
of prehistoric and ancient times.
The terrace gardens overlooking the
Seine were designed by Le Nôtre and
inspired Impressionist painter Alfred
Sisley (1839–99).

Basilique de St-Denis ❻

Address: www.monuments-nationaux.fr
Tel: 01 48 09 83 54
Opening Hrs: Apr–Sept Mon–Sat
10am–6.15pm, Sun noon–6.15pm,
Oct–Mar Mon–Sat 10am–5pm, Sun

FACT

During the Revolution,
the tombs in St-Denis
were vandalised and the
royal bodies thrown into
a pit. However, they were
secretly rescued and
finally returned to their
original resting places in
restored tombs by Louis
XVIII in 1816.

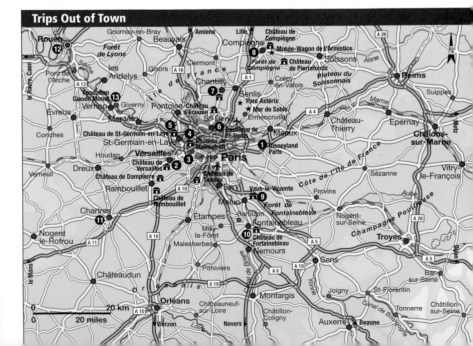

Trips Out of Town

noon–5.15pm
Entrance Fee: charge
Transport: Metro line 13 (Basilique-St-Denis), RER D, Tramway line T1

Less than 4km (3 miles) north of Paris stands the final resting place of France's kings and queens. Revered as an early masterpiece of Gothic architecture, the basilica was mainly built by the charismatic Abbot Suger, close friend of Louis VII, in the 12th century on the site of an abbey church. According to legend, this is the spot reached by St Denis, first bishop of Lutetia, when he walked out of Paris carrying his head, after being beheaded on Montmartre. Monarchs from as far back as Dagobert I (628–37) are buried here, and the medieval and Renaissance tomb sculptures are some of the finest in France.

NORTH TO CHANTILLY AND COMPIÈGNE

Chantilly, about 50km (30 miles) away from Paris, is famous for horse racing, but also has a sumptuous palace, a magnificent park created by Le Nôtre and the splendidly palatial 18th-century **Grandes Ecuries**,

Chantilly curio.

Inside the Gothic Basilique de St-Denis.

stables built by Prince Louis-Henri de Bourbon, who believed that he would be reincarnated as a horse.

Château de Chantilly

Address: www.domainedechantilly.com
Tel: 03 44 27 31 80
Opening Hrs: Apr–Oct daily 10am–6pm, Nov–Mar Wed–Mon 10.30am–5.00pm
Entrance Fee: charge
Transport: SNCF from Gare du Nord, RER D (Chantilly-Gouvieux).

This fairytale castle is nestled in a forest grove, its white walls topped by a blue-slate roof, and wild ducks bustling around the moat. Inside, the **Musée Condé** holds works by Botticelli, Raphael, Giotto and Holbein.

You don't have to be a horse-racing enthusiast to enjoy the **Musée Vivant du Cheval** (Wed–Mon Mar–Nov 10am–5pm, Dec 1.30–5pm;), under the impressive dome of the Grandes Ecuries, with various breeds on show and many exhibition rooms – these stables once housed 240 horses and 500 dogs. Riding displays are held on the first Sunday of each month. The Chantilly racecourse is the most fashionable in France, and high society

gathers here in June for the prestigious flat-racing trophies.

Compiègne and its forest

The town of **Compiègne** ❽, 30km (20 miles) northeast of Chantilly and 80km (50 miles) northeast of Paris (SNCF from Gare du Nord), sits between the Oise River and one of France's largest forests. Its Hôtel de Ville has the oldest bell in the country in its clock tower, and picantins (little figures) strike every hour. The **Château de Compiègne** (http://palaisdecompiegne.fr; tel: 03 44 38 47 02; Wed–Mon 10am–6pm) was once the favourite residence of Napoleon III and has three museums (one of vintage cars).

If you enjoy walking, make your way on foot to **Les Beaux Monts**, just outside the town, for a spectacular view of the château and the Oise. From here, a circular walk, lasting between one and two hours, has been marked out, guiding you through the beautiful **Forêt de Compiègne**, an ancient royal hunting forest full of old oaks and beech trees. By car or SNCF bus from Compiègne station, you can also visit the **Musée**

Wagon de l'Armistice (www.musee-armistice-14-18.fr. tel: 03 44 85 14 18; Apr–mid-Sept Wed–Mon 10am–6pm, mid-Sept–Mar Wed–Mon 10am–5.30pm) in the Clairière de l'Armistice (Armistice Clearing), where the 1918 Armistice between Germany and the Allies was signed, and where Hitler humiliated the French by making them surrender in the same place on 22 June 1940.

On the eastern edge of the forest is Napoleon III's hunting lodge, the **Château de Pierrefonds** (www.monuments-nationaux.fr; tel: 03 44 42 72 72; May–Sep daily 9.30am–6pm, Sept–Apr Tue–Sun 10am–1pm, 2–5.30pm). Entirely reconstructed in the 19th century in Romantic medieval style by Viollet-le-Duc, with drawbridge, moat and towers, it is a remarkable architectural oddity. Inside, the fanciful architect allowed his imagination free rein.

SOUTHEAST TO FONTAINEBLEAU

Vaux-le-Vicomte ❾

Address: www.vaux-le-vicomte.com
Tel: 01 64 14 41 90

Admiring the collection of paintings in the Château de Chantilly.

The duchess's blue bedroom in the Château de Chantilly.

The charming Château de Chantilly is surrounded by a moat.

Vaux-le-Vicomte, complemented by Le Nôtre's elegant French-style gardens.

Opening Hrs: Mar–Nov daily 10am–6pm, gardens open some weekends Nov–Mar
Entrance Fee: charge
Transport: SNCF from Gare de Lyon to Melun

Some 40km (25 miles) south of Paris outside Melun is this luxurious 17th-century château, built by Louis XIV's powerful treasurer Nicolas Fouquet, a devoted patron of the arts. The impeccable house, along with a beautiful garden *à la française* – the

first created by Le Nôtre – was his undoing: jealous advisers whispered to the king that Fouquet had paid for it with treasury funds. After a grand house-warming party for the young monarch, Fouquet was imprisoned at Vincennes, and the upstaged Louis set out to build something even more splendid – Versailles – using the very same architect and designers.

The château and grounds provide an intriguing visit. One room traces the history of its owners, others are decorated in sumptuous period style, with coffered, painted ceilings and Gobelins tapestries, and the kitchen equipment is fascinating. The candle-lit tour on Saturday evening (May–mid-Oct 8pm–midnight) gives an added atmospheric dimension.

Château de Fontainebleau ⑩

Address: www.musee-chateau-fontainebleau.fr
Tel: 01 60 71 50 70
Opening Hrs: Wed–Mon Apr–Sept 9.30am–6pm, Oct–Mar until 5pm
Entrance Fee: charge

Transport: SNCF from Gare de Lyon to Fontainebleau-Avon, then bus

Melun sits on the edge of the **Forêt de Fontainebleau**, which was once a royal hunting ground and is now the haunt of cyclists, mushroom hunters, birdwatchers, picnickers and rock climbers, attracted by the giant rock formations. The town of Fontainebleau lies just 15km (9 miles) away, and is dominated by the first of France's purpose-built royal châteaux, residence of French sovereigns from François I to Napoleon III. Each one added something to the palace, creating a mixture of styles, but Napoleon I outdid them all by building an ornate throne room – his *grands appartements* are definitely worth seeing.

The artists' village: Barbizon

Barbizon, 7km (4 miles) away on the eastern edge of the forest, is a village that has attracted landscape painters since the 1840s, when Théodore Rousseau (1812–67) and Jean-François Millet (1814–75) fled to the woods to escape the Industrial Revolution and rediscover nature. The Office du Tourisme is set in Rousseau's former house, and his workshop is now a museum to the **Ecole de Barbizon** (www.musee-peintres-barbizon.fr; tel: 01 60 66 22 27; Wed–Mon 10am–12.30pm, 2–5.30pm, Jul–Aug until 6pm).

FACT

As well as designing some of the most famous gardens in France, his most celebrated at Versailles, André Le Nôtre (1613-1700) drew up designs for a parterre at Greenwich Park in London (uncompleted) and designed the gardens of the castle of Racconigi near Turin.

Inside the Château de Fontainebleau.

The majestic entrance to the Château de Fontainebleau.

EAT

The Musée des Impressionnismes has a café, Terra Café, where the menu focuses on regional specialities from Normandy; snacks and drinks are available too. There is a lovely garden terrace for fine days.

SOUTHWEST TO CHARTRES

A trip to **Chartres ⓫** – 89km (55 miles) from Paris – can be taken slowly, stopping off at the châteaux of **Dampierre** and **Rambouillet** (see box) on the way, or you can go straight there by train (SNCF from Gare Montparnasse). The two spires of the magnificent Gothic **Chartres Cathedral** (www.cathedrale-chartres. org; tel: 02 37 21 59 08; daily 8am– 7.30pm; Jul–Aug Mon Fri Sun until 10pm; entrance charge for towers) soar above the surrounding fields. Originally Romanesque, the cathedral dedicated to the Virgin Mary was destroyed by fire in 1194, but everyone from peasant to lord contributed straightaway to the rebuilding, with labour or money. The famous rose windows, together with 170 more of Europe's finest original stained-glass windows, fill the cathedral with changing colours. Behind the cathedral is the **Musée des Beaux-Arts** (tel: 02 37 90 45 80; Nov–Apr Wed–Sat 10am–12.30pm, 2–5pm, Sun 2–5pm, May–Oct until 6pm), with Renaissance and 18th-century paintings and some fine tapestries.

Claude Monet, the father of Impressionism.

La Maison Picassiette (22 rue du Repos; 02 37 34 10 78; Apr–Oct Wed–Mon 10am–12:30. 2–6pm) was built by Raymond Isidore from broken bits of tile and glass from 1938-1962; it is considered a fine example of naïve art and is a listed building.

WEST TO MONET'S GIVERNY

For a longer break from Paris, head for **Rouen ⓬**, which is on the Seine about 110km (70 miles) along the N13 from Paris (or by SNCF from Gare St-Lazare). Once the capital of Normandy, Rouen has a wealth of picturesque timber-frame houses, narrow streets and many of France's finest Gothic buildings, both civic and religious, despite the damage it suffered during World War II. The city is centred on the impressive, soaring Gothic cathedral, which was much loved and much painted by Claude Monet. Joan of Arc was burned at the stake in the city in 1431, on a site that is now one of Rouen's liveliest squares.

Exquisite stained-glass window, Chartres cathedral.

The road to Rouen passes not far from **Giverny**. Set on a hillside just above the Seine, this small village is where Claude Monet lived and worked for 43 years until his death in 1926, at the age of 86.

Fondation Claude Monet

Address: www.fondation-monet.com
Tel: 02 32 51 28 21
Opening Hrs: Apr–Oct daily 9.30am–6pm
Entrance Fee: charge
Transport: SNCF from Gare St-Lazare to Vernon 6km/3 miles away, then bus

Monet's house is now a museum and memorial beautifully restored and redecorated in the same colours the painter loved. The gardens that the father of Impressionism designed and drew inspiration from are a living work of art – at their colourful best during May, June and July – with the Japanese bridge and the famous water lilies on the pond. Arrive early, though, to try to avoid the crowds, and if possible go on a weekday.

Only copies of Monet's works are on display at Giverny but, nearby, the **Musée des Impressionnismes** (www.

Monet's garden in Giverny.

mdig.fr; tel: 02 32 51 94 65; Apr–Oct daily 10am–6pm) celebrates the work of the Impressionists and puts on temporary exhibitions.

You can also head for the **Forêt de Lyons**, northeast of Giverny (buses run from Rouen and Vernon). The centennial beech trees make a walk or cycle ride a particular pleasure, with fine views of Norman villages and their half-timbered houses.

Château de Sceaux.

CHÂTEAUX AROUND PARIS

The Ile-de-France region is rich in châteaux, many built in the wake of the Sun King's extravagance at Versailles. The **Château de Sceaux** (tel: 01 41 87 29 50; http://domaine-de-sceaux.hauts-de-seine.fr), 7km (4 miles) south of Paris, was built in 1670 for Fouquet's successor Colbert, with a beautiful park and gardens by Le Nôtre. Rebuilt in 1856, it now hosts the Musée de l'Ile-de-France. More Le Nôtre gardens are found at the **Château de Dampierre** (tel: 01 30 52 53 24; www.chateau-de-dampierre.fr), 35km (22 miles) southwest, which has a touch of Versailles about it. The president's summer residence, **Rambouillet** (www.rambouillet-tourisme. fr; tel: 01 34 83 21 21), 15km (9 miles) further on, was once a feudal castle and is open when the president is away. The **Château d'Ecouen** (www.valdoise-tourisme.com; tel: 01 34 38 38 50), 19km (11 miles) north, is a masterpiece of Renaissance architecture, now the Musée National de la Renaissance, with the finest tapestries in France. **Maisons** (www. tourisme-maisonslaffitte.fr; tel: 01 39 62 63 64) at Maisons-Laffitte, near St-Germain-en-Laye, is a small gem designed in 1641 by François Mansart for René de Longueil, future finance minister of Louis XIV; the town itself is well known for its horse racing.

VERSAILLES

Paris was not always the capital of France – for a while, the country was run from a sumptuous palace at Versailles, to the southwest of the city.

The Château de Versailles is the ultimate expression of the French monarchy's power and ostentation prior to the Revolution. Built in 1624 as a hunting lodge for Louis XIII, the building was developed by Louis XIV, who employed the celebrated creative trio of Le Vau, Le Nôtre and Le Brun, as well as the no less illustrious architect Mansart. Versailles became the capital of France, and, by 1774, following alterations by Louis XV and XVI, the palace had 2,143 windows and 67 staircases, and was home to 10,000 courtiers and servants. The gardens were designed by Le Nôtre on the same grand scale as the château itself, and adorned with statues and fountains. The Royal Family left Versailles for the Tuileries in 1789 and in 1790 it was emptied of its furniture, which was eventually sold off. After the arrest of Louis XVI in 1791, the palace was sealed by the National Constituent Assembly. In 1793 it became a depository for seized artworks and was then turned into a museum, which was closed when Napoleon came to power and reopened in the 1830s by Louis-Philippe. Its preservation for the nation has been ongoing since then.

The landscaped gardens cover a vast area: 8 sq km (3 sq miles).

The Essentials

Address: www.chateau versailles.fr
Tel: 01 30 83 78 00
Opening Hrs: Château: Tues–Sun Apr–Oct 9am–6.30pm, Nov–Mar until 5.30pm.
Entrance Fee: charge
Transport: RER C5 to Versailles-Rive Gauche, Bus 171

The sculptures are one of the gardens' many attractions – but note that they're all covered during the winter months.

THE SUN KING

Louis XIV, the Sun King.

Louis XIV came to the throne at the age of five, in 1643, and his reign lasted 72 years – the longest in the history of France. He believed in the divine right of kings and it was because everything revolved around him that he later became known as The Sun King. It was a golden age of literature and art, and of French international expansion: Louis waged an aggressive foreign policy, built up a navy and reorganised the army into the most formidable fighting force on the Continent. His energy was prolific, and he served as his own prime minister – hence his famous comment *"L'Etat, c'est moi"* ("I am the state"). But for all the show of luxury and accomplishment, he was far from a benevolent monarch: in 1685 he revoked the Edict of Nantes, which brought about the bloody persecution of Protestants. He died aged 76 in 1715 and was succeeded by his five-year-old grandson, Louis XV.

There's an extra charge to enter the gardens on Saturdays and Sundays between April and September, when the fountains come to life and 17th-century music plays over the flower beds and pathways. But although it's fabulous to see the gardens in such watery splendour, Sunday is the worst day to visit the inside of the château, as it can become unbearably overcrowded.

This beautiful gilded clock face is one of many Versailles adornments with the Sun King's effigy.

The view northwest from the château along the gardens' central aisle. The fountain in the foreground is the centrepiece of the Bassin d'Apollon (Apollo's Fountain).

The scale and glory of the château are apparent right from its main entrance – the Cour de Marbre (Marble Courtyard).

The highlights

The château's main tour, plus the gardens, can be covered in a day; but to savour fully the wealth of historic and architectural heritage, allow two days.

The main tour

The main part of the château, which can be accessed without a guide, are the lavish King and Queen's State Apartments (*Grands Appartements*), notably the King's State Bedroom. Also included are the Queen's bedchamber and the vast Hall of Mirrors. Other highlights of the main tour include, in the Hercules Room, François Lemoyne's fresco *The Apotheosis of Hercules*, and, in the salle du Sacre dedicated to Napoleon I, a replica of Jacques-Louis David's colossal *Coronation of the Emperor Napoleon I*. There are guided tours (an additional €7, Tel 01 30 83 78 00) of the private apartments of the kings and the Jeu de Paume rooms.

The Trianons and Hameau

The single-storey, Italianate Grand Trianon was built for Louis XIV as a miniature palace in which he could escape the formality of the château. The Petit Trianon was built as a retreat for Louis XV and his mistresses. A cluster of thatched cottages, the Hameau ("Hamlet") is associated with Marie-Antoinette; they were the queen's fairy-tale farm and milking parlour.

The best ticket is the Passport, valid for one (€18) or two days (€25), which allows entry to the main palace (with an audioguide), the Trianon palaces, Marie-Antoinette's farm and the gardens. Musical Fountains Show, Musical Gardens (Apr-Oct) and exhibitions are included.

The Hameau de la Reine (Queen's Hamlet) was built in 1783 at the request of Marie-Antoinette, who wanted a refuge from the routines of the château. It was a working farm, with orchards and fields that produced food for the royal table.

The impossibly lavish Galerie des Glaces (Hall of Mirrors). The unification of Germany was ratified here in 1871, as was the Treaty of Versailles in 1919.

Marie-Antoinette.

AN UNPOPULAR QUEEN

Marie-Antoinette has always had a bad press. On the one hand, there's the apparent heartlessness of her almost certainly fictitious comment "Let them eat cake"; on the other, the frivolity of her antics at her model farm, Le Hameau de la Reine, where she and her servants dressed as farm hands and milked carefully washed cows and goats into Sèvres porcelain buckets. What's more, she was Austrian, a lifelong handicap in the French court where she was known as *l'autrichienne* (that Austrian woman). For many courtiers, the unfortunate queen could do nothing right; Versailles was a vipers' nest of intrigue, and she was continually criticised – unfairly for the most part. In the 1780s, she was thought to be involved in a scheme to defraud the crown jeweller out of the fee for an elaborate diamond necklace, an unproven incident which tarnished the monarchy in the eyes of the public. Losing her life on the guillotine in 1793 was the crowning misfortune.

As Premier peintre du Roi, or Chief Painter to the King, Charles Le Brun (1619–90) directed the team of artists who decorated the ceilings at Versailles.

The magnificent Baroque Royal Chapel, adorned with carved white marble, gilding and murals. The royal family worshipped from the gallery.

The King's State Bedroom, created in 1701 – a place for day-to-day business, not sleep.

TRAVEL TIPS
PARIS

TRANSPORT

GETTING THERE AND GETTING AROUND

GETTING THERE

By Air

Most major international airlines fly regularly to Paris's Roissy-Charles de Gaulle airport (Paris-CDG), northeast of the city. Air France naturally has the largest number of flights from North America and within Europe. British Airways have frequent flights from various UK airports, and the low-cost airlines easyJet, Flybe and Jet2 also fly to Charles de Gaulle from airports around the UK, including Belfast.

Travellers from the US and Canada can fly direct to Paris-CDG or to the larger provincial cities such as Nice and Lyon on Air France, Air Canada and many US airlines. Many French domestic, and some international flights, use Orly airport in the south of the city. Low-cost operator Ryanair fly to Beauvais, 88 km (55 miles) north of Paris, from Edinburgh, Glasgow Prestwick, Manchester, Dublin and Knock.

A big range of fare options can be found on the internet. For flights originating in the UK, check out Cheap Flights (www.cheap flights.co.uk) or the Travel Super-market (www.travelsupermarket. com); from North America, try www.flightcenter.com or www.euro

vacations.com. In France, Nou-velles Frontières (www.nouvelles-frontieres.fr) or Last minute (www. lastminute.com) offer competitive fares on both scheduled and charter flights, and Opodo (www.opodo.com) is a pan-Euro-pean alliance of several major air-lines that offers a broad range of fares.

Students and anyone under 26 can also get discount flights through specialist travel agen-cies. In the UK, try STA Travel, with over 46 branches, tel: 0871 230 0040, www.statravel.co.uk; in the US, STA Travel also has branches across the country, tel: 1 800 781 4040, www.statravel.com.

By Sea or Tunnel

Ferries

Ferries from the UK, Ireland and the Channel Islands to France have cut prices since the Channel Tunnel opened. Catamaran-style

AIRLINES

Aer Lingus: tel: 0333 006 6920 (UK), 1890 800270 (Ireland), 516 622 4226 (US), 0821 23 02 67 (France), www.aerlingus. com
Air Canada: tel: 0871 220 1111 (UK), 1 888 247 2262 (Canada/US), 08 25 88 08 81 (France), www.aircanada.ca
Air France: tel: 0207 660 0337 (UK), 800 237 2747 (US), 36 54 (France), www.airfrance.com
American Airlines: tel: 0207 660 2300 (UK), 800 433 7300 (US), 0821 980 999 (France), www.aa.com
British Airways: tel: 0844 493 0787 (UK), 800 247 9297 (US), 08 25 82 54 00 (France), www.ba.com
Delta Airways: tel: 0207 660

0767 (UK), 800 221 1212 (US), 0892 702 609 (France), www.delta.com
United Airlines: tel: 0845 607 6760 (UK), 800 864 8331 (US), 01 71 23 03 35 (France), www.united.com
Budget Airlines
easyJet: tel: 0330 365 5000 (UK), 0820 420 315 (France), www.easyjet.com
flybe: tel: 0871 700 2000 (UK), 00 44 1392 683152 (from out-sideUK), www.flybe.com
Jet2: tel: 0800 408 1350 (UK), 0821 230 203 (France), www.jet2.com
Ryanair: tel: 0871 246 0000 (UK), 1520 444 004 (Ireland), 08 92 562 150 (France), www.ryanair.com

Helpful signs in Beaubourg.

"fast ferries" offer the quickest service, but are sometimes cancelled if the sea is really rough. Boulogne, Calais and Le Havre all have motorway links to Paris. Trains meet connecting ferries at Dover, Calais and some other Channel ports.

The following companies operate from the UK and Ireland: **Brittany Ferries**, tel: 0330 159 7000 (UK), 08 25 82 88 28 (France), www.brittany-ferries.com. Portsmouth to Caen, Cherbourg and St-Malo: Poole to Cherbourg, and Plymouth and Cork to Roscoff.
Condor Ferries, tel: 01202 207216 (UK), 08 25 13 51 35 (France), www.condorferries.co.uk. Poole to St-Malo, Weymouth to St-Malo and Portsmouth to Cherbourg, via the Channel Islands.

The Eurostar.

Irish Ferries, tel: 0818 300 400 (Ireland), 01 70 72 03 26 (France), www.irishferries.com. Services from Dublin to Cherbourg, Rosslare to Cherbourg and Roscoff.
LD Lines, tel: 0844 576 8836 (UK), 08 25 30 43 04 (France), www.ldlines.com. Dover to Calais and Dunkerque, Newhaven to Dieppe.
DFDS, tel: 0871 574 7235 (UK), 02 32 14 68 50 (France), www.dfdsseaways.co.uk. Dover to Calais and Dunkerque, Newhaven to Dieppe.
P&O Ferries, tel: 0800 130 0030 (UK), 03 66 74 03 25 (France), www.poferries.com. Sails from Dover to Calais.

The Channel Tunnel

The alternative to ferries for those driving from the UK, **Eurotunnel** takes cars and passengers from Folkestone to Calais on a drive-on, drive-off service, known as *Le Shuttle*, taking 35 minutes platform to platform and about an hour from motorway to motorway. Payment is made at toll booths, which accept cash or credit cards, and the price applies to the car, regardless of the number of passengers. You can book in advance via tel: 08443 35 35 35 (UK), 08 10 63 03 04 (France), or www.eurotunnel.com, or simply turn up and take the next available service. Unlike the ferries, *Le Shuttle* is never affected by bad weather, and runs 24 hours a day, all year.

By Rail

The fast, frequent train service from London St Pancras to Paris (Gare du Nord), runs about 16 times a day, and takes around two hours 15 minutes. For reservations, contact Eurostar, tel: 03432 186 186 (UK) or 0892 35 35 39 (France) or www.eurostar.com. There are frequent fare offers, and lower fares for children aged 4–11; those under 4 travel free but are not guaranteed a seat.

Paris has six mainline railway stations, with lines radiating across France and Europe. Each connects with several Métro or RER lines, and all have left-luggage facilities *(consignes)* and coin-operated lockers *(consignes automatiques)*.The SNCF's *Train à Grande Vitesse* (TGV) high-speed trains offer fast, comfortable services from Paris to cities around France and other European countries. They are not cheap, so it pays to travel off-peak: you must reserve TGV tickets in advance. Information and reservations are available outside France from Rail Europe, (UK) tel: 0844 848 4064, http://uk.voyages-sncf.com, or (US) tel: 1 800 622 8600. You can also contact French Railways (SNCF) direct, tel: 36 35 (France), www.sncf.com.

Note that before boarding an SNCF train you must have your ticket date-stamped *(composté)* for it to be valid. Simply insert your ticket in the orange *composteur* machine at the platform entrance.

By Bus

Eurolines is a consortium of around 30 European coach companies, which has daily services from London (Victoria Coach Station) to Paris that represent one of the cheaper ways to get to the French capital. The ticket includes the ferry crossing (via Dover), and there are discounts available for under-26s and senior citizens, and passes that give unlimited travel for a month or longer. For more information, contact **National Express-**

BETWEEN AIRPORTS

RER line B runs from Roissy-Charles de Gaulle to Antony station, from where the fast Orlyval shuttle trains (www.orlyval.com) run to Orly airport. An Air France bus also links Roissy-Charles de Gaulle and Orly every 30 minutes, from 6.20 am to 10.20pm.

Eurolines, tel: 0871 781 8177 (UK), www.eurolines.co.uk, or **Eurolines France** at Gare Routière-Coach Station Galliéni, 28 avenue du Général de Gaulle, Porte de Bagnolet (Métro Galliéni), tel: 08 92 89 90 91, www.eurolines.fr. OUI-BUS (www.ouibus.com) is a bus company operated by SNCF (French railways) which offers luxurious services to London and other European destinations from its terminal at Gare de Bercy. Megabus (http://uk.megabus.com) is a low-cost bus operator offering connections from most UK cities to Paris.

GETTING AROUND

From the Airports

From Roissy-Charles de Gaulle

Train
Trains are the quickest and most reliable way to get to central Paris.

Beware of imposters – hail a genuine taxi, one with a light on the roof.

Having a coffee before getting the train.

RER line B trains go direct from Terminal 2; there is a free connecting shuttle bus *(navette)* *between terminals*. Trains run every 7–8 minutes between about 6am and 0.30am, calling at Gare du Nord and Châtelet-Les Halles, the hub of the Métro network. The average journey time is about 30 minutes.

Bus
The Roissybus runs between the airport and Rue Scribe, near Place de l'Opéra. It runs every 15–20 minutes from 5.15am to 0.30am and takes about 75 minutes. Alternatively, there are Air France buses (http://en.lescarsairfrance.com) direct to northwest Paris (Porte Maillot and Charles de Gaulle-Etoile), every 30 minutes, 6am–11pm, and to southern Paris (Gare de Lyon, Gare Montparnasse), every 30

minutes, 6.20am–10.30pm. For recorded information on Air France buses in English, French, German or Italian, tel: 08 92 35 08 20. All bus services call at both airport terminals. Alternatively, take public buses 350 (to Paris Gare de l'Est, from 6am to 10.30pm) and 351 (to Paris-Nation, from 7am to 9.30pm). Night buses (N140 and N143) to Gare de l'Est operate between 0.30 and 5.30am.

Taxi
Taxis are by far the most expensive, but unquestionably the easiest way, to get to Paris from the airport. This can take from 30 minutes to over an hour, depending on traffic. The cost (usually €50–60) is shown on the meter.

From Orly

Train
Shuttle buses run from the two Orly terminals (Orly-Sud and Orly-Ouest) to the Pont de Rungis rail station, on RER line C, which stops at Gare d'Austerlitz, St-Michel-Notre-Dame and the Musée d'Orsay. It runs every 15 minutes from 5am to 1.30pm and takes approximately 45 minutes to Gare d'Austerlitz.

The more expensive Orlyval (www.orlyval.com) automatic train runs to Antony station on RER line B, which has frequent trains to Châtelet-Les Halles and Roissy-Charles de Gaulle airport. It runs

about every 5–7 minutes from 6am to 11pm daily, and takes 35 to 50 minutes depending on the final destination.

Tramway 7 links the airport with Villejuif-Louis Aragon station connected with the Metro line 7. It operates daily from 5.30am till 0.30am and the journey takes 45 minutes.

Bus

Air France buses run from both Orly terminals to Invalides, Etoile and Gare Montparnasse, every 20–30 minutes, 6am to 11.30pm, and take 45–60 minutes. Tickets are available from the Air France terminus.

The Orlybus also runs from both terminals to Place Denfert-Rochereau. There are services every 8–15 minutes, from 6am to 0.30am every day. Bus 183 runs every 15–40 minutes from the airport to Porte de Choisy in Paris from 6am to 0.20am. Night buses (N22, N31, N131, N144) go to/from the city between 0.30 and 5am.

Taxi

Taxis are available outside the terminal buildings at any time. The journey from Orly to the city centre takes 20–40 minutes, depending on the traffic.

Down to the Métro.

Public Transport

Métro and RER

Run by the Régie Autonome des Transports Parisiens (RATP), the Paris Métro is one of the world's oldest subway systems. Used by around 9 million people every day, it is quick and efficient.

The Métro operates Mon–Thu from 5.30am, with the last train leaving end stations at around 12.30am (till 1.30am Fri–Sun and public holidays). You can pick up a free map at any Métro station. Follow the orange correspondance signs to change Métro lines.

The Métro operates in conjunction with the RER (suburban regional express train networks), which has five main lines: A, B, C, D and E, that run out into the suburbs. RER trains run daily about every 12 minutes from 5.00am to midnight (1am Friday–Saturday). They have fewer stops than the Métro in central Paris, and so can be significantly faster.

Buses and Trams

Taking the bus is a pleasant way to see the city, but is much slower than the Métro because of often heavy traffic. The same tickets are used as for the Métro and RER, but you must remember to punch single tickets (though not travel cards) in the *composteur* machine by the entry doors and behind the driver every time you board a bus.

Buses don't automatically halt at every bus stop, so when you want to get off press one of the request buttons and the *arrêt demandé* (bus stopping) sign will light up. Each bus has a map of its route posted at the front and back and at every bus stop. Most routes run from 6.30am to 8.30pm Monday to Saturday, although some routes continue until 12.30am, and some routes run all day on Sunday.

From 12.30am to 5.30am nightly over 40 *Noctilien* night bus

TAXIS

Taxis are readily available at airports and railway stations. In the city itself there are almost 500 taxi ranks, but be careful to hail only a genuine taxi – one with a light on the roof – as other operators may charge exorbitant fares. The white light will be on if a cab is free, while a glowing orange light means that the taxi is occupied. Paris taxis operate on three fare rates at different times:

Tariff A 10am–5pm Monday to Saturday, in the city.

Tariff B 5pm–10am Monday to Saturday, 7am–midnight Sunday, and 7am–7pm Mon–Sat in the suburbs (all areas outside the *Boulevard Périphérique*).

Tariff C midnight–7am Sundays in the city, and 7pm–7am in the suburbs.

The website www.taxi-paris.net provides comprehensive information on Paris's cabs. The following companies take phone bookings 24 hours a day:

Alpha: 01 45 85 85 85; www.alphataxis.fr

G7: 3607; www.taxisg7.fr

Taxis Bleus: 08 91 70 10 10; www.taxis-bleus.com

If you have a complaint about a taxi, send it (with the cab licence number) to: Service des Taxis, Préfecture de Police, 36 rue des Morillons, 75015, tel: 01 55 76 20 05.

Tram line T3 – the only line so far inside the city limits.

routes operate around Paris and its region, including one that makes a circuit around the main railway stations. Tickets are the same as for daytime services. Full details of night buses can be found on www.noctilien.fr.

Another service is the *Balabus*, a special sightseeing bus that runs up and down from Gare de Lyon to La Défense, passing many of Paris's major attractions. It runs only on Sundays and on public holidays between 11 April and 26 September, from 12.30 to 8pm. The tour lasts about 50 minutes, and tickets are the same as for regular buses. Look out for bus stops marked *Balabus* or *Bb*.

Paris also has a Tramway system, which was reintroduced in 1992, the city's original tram network having closed in 1938. Currently, it consists of seven lines (T1–T8) with only one, T3, running through the city centre. Two more lines (T9 and T10) are scheduled to become operational by 2021. For routes and timetables see www.ratp.fr/en/ratp/c_5045/tramway.

Tickets and Fares

The Métro, RER, city buses and trams all use the same tickets (€1.80 for a single fare). A book or *carnet* of 10 tickets offers a considerable saving at €14.10.

Single tickets and *carnets* can be bought at Métro stations, tourist offices, tobacco shops, newsstands and some other shops. Only single tickets can be bought on board buses, so to use another ticket type you must buy it in advance at one of the other ticket outlets. With one ticket you can make a journey of any distance within fare zones 1 and 2, which includes the whole of central Paris and the Métro system, no matter how many times you change lines or whether you use the RER. However, every time you board a bus you must use a new single ticket.

All public transport in Paris is free for children under 4, and half-price for those aged 4–11.

A range of travel passes provide good-value, time-saving alternatives to buying single tickets or *carnets*. The most popular is the *Paris Visite* card, giving unlimited travel for one, two, three or five consecutive days on the Métro, buses and railways in Paris and the Ile de France. The cards are valid for a combination of fare zones, beginning with zones 1–3 (all of central Paris), approximate prices for which are €11, €18, €25 and €36 for adults, children aged 4–11 pay half price. *Paris Visite* holders also obtain discounts at several attractions, shops and restaurants. Cards can be bought from Métro, RER and SNCF stations and several other outlets; for full current details, check www.parisvisite.com.

Another option is the *Mobilis* card, which gives unlimited travel for one day on the Métro, buses, RER and other local networks, without the other benefits of the *Paris Visite*. It can be bought at all the usual ticket outlets and from all Métro stations; prices range from €7 for zones 1 and 2 to €17 for 5 zones. *Mobilis* cards are not valid for trips to either Paris airport.

Note that *Paris Visite* and *Mobilis* cards are valid for one calendar day (or series of them), not for 24 hours from the time you buy them, so to take full advantage it's best to start using them first thing in the morning.

For anyone spending longer in Paris the most useful option is the Forfait Navigo travel pass, which gives unlimited travel on all services in the zones of your choice for a month (*Navigo Mois*, approximately €70, all zones) or a week (*Navigo Semaine*, €21). To buy either you need to take a passport photograph to any Métro or SNCF station, and must

Make sure to validate your tickets before getting on the train.

fill in a brief form and sign your name on the card. There are also special youth and senior travel cards. For further information on all Paris transport services and fare options, check www.ratp.fr or www.parisinfo.com.

Private Transport

Driving in Paris requires confidence and concentration. In fact, the best thing to do with a car in the city is to leave it in a car park and take public transport.

If you do intend to drive, here are a few guidelines. Seat belts are obligatory in the front and back of the car, and the speed limit in town is 50kph (30mph). Do not drive in bus lanes at any time, and at unmarked junctions give priority to vehicles approaching from the right. This applies to some roundabouts, where cars on the roundabout stop for those coming onto it. Helmets are compulsory for motorbike riders and passengers. Street parking is very difficult to find; most spaces are metered Monday–Saturday 9am–7pm (paid for not with coins but a *Paris Carte*, currently €15 or €40, purchased from a *tabac*) and the maximum stay is two hours. Most car parks are underground; see www.parkingsdeparis.com. Illegally parked cars may be towed away. Do not leave any possessions on show, as theft from cars is common.

Traffic on Place de l'Etoile is chaotic.

Petrol can be hard to find in the city centre, so if your tank is almost empty head for a *porte* (exit) on the *Périphérique* (the multi-lane ringroad), where there are petrol stations open 24 hours a day all year-round.

Drivers are liable to on-the-spot fines for speeding or drunk driving. The limit in France is 50mg/litre of alcohol in the blood (equivalent to about two glasses of wine) and is strictly enforced.

Car Hire

The minimum age for hiring a car varies from 21 to 23, depending on the company. The hirer must have held a full licence for at least a year, and must have a credit card.

Central reservation services of major car hire firms are:
Auto Europe, (UK) www.autoeurope.co.uk, (US) www.

autoeurope.com. Online bookings in France and across Europe, at competitive rates.
Avis, tel: 0821 230 760, www.avis.fr.
easycar, www.easycar.com.
Europcar, tel: 08 25 35 83 58, www.europcar.fr.
Hertz, tel: 0825 800 900, www.hertz.fr.

Bicycles

If you know Paris reasonably well and have nerves of steel, a bicycle is an excellent way to explore. You can hire bicycles from:
Gepetto & Velos, 59 rue du Cardinal Lemoine, 5th, tel: 01 43 54 19 95, www.gepetto-velos.com.
Paris à Vélo c'est Sympa, 22 rue Alphonse-Baudin, 11th, tel: 01 48 87 60 01, www.parisvelosympa.com.

Vélib (www.velib.paris.fr) is Paris's bike transit system. You can pick up and drop off your bike at 750 locations throughout the city. Bikes are available round the clock with a credit card. You can also buy a one day (€1.70) or a 7-day ticket (€8). First half an hour is always free of charge.

Hitchhiking

It can be difficult to get a lift out of the Channel ports, so take a bus or train for the first leg of the journey. Hitching is forbidden on autoroutes (motorways), but waiting at toll booths is allowed.

Allostop aims to connect hitch hikers with drivers. You simply pay a registration fee and a contribution towards the total petrol cost. Visit www.allostop.net.

Vélibs waiting for customers.

A – Z

AN ALPHABETICAL SUMMARY OF PRACTICAL INFORMATION

A

Accommodation

It is always advisable to reserve accommodation in advance, either direct with the hotel, through a booking service or via the Paris Tourist Office (www.paris-info.com). Tourist offices will also book your first night's accommodation if you arrive in person without a room, for a small fee.

Hotel prices are not subject to controls and can change without notice, so check when booking. The majority of hotels also vary prices by season; low season is generally November to March, high season April to October, but this can vary, as many hotels are particularly busy (and so have higher rates) during certain winter trade fairs and fashion weeks. State your arrival time if you book online or by phone, or your room will not be held after 7pm.

Addresses

Paris is divided into numbered districts – *arrondissements* – and people refer to them by number, saying, for example, that they live "in the 5th". Street names are followed by a five-digit postcode, in which the last digits are the *arrondissement* number, so an

address with a 75008 code will be in the 8th *arrondissement*, and 75012 in the 12th.

Admission charges

Most national museums charge an entrance fee for temporary exhibitions (permanent collections are free), but are often free for under-18s (also for under 25 in case of EU citizens and disabled persons with their companions), and municipal museums are free for all (except for temporary exhibitions). Entrance at national museums is free for all on the first Sunday of each month. There are also reductions at most museums for senior citizens, and students with a valid student card.

If you plan to visit several museums during your stay, buying a Paris Museum Pass means you need queue only once to visit over 60 museums or monuments – including all the most famous ones – in Paris and the Ile-de-France region, and also saves a great deal of money on entrance prices. Tickets are available for two, four or six days, and cost €42 / €56 / €69 per person. They are sold at tourist offices and the participating museums. For full details, see www.parismuseumpass.com.

As a rule, national museums are closed on Tuesday, and

municipal museums on Monday. Most museums stay open throughout the day.

B

Budgeting for Your Trip

The price of accommodation ranges across the spectrum. You can get a double room in a small pension for under €60 a night, or you can pay €500 in a luxury hotel. An average price, however, for an en suite double room in a centrally located, comfortable hotel is around €100–150.

Meals also cover a wide price

Most cafés and bistros offer a formule – set menu.

range, but on average expect to pay €35-50 for a three-course meal with a half-bottle of house wine. In French restaurants the most economical (and most usual) way to order food is from a *prix fixe* set menu (also called a *menu* or a *formule*), which gives two, three or four courses, and coffee, for a set price. Drinks are not usually included. *Menus* are a real bargain, with many for €20–30 or less. Ordering *à la carte* is always more expensive. Note too, that many restaurants only offer bargain menus for lunch, so it will be more economical to eat at midday than in the evening. A beer will cost around €6 but a glass of house wine can cost as little as €3 while soft drinks are about €5.

A taxi from the airport will cost around €45–70, depending on traffic, plus €1 per bag and a tip of about 5 percent. Single Métro and bus fares cost €1.80, or €14.10 for a *carnet* of 10 tickets, but, again, it's much more economical to take advantage of the various travelcards available on Paris's transport system. For details, see page 274.

Business Visitors

Business travel accounts for about a third of French tourism revenue. This important market has led to the creation of a special Conference and Incentive Department at French tourist offices in London and New York. This department deals with business travel enquiries, and helps organise hotels, conference centres and incentive deals.

Conferences and Exhibitions

Paris is a world leader for conferences, exhibitions and trade fairs, and La Défense is the largest business district in Europe. For further information, call Info-Défense, tel: 01 47 74 84 24, or visit www.ladefense.fr.

For lists of exhibitions and details on participating, contact

Promo Salons agency, via www.promosalons.com, with many offices around the world.

Many châteaux and hotels offer luxurious accommodation for smaller gatherings, and it's even possible to organise a congress at Disneyland Paris.

Trade Fair Venues

Palais des Congrès, Porte Maillot, 17th, tel: 01 40 68 22 22, www.viparis.com.
Paris-Expo, Porte de Versailles, 15th, tel: 01 40 68 22 22, www.viparis.com; Paris's biggest trade fair complex.
Parc des Expositions de Paris-Nord, Villepinte, near Roissy-Charles de Gaulle airport, tel: 01 40 68 22 22, www.viparis.com. CNIT, La Défense, tel: 01 47 73 54 44, www.les4temps.com; has links to other salons at Porte de Champerret and Carrousel du Louvre.

Chambers of Commerce

An excellent source of information on local companies, export and import technicalities, translation agencies and conference centres is the **Chambre de Commerce et d'Industrie de Paris**, 27 avenue de Friedland, 8th, tel: 0820 012 112, www.cci-paris-idf.fr. The **Franco-British Chamber of Commerce** is at 10 Rue de la Bourse, tel: 0825 595 702, www.francobritishchambers.com. There are also French Chambers of Commerce in key cities around the world. In London, the Chamber is at Lincoln House, 4th floor, High Holborn, London, WC1V 7JH, tel: 020 7092 6600, www.ccfgb.co.uk.

C

Children

Paris is most definitely a child-friendly city and there are plenty of activities and sights that they will enjoy. Children under 18 usually go free in museums, even if there's a charge for adults. Many restaurants will have high chairs

and children's menus while hotels will have family rooms and can often supply cots with advance notice. Larger hotels will usually have a baby-sitting service; alternatively try Mababysitter (tel: 09 66 98 08 25, www.baby-sitter-paris.fr) which provides qualified child carers for around €22 per hour.

To find out details of current activities and entertainments available in Paris that should appeal to children, such as plays, films, puppet shows and circuses, refer to *L'Officiel des Spectacles* and *Pariscope*.

Climate

France is the only European country that is both North European and Mediterranean. In Paris, the climate is similar to that of southern England, but less changeable, and temperatures can be higher in mid-summer. The average maximum in July and August is 25°C (76°F), the average minimum 15°C (58°F), but 27°C (80°F) is not unusual. In January, expect a maximum of 6°C (43°F), a minimum of 1°C (43°F). To check the weather for your visit, see www.weather.com.

When to Visit

Spring, when the temperature is ideal for sightseeing, is probably the best time to visit Paris,

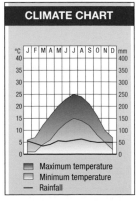

CLIMATE CHART

Maximum temperature
Minimum temperature
Rainfall

although you should be prepared for showers. Autumn mornings can be sharp, but by midday the skies are usually clear and bright. Some believe that winter light shows Paris at its best.

What to Wear

Paris is a great city to explore on foot, so comfortable walking shoes are essential. Bring warm clothes if you're coming to Paris in winter, as the weather can be very chilly, and remember to have something waterproof (or at the least an umbrella) with you in spring or autumn, as showers are quite common.

Most Parisians are very style-conscious, and won't brave even the corner shop without displaying a fair amount of sartorial élan. Casual tourists might therefore consider taking a smart change of clothes – in case, for example, you might want to try a night out at one of the city's many upmarket restaurants, where smart dress is de rigueur.

Crime and Safety

Police

In the event of loss or theft, a report must be made in person at the nearest police station (commissariat) as soon as possible after the event. This will also be required if you wish to claim from your insurance company. Visit www.prefecturedepolice.interieur.gouv.fr for station locations, or for emergency help tel: 17 or 112.

Security

If you take sensible precautions with your possessions, you should be safe in Paris. There is a problem with pickpockets in some of the Métro stations. Obvious centres of prostitution (such as Les Halles and parts of the Bois de Boulogne) are best avoided at night. As anywhere else, use care when withdrawing money with debit or credit cards at a bank, currency exchange office or ATM machine, and make sure others

cannot see your PIN. It's always a good idea to keep a photocopy of your passport in case of theft (see also Emergencies).

Customs Regulations

There are no official restrictions on the movement of goods within the European Union, provided that the goods were purchased within the EU. However, people of all nationalities must declare, upon arrival or departure, sums of cash exceeding €10,000.

Duty-paid goods

If you are an EU resident and buy goods in France on which you pay tax, there are no longer any restrictions on the amounts you may take home with you. However, EU law has set "guidance levels" on the amounts that are acceptable of the following:
Tobacco 800 cigarettes, or 400 cigarillos, or 200 cigars, or 1kg of tobacco
Spirits 10 litres
Fortified wine/wine 90 litres (not more than 60 litres may be sparkling wine)
Beer 110 litres
If you exceed these amounts you must be able to show that the goods are for personal use, for example a family wedding.

Duty-free goods

If you are from outside the EU and buy goods duty-free in France, the following limits still apply (these quantities may be doubled if you live outside Europe):
Tobacco 200 cigarettes, or 100 cigarillos, or 50 cigars, or 250g of tobacco
Alcohol 1 litre of spirits or liqueurs over 22 percent volume, or 2 litres of fortified, sparkling wine or other liqueurs, 4 litres of still wine and 16 litres of beer.
Perfume 50g of perfume, plus 250ml of eau de toilette.
There are no restrictions on the amount of currency you can take into France (however sums over €10,000 must be declared).
For more information contact

Centre de Renseignements des Douanes, tel: 08 11 20 44 44, or check www.douane.gouv.fr.

D

Disabled Travellers

Travellers with mobility problems are advised to book accommodation in advance. Official hotel lists use a symbol to denote wheelchair access, but it's a good idea to check with the hotel regarding the exact facilities available. Information on hotels with good access facilities can be found on the Paris Tourist Office website, www.parisinfo.com.

Hotels in the Accor group (www.accorhotels.com) and Louvre Hotels group (www.louvrehotels.com) have at least one room for disabled guests in a variety of chains to suit all budgets.
Fédération Française des Clubs UNESCO, 173 rue de Charenton, 12th, tel: 01 42 58 68 06; www.ffpunesco.org, has accommodation for disabled young people.

Wheelchairs to rent

CRF Matériel Médical, 153 boulevard Voltaire, 11th, tel: 01 43 73 98 98, www.go2sante.fr.

French Organisations

Association des Paralysés de France, 17 boulevard Auguste-

MORE INFORMATION

The following guides are useful for people with disabilities:
Access in Paris A guidebook that provides essential information for anyone with a mobility problem, including the elderly or parents travelling with young children. It can be obtained from Access Project, 39 Bradley Gardens, West Ealing, London W13 8HE, www.accessinparis.org.
Can be Done The UK travel operator catering for disabled people. www.canbedone.co.uk

EMBASSIES AND CONSULATES

Australia
4 rue Jean-Rey, 15th
Tel: 01 40 59 33 00
www.france.embassy.gov.au
Canada
35 avenue Montaigne, 8th
Tel: 01 44 43 29 00
www.canadainternational.gc.ca/
france
New Zealand
7ter rue Léonard-de-Vinci, 16th
Tel: 01 45 01 43 43
www.nzembassy.com/france
Republic of Ireland
12 avenue Foch, 16th
Tel: 01 44 17 67 00
www.embassyofireland.fr
South Africa
59 quai d'Orsay, 7th
Tel: 01 53 59 23 23
www.afriquesud.net
UK
35 rue du Faubourg-St-Honoré,
8th, tel: 01 44 51 31 00
Consular services: 18bis rue
d'Anjou, 8th, tel: 01 44 51 31 00
http://ukinfrance.fco.gov.uk
US
2 avenue Gabriel, 8th
Tel: 01 43 12 22 22
http://france.usembassy.gov
Office of American Citizen Services (consular services for US
travellers or residents): 4 avenue Gabriel, 8th

French Embassies

Australia
6 Perth Avenue, Yarralumla ACT
2600, Canberra
Tel: (02) 6216 0100
www.ambafrance-au.org
Canada
42 promenade Sussex, Ottawa,
Ontario K1M 2C9
Tel: (613) 789 1795
www.ambafrance-ca.org
New Zealand
Etages 12 et 13 Soverign
House, 34-42 Manners Street,
Wellington, 6142
Tel: (04) 384 25 55
www.ambafrance-nz.org
Republic of Ireland
66 Fitzwilliam Lane,
Dublin 2
Tel: 1 277 5000
www.ambafrance-ie.org
South Africa
250 Melk Street, Nieuw Meuck-
leneuk, 0181 Pretoria
Tel: (0) 12 425 1600
www.ambafrance-rsa.orgUK
58 Knightsbridge, London,
SW1X 7JT
Tel: 0207 073 1000
www.ambafrance-uk.org
US
4101 Reservoir Road NW,
Washington DC20007
Tel: 202 944 6000

UK Organisations
Disability Rights UK, Ground Floor,
CAN Mezzanine 49-51 East Rd, London N1 6AH, tel: 020 7250 8181,
www.disabilityrightsuk.org. Provides
helpful and friendly advice.
Disabled Motoring UK, tel:
01508 489449, www.disabledmo-
toring.org.

US Organisations
**Society for Accessible Travel
and Hospitality** (SATH), 347 Fifth
Avenue, Suite 605, New York, tel:
212-447 7284, www.sath.org. A
non-profit organisation that represents travellers with disabilities,
and can also provide information.
MossRehab Resource Net www.
mossrehab.com. A website with a
very wide range of information on
travelling and other disability-
related issues.

E

Eating Out

France's dedication to the gastronomic arts is legendary, and the
respect for food in all its forms is
still strongly in evidence in the capital. Granted, it may not be as
cheap as it once was to dine out
here – even the classic set menus
can seem pricey these days – but
that doesn't seem to have
deterred either Parisians or tourists. The city is peppered with great
eateries, from bistros, brasseries
and glitzy Michelin-starred restaurants to Breton crêperies and
Moroccan couscousseries and
top-notch Asian restaurants, all of
which affords plenty of opportunity
to sample life as a true bon viveur.
Note that in up-market restaurants
there is often a dress code, with a
jacket requested and tie preferred
for men. Note, too, that many restaurants close on Sunday evening
(brasseries excepted) and for the
whole of August.

Electricity
The standard voltage is 220 volts.
Round-pin plugs are used, so

Blanqui, 13th, tel: 01 40 78 69
00, www.apf.asso.fr.
The association may be able to
answer specific enquiries and can
provide branch addresses.
CIDJ (see page 285, Study in
France) youth information service
has extensive information on services for less-able young travellers. It publishes *Vacances pour
Personnes Handicapées* and leaf-
lets on activity and sports holidays for young disabled people.
**Union Nationale des Associa-
tions de Parents d'Enfants Ina-
daptés** (UNAPEI), 15 rue
Coysevox, 18th, tel: 01 44 85 50
50, www.unapei.org. Parents may
wish to contact this organisation
for information about facilities for

children with disabilities.
**Comité de Liaison pour le Trans-
port des Personnes Handicapées** (http://info-handicap.com),
Conseil National des Transports,
34 avenue Marceau, 8th, tel: 01
53 23 85 85. Gives brief information on accessibility and arrange-
ments for less-able passengers
on public transport, and contacts
for special transport schemes in
France.
Ptitcar, 27-29 rue Raffet, 16th, 09
83 200 169, www.ptitcar.com, is an
excellent transport company that
operates a fleet of wheelchair-
accessible vehicles for transport
and tours. They also prepare vaca-
tion itineraries for wheelchair users,
and offer other helpful services.

pack an adaptor. Visitors from North America with 110v equipment will also need a transformer for the higher voltage.

Etiquette

If you walk into a small shop or restaurant with people in it, it is usually polite to say "bonjour". And if someone says "bonjour" to you it is polite to reciprocate; it is nice to add "monsieur" or "madame" or "mademoiselle" (for young women) after it eg. "bonjour, madame". If you enter a church or other place of worship, be sure to cover up with no bare shoulders, cleavage or legs on show for women.

F

Festival and Events

A listing of all major events in Paris is available from the Tourist Office (see page 286). Here are just some of the festivals and events that occur every year:
January sales
February–March *Six Nations Rugby Tournament* International rugby extravaganza running for three weekends.
late February–early March *Salon de l'Agriculture* (www.salon-agriculture.com). Rural France comes to Paris in a huge agricultural and food fair.

April Paris Marathon
April–early June *Foire du Trône* (www.foiredutrone.com). France's biggest funfair; Pelouse de Reuilly, Métro: Porte Dorée.
May *Carré Rive Gauche* (www.carrerivegauche.com). Open days at the Left Bank antiques enclave.
late May–early June French Tennis Open (www.rolandgarros.com); Stade Roland Garros, Métro: Porte d'Auteuil
early June Champs-Elysées Film Festival (www.champselyseesfilmfestival.com).
June *Fête de la Musique* (21 June). Huge street music festival; free concerts and dances all across Paris. Fete du Cinema (http://feteducinema.com). A four day film feast for cinema buffs that usually starts on the last week of the month.
June-September Opéra côté Cour. Summer open-air opera festival held in Bercy Village with short performances and singing workshops. End of June Paris Air Show at Le Bourget. Over a hundred years old, this is arguably the most important international aerospace trade show in the world.
July Bastille Day. Celebrations begin at the Bastille on the evening of 13 July; on the 14th, a military parade starts at 10am on the Champs-Elysées. Fireworks follow at the Trocadéro.
mid-July–mid-August *Paris Quartier d'Eté* (www.quartierdete.

EMERGENCIES

Ambulance: 15
Police: 17
Fire service: 18
Emergency calls from a mobile phone: 112
SOS Help English-language helpline (daily 3–11pm): 01 46 21 46 46

com). Summer arts festival: contemporary dance, street theatre, world music and outdoor jazz provide cultural entertainment when the theatres and concert halls close down for the summer. See page 107. *Cinéma en Plein Air*. Classic movies on a giant screen at the free outdoor film festival at La Villette.
September *Journée du Patrimoine* (3rd weekend). Open day at otherwise off-limits government and private buildings. *Festival d'Automne* (until Dec; www.festival-automne.com). Annual festival of theatre, music and dance.
October (1st Sat) *La Nuit Blanche*. Stay up all night for artistic happenings in museums and venues all over town.
November The arrival of Beaujolais Nouveau is celebrated in bars and cafés (3rd Thursday of the month).
December Notre-Dame is packed for the Christmas Eve service. On New Year's Eve, crowds fill the Champs-Elysées, and there's a giant fireworks display at Trocadéro.
mid December–late January *Patinoire de Noël*. Ice-skating in a spectacular setting: Champs-Élysées.

G

Gay Travellers

The Marais (the 4th *arrondissement*) is the most gay-friendly district in Paris, with gay-oriented restaurants, wine bars, boutiques, bookstores, beauty salons, hotels, bars and discos. For more information check out the websites www.parismarais.

The Marais is the most gay-friendly neighbourhood in Paris.

com, www.gay-france.net and http://paris.gaycities.com. There are various free magazines you can pick up in most gay bars in the 3rd and 4th *arrondissements*. The gay magazine *Têtu* (www.tetu. com) is a useful source of information, and can be bought at most news kiosks in the city.

H

Health & Medical Care

If you are an EU national and you fall ill in France, you can receive emergency medical treatment from doctors, dentists and hospitals. You will have to pay the cost of this treatment, but are entitled to claim from the French *Sécurité*

Sociale, which refunds up to 70 percent of your medical expenses. To receive a refund you must have a **European Health Insurance Card** (**EHIC**). These are available online at www.ehic. org.uk or can be ordered through post offices and health centres.

If you need to see a doctor, expect to pay at least €23 per consultation, with prescription charges on top. The doctor will provide a statement of treatment *(feuille de soins)*. With this, EU citizens can reclaim around 70 percent of the cost of treatment. If you buy any medicines on prescription, check that the price stamp *(vignette)* is attached to the *feuille de soins* by the chemist, so that you can reclaim part of this cost too. When complete, the *feuille de*

Pharmacy sign.

soins and prescription should be sent as soon as possible to the local *Caisse Primaire d'Assurance Maladie* (the doctor or chemist will have the address, or see the phone book under *Sécurité Sociale*) for your refund. It can also be a good idea to include a photocopy of your EHIC, and keep copies yourself of the other documents. The refund will be sent to your home, which will take about a month. If you have any difficulties, contact the **Caisse Primaire d'Assurance Maladie de Paris**, 27 rue Georges Auric, 75019 Paris, www.ameli.fr or in the UK call tel: 0191 218 1999.

For more information, consult the leaflet **Health Advice for Travellers** (available from post offices, online at www.dh.gov.uk or by tel: 020 7210 4850). Reciprocal EU health agreements do not cover all medical expenses, such as the cost of bringing a sick person back to the UK, so the Department of Health advises travellers also to take out private insurance. If you plan to drive in France, you should check that your motor insurance covers you for accidents abroad.

For travellers from North America, a comprehensive travel insurance policy with full medical cover is essential. You can also contact the **International Association for Medical Assistance to Travellers (IAMAT),** based in Guelph, Ontario, tel: 519 836 0102/416 652 0137, www.iamat.org. This non-profit-making group offers

WHAT'S ON AND WHERE TO GET TICKETS

The listings magazines *L'Officiel des Spectacles* and *Pariscope* (www.premiere.fr) provide full details of cultural events and venues in and around the city. *Figaroscope*, the Wednesday supplement of *Le Figaro* national newspaper (http://evene.lefigaro.fr), is another very useful source of entertainment information.

Music, theatre and tickets for a big range of other events in Paris can also be booked at discounted prices through various local websites; try www.billetreduc.com, www.ticketac.com or www.promotheatre.com. All are in French only; normally, once you make the booking by credit card you will be sent an email or a text message to a mobile phone with a booking number, which you must show at the venue (about 30 minutes before the performance) to collect your tickets.

The Paris tourist office website provides a great deal of up-to-date information in several languages on what's on in the city in theatre, music, exhibitions and other attractions,

together with news of upcoming programmes and festivals, on www.parisinfo.com.
Main ticket agencies
FNAC Billeterie, at FNAC stores: 1–7 Forum des Halles, rue Pierre-Lescot, 1st; 77–81 boulevard. St-Germain, 6th; 136 rue de Rennes, 6th; 74 avenue des Champs-Elysées, 8th; passage du Havre, 109 rue St-Lazare, 9th; Centre Commercial Italie, 30 avenue d'Italie, 13th; 26–30 avenue des Ternes, 17th. Bookings can also be made online at www.fnac.com.
Kiosque Madeleine, Place de la Madeleine, 8th, Kiosque Ternes, 17th, www.kiosque theatre.com; and **Kiosque Montparnasse**, Parvis de la Gare Montparnasse, 14th; these kiosks sell tickets for performances the same day at half-price. Tue–Sat 12.30–8pm, Sun 12.30–4pm.
CROUS (Centre Régional des Œuvres Universitaires et Scolaires), 39 avenue Georges-Bernanos, 5th, tel: 01 40 51 62 00, www.crous-paris.fr. Reduced-price seats for students (with valid student cards).

HOSPITALS

All state hospitals have casualty departments (urgences). A complete list is available on www.aphp.fr. Below are some of the larger ones:

Hôpital Bichat
46 rue Henri-Huchard, 18th
Tel: 01 40 25 80 80

Hôpital Fernaud-Widal
(poisons control centre)
200 rue du Faubourg St-Denis, 10th
Tel: 01 40 05 45 45

Hôpital Hôtel-Dieu
1 place du Parvis-Notre-Dame, 4th
Tel: 01 42 34 82 34

Hôpital Necker
(children's hospital)
149 rue de Sèvres, 15th
Tel: 01 44 49 40 00

Hôpital de la Pitié-Salpêtrière
47 boulevard de l'Hôpital, 13th
Tel: 01 42 16 00 00

Hôpital St-Louis
1 avenue Claude-Vellefaux, 10th
Tel: 01 42 49 49 49

members fixed rates for treatment from participating physicians. Members receive a passport-sized medical record and a directory of English-speaking IAMAT doctors in France. Membership is free, but a donation is requested.

In Paris, you can find English-speaking health services at the highly regarded but expensive private **American Hospital** (Hôpital Américain de Paris, tel: 01 46 41 25 25, www.americanhospital.org), or the **British Hospital** (Hôpital Franco-Britannique, tel: 01 46 39 22 00, www.british-hospital.org), which is covered by the French social security system. However, not all the staff are bilingual, and the hospital is mainly known for its maternity unit.

Pharmacies

Most pharmacies display flashing green neon crosses, and are open from 9 or 10am to 7 or 8pm. At night, they all post the addresses of the nearest late-opening pharmacies in their windows. Staff can provide basic medical advice and services. The following pharmacies also open late every night:

Dhéry, 84 avenue des Champs-Elysées, 8th (Métro George V), tel: 01 45 62 02 41. Open 24 hours.

Pharmacie Européenne de la Place de Clichy, 6 place de Clichy, 9th (Métro Place de Clichy), tel: 01 48 74 65 18. Open 24 hours.

Pharmacie des Halles, 10 boulevard de Sébastopol, 4th (Métro Châtelet), tel: 01 42 72 03 23, fax: 01 42 72 52 10. Mon–Sat 9am–midnight and Sun 9am–10pm.

Publicis Drugstore, 133 avenue des Champs-Elysées, 8th (Métro Etoile), tel: 01 47 20 39 25. Open daily till 2am.

I

Internet

WiFi (pronounced "wee-fee" in France) is now widely available in French hotels, although there is often a charge. For a list of free Wi-Fi spots around the city, including public buildings, parks and squares see www.paris.fr. A list of cafés with free Wi-Fi can be found here http://myparisianlife.com. There are cyber cafés all over the city – ask at the tourist office for current ones or see www.parisinfo.com.

There is an enormous wealth of information available over the web, from pages telling you how to get to your destination, to how to speak the language when you get there. The following entries are only the tip of the iceberg:

www.parisinfo.com official site of the Paris Tourist Office, with information on hotels, sites, events, exhibitions, transport, weather and more
www.rendezvousenfrance.com official site of the French Tourist Office, Maison de la France, for general information on France
www.paris.fr site of the Mairie de Paris, the Town Hall

www.ratp.fr the Paris transport system site
www.culture.fr official site of the Ministry of Culture
www.monuments-nationaux.fr official site of France's Department of National Monuments
www.rmn.fr guide to national museum exhibitions
www.meteofrance.com weather online
www.pagesjaunes.fr the French Yellow Pages
www.lemonde.fr France's most respected newspaper
www.mondediplo.com Le Monde's supplement Le Monde Diplomatique in English
http://evene.lefigaro.fr online edition of Le Figaro's weekly Paris arts and restaurant supplement
www.timeout.com/paris Time Out city guide for Paris
www.gogocityguides.com a guide to what's hip and happening in the city
www.girlsguidetoparis.com a guide to Paris for women with a focus on shopping

M

Maps

Essential Paris (Editions de l'Indispensable) is the most useful map for visitors. It can be bought for about €5 at any of the ubiquitous news-stands and kiosks around the city or on-line (www.massin.fr). You may also be able to get by on the tourist office maps. Free maps of the public transport network can be picked up in the metro stations.

Media

Newspapers

The two main national dailies are Le Monde, the most influential paper in the country, which has a rather dry and leftish slant on politics and economic news, and sells about 330,000 copies daily. The more conservative Le Figaro sells about the same number of copies.

TRANSPORT

Le Parisien, the most popular daily newspaper in France.

The paper representing the Communist Party is *L'Humanité*, and not veering so heavily left is Jean-Paul Sartre's brainchild, *Libération*. The major weekly news magazines are *Le Point* (right), *L'Express* (centre) and *Le Nouvel Observateur* (left), which each sell around 350,000–500,000 copies. British, American and other European dailies are available on the same day at city-centre kiosks and shops showing *journaux* or *presse* signs.

The *International Herald Tribune*, published in Paris, has listings for the city. To find out what is going on in Paris, try *L'Officiel des Spectacles* (www.offi.fr) or *Pariscope* (both out on Wednesday), which give listings of movies, clubs, exhibitions, concerts, theatres and more.

Radio

France Inter (87.8 MHz; www.franceinter.fr) is the biggest station, offering something to suit all tastes. Radio Classique (101.1 MHz) plays non-stop lightweight classical music.

For something a bit less mainstream, try France Musiques (91.7 and 92.1 MHz; www.francemusique.fr). RTL (104.3 MHz; www.rtl.fr), a popular station throughout France, plays music from the charts interspersed with chat.

Europe 1 (104.7 FM; http://www.europe1.fr) is the best for morning news coverage, while France Info (105.5 FM; www.franceinfo.fr) is a non-stop French news channel.

Television

TF1, France 2, France 3, France 5, Arte and M6 are the five main television stations. There is also a huge choice of cable channels, which are often available in larger hotels.

Canal+ is a subscription channel, which shows big-name films. CNN and BBC World are also available in many hotels.

Money

Currency

The euro (€) is the official French currency and is available in 500, 200, 100, 50, 20, 10 and 5 euro notes, and 2 euro, 1 euro, 50 cent, 20 cent, 10 cent, 5 cent, 2 cent and 1 cent coins. There are 100 cents to 1 euro.

Credit Cards

Most large shops and restaurants and almost all hotels accept credit cards. The most common in France are Visa, MasterCard and Carte Bleue (often called "CB"). American Express (Amex) and Diner's Club (DC) are widely recognised, and many places also accept Maestro and Cirrus, but if you don't see a card's sticker in a hotel or restaurant window, it's advisable to double-check.

Exchange

Bureaux de change at train stations vary their hours in high or low seasons, but most are open Monday to Friday 7am–7pm. In banks, separate exchange counters are increasingly rare.

Exchange offices at **Roissy-Charles de Gaulle** (terminals 2A, 2B and 2D) and **Orly Sud** airports are open daily until 11pm.

Travelex at 194 rue de Rivoli, 1st, tel: 01 47 03 49 52, or for other locations visit: www.travelex.fr. Mon-Sat 9.15am-7.30pm, Sun 10.45am-5.45pm.

Multi Change at 180 boulevard St-Germain, 6th, tel: 01 42 22 41 00, www.multi-change.com. Mon-Sat 9.30am-6.30pm. Take your passport if you want to cash travellers' cheques.

Cash Machines

You can draw cash from bank dispensing machines (ATMs) using a credit card or European bank cashpoint card, using your PIN if your card is one of the following: Visa, MasterCard, Maestro or Cirrus. Be sure to confirm with your home bank that both your card and PIN can be used abroad.

A – Z

LOST PROPERTY

If your documents, cash, credit cards or other belongings are lost or stolen, go to the *commissariat de police* closest to the scene of the incident as soon as possible – even before contacting your credit card company or your consulate. If you lose your passport, report it to your consulate immediately after notifying the police. There is a complete list of consulates in the local Yellow Pages (*Pages Jaunes*). If credit cards are lost or stolen, local numbers are: **American Express**, tel: 0800 83 28 20

Diners Club, tel: 0810 82 01 43 **MasterCard**, tel: 0800 90 13 87

Visa, tel: 0800 901 179 To reclaim anything else lost in Paris, go (with ID) to the **Bureau des Objets Trouvés**, 6 rue des Morillons, 15th, tel: 08 21 00 25 25 (Métro Convention); Mon–Thu 8.30am–5pm, Fri 8.30am–4.30pm.

LANGUAGE

Tipping

Restaurants By law, restaurant bills must include a service charge, which is usually 12 or 15 percent. Nevertheless, it is common to leave a small additional tip (not more than 5 percent) for the waiter if the service has been especially good. Address waiters as *Monsieur* (never *garçon*) and waitresses as *Mademoiselle*, if they are young, or *Madame*, if they are older.

Taxis Rounding up to the nearest euro is the norm.

O

Opening Hours

Office workers normally start early (8.30am is not uncommon) and often stay at their desks until 6pm or later. This is partly to make up for the long lunch hours (two hours, from around noon) traditional in public offices. Many companies are changing to shorter lunch breaks, as employees appreciate the advantages of getting home earlier in the evening.

Traditionally **banks** open from Monday to Friday 9am to 5pm and are closed on Saturday and Sunday. However, many banks now close on Monday instead, and open on Saturday morning.

Food shops, especially bakers, tend to open early. Most boutiques and department stores open about 9am, but some do not

Postboxes are yellow.

open until 10am. Traditionally most French shops close from around noon to 2.30pm, but in Paris many remain open until 7 or 7.30pm. Big department stores do not close at lunchtime, and open until 9 or 10pm on Thursday. Most shops close on Sunday, but bakers and patisseries are usually open in the morning.

Suburban hypermarkets are usually open all day until 8 or 9pm (except Sunday).

P

Postal Services

The French post office is run by the PTT (*Poste et Télécommunications*). The main branches are open on average Mon–Fri 8am–7pm and Sat 8am–noon. The central post office at 52 rue du Louvre, 1st, tel: 36 31, www.laposte.fr, operates a daily 24-hour service. Another large post office is at Place de la Bourse, 2nd, tel: 36 31, Mon–Fri 8.15am–8pm, Sat 9.30am–1pm. Fax and photocopying facilities and limited Internet access are available in all larger post offices.

Stamps *(timbres)* are available at most *tabacs* (tobacconists) and other shops selling postcards and greetings cards. For postcards and letters weighing up to 20 grams, postage costs €0.76 within France and €0.95 to the rest of the EU. Sending a letter airmail to Australia, the US and Canada costs €1.20.

R

Religious Services

Most religious believers in France are Catholic, and Paris's many churches, including Notre-Dame, are open to the public. For a list of all denominational churches, mosques, temples and synagogues, look out for the guide Essential Paris from a kiosk or bookshop. For information on

New Year's Day, Easter Monday, 1 May (Labour Day), 8 May (end of World War II in Europe), Ascension Day – mid/late May, Whit Monday – late May, 14 July (Bastille Day), 15 August (Feast of the Assumption), 1 November (All Saints' Day), 11 November (Armistice Day, 1918), 25 December (Christmas).

catholic services contact the **Service d'Information Religieuse** www.paris.catholique.fr.

There are services in English around Paris, notably in the **American Church**, 65 quai d'Orsay, 7th, tel: 01 40 62 05 00, or visit www.acparis.org.

S

Student Travellers

Students and young people under the age of 26 can get cut-price travel to Paris. For a prolonged stay, it may be worth finding out about an exchange visit or study holiday. The following organisations provide information or arrange visits.

UK Services

The **British Council** provides opportunities for international youth experience, exchange and other projects. Go to www.britishcouncil.org to find out about the latest opportunities.

Those who can speak French could approach UK-based camping holiday operators, such as **Holidaybreak** (Hartford Manor, Greenbank Lane, Northwich, Cheshire CW8 1HW, tel: 0844 346 1470, www.holidaybreakjobs.com, which often employ students as site attendants in France and other European countries in summer.

US Services

American Council for International Studies (ACIS), Boston Regional Office, 343 Congress

TRANSPORT

Street, Suite 3100, Boston, MA, 02210, tel: 1 800 888 ACIS, www. acis.com.
Council on International Educational Exchange (CIEE), 300 Fore Street, Portland, ME 04101, tel: 207 553 4000, www.ciee.org. Work and study programmes overseas.
Youth for Understanding, 2141 Wisconsin Ave, NW Suit D2, Washington, DC 20007 www.yfu. org. One of the world's oldest and largest international exchange organisations.

Study in France

Several French tour operators can organise study tours and language courses.
Office National de Garantie des Séjours Linguistiques, 8 rue César-Franck, 15th, tel: 01 42 73 36 70, www.loffice.org, is a national association that quality-check all its members that offer language courses. Write for a list of schools, or try the following organisations:
Centre d'Information et de Documentation Jeunesse (CIDJ), 101 quai Branly, 15th, tel: 01 44 49 12 00 (from Monday to Friday 1–6pm, Sat 1-5pm), www.cidj. com. A national organisation that disseminates information on youth and student activities.
CROUS, 39 avenue Georges-Bernanos, 5th, tel: 01 40 51 62 00, www.crous-paris.fr. Provides information on student accommodation, Resto-U canteens and courses and enrolment for British students studying in France.

T

Telephones

All telephone numbers in France have 10 digits. Paris and Ile de France numbers begin with 01, while the rest of France is divided into four zones: Northwest 02; Northeast 03; Southeast and Corsica 04; and Southwest 05. Toll-free phone numbers begin with 0800; all other numbers beginning with 08

are charged at variable rates; and 06 numbers are mobile phones. You get 50 percent more call-time for your money if you ring between 10.30pm and 8am on weekdays, and from 2pm at weekends.
The main mobile networks in France are Orange, SFR, Bouygues Télécom and Free they are compatible with GSM 900 and GSM 1800 phones. It is a good idea to check with your network provider that your phone is set up for roaming before you head to France and also to find out the cheapest way to make and receive calls while abroad. If you plan to make a lot of calls, especially within France, it will be cheaper to buy a French pay-as-you-go (*prépayé*) SIM card with a French number to use in your phone during your stay. It is also possible to hire SIM cards and phones from a wide variety of specialist companies in the UK and US for a trip. The recently introduced LEBARA SIM cards sold at most metro stations are worth considering as they're cheap and come with generous data allowance (3GB).
Most public phone boxes in Paris are now operated with a card (*télécarte*). A *télécarte* can be bought from kiosks, *tabacs* and post offices for 50 or 120 units (currently €8 or €15). Insert the card and follow the instructions on the screen. You can only receive calls at phone boxes displaying a blue bell sign.
You can also phone from post offices. To call long-distance, ask at the counter and you you will be assigned a booth – you pay when the call is over. Cafés and *tabacs* often also have public phones, which usually take coins or *jetons*, coin-like discs bought at the bar.
To dial Paris from the UK: 00 (international code) + 33 (France) + 1 (Paris) + an eight-figure number. To call other countries from France, first dial the international code (00), then the country code: Australia 61, UK 44, US and Canada 1. If using a US credit phonecard, call the company's access number: Sprint, tel: 08 00 99 00 87; AT&T, tel: 08 00 99 00 11; MCI, tel: 08 00 99 00 19.

Time Zone

France is one hour ahead of Greenwich Mean Time (GMT) and six ahead of Eastern Standard Time. Most French people use the 24-hour clock, so 1pm appears as 13h00 on timetables and is referred to as *treize heures*.

Tour Operators

In the UK
British Airways Holidays, tel: 0844 493 0787, www.britishairways.com. Short breaks by plane.
Cresta, tel: 0844 800 7020, www.crestaholidays.co.uk. Breaks to Paris by plane or Eurostar.
Eurostar, tel: 03432 186 186, www.eurostar.com. Booking a train and hotel together usually saves money.
Railbookers, tel: 0203 780 2222, www.railbookers.com, 14 Bonhill Street, London, EC2A 4BX, tel: 0203 327 0800. Short breaks to Paris by train.
Riviera Travel, New Manor, 328 Wetmore Road, Burton-on-Trent, Staffs, DE14 1SP, tel: 0128 374 2300, www.rivieratravel.co.uk. Escorted four-day trips to Paris by Eurostar.
Travel Editions, 69-85 Tabernacle Street, London, EC2A 4BD, tel: 0207 251 0045, www.travel editions.co.uk. Escorted short

USEFUL NUMBERS

Directory Enquiries
118 218
International Directory Enquiries
32 12
International Operator
32 12 + country code
Reverse charges/collect calls: You cannot normally make reverse-charge calls within France, but you can to other countries where such calls are accepted. Go through the international operator and ask to make a PCV (pay-say-vay) call.

A – Z

LANGUAGE

Sightseeing on the Seine.

theme breaks by Eurostar: Gastronomic Paris and Secret Paris on Foot.
Travelsphere, tel: 0185 889 8756, www.travelsphere.co.uk. Escorted short breaks to Paris by coach.

In the US

Academic Travel, 1155 Connecticut Ave NW, Ste 300 Washington, DC 20036-4355, tel: 800 566 7896, www.academic-travel.com. Educational tours for adults.
Adventures and Voyages, PO Box 352, Lincoln, California 95648, tel: 888 868 5688, www. adventuresandvoyages.com. Personalised itineraries to Paris.
France Journeys, 12381 Fenton Road, Fenton, MI 48430, tel: 888 357 6978 or 810 714 3803, www.francejourneys.com. Organises individual breaks to Paris and elsewhere in France.
Tour Vacations to Go, 5851 San Felipe, Suite 500, Houston, TX 77057, tel: 832 252 2265, www.tourvacationstogo.com. Individual and escorted tours to Paris for all budgets.

In Paris

Cityrama, 2 rue des Pyramides, 1st, tel: 01 44 55 61 00, www.parisvision.com. Excursions to Versailles, Giverny, Normandy, the Loire and elsewhere in France.
FcomFrance, 11 avenue de l'Opéra, 1st, tel: 01 42 61 24 64, www.fcomfrance.com. Coach excursions to Versailles, Giverny and the châteaux of the Loire.
France Tourisme, 33 quai des Grands Augustins, 6th, tel: 01 53 10 35 36, www.francetourisme.fr. Excursions include Champagne, Normandy beaches and Fontainebleau.

Tourist Offices

Atout France Lincoln House, 300 High Holborn, London WC1V 7JH, tel: 0906 824 4123 (calls 60p per minute), http://uk.rendezvousenfrance.com. Mon–Fri 10am–4pm. Useful source of information before you travel.
Tourist Offices in Paris
All provide ample information and can book hotels. Most are closed 1 May and 25 Dec.
25 rue des Pyramides, 1st, Métro: Pyramides. May–Oct daily 9am–7pm, Nov–Apr Mon–Sat 10am–7pm.
Champs-Elysées, corner of avenue Marigny, 8th, Métro: Champs Elysées-Clémenceau. May–Oct daily 10am–7pm.
Gare de Lyon, 20 boulevard Diderot, 12th, Métro: Gare de Lyon. Mon–Sat 8am–6pm.
Gare du Nord, 18 rue de Dunkerque, 10th, Métro: Gare du Nord. Daily 8am–6pm.
Anvers, outside 72 boulevard Rochechouart, 18th, Métro: Anvers. Daily 10am–6pm.
Montmartre, 21 place du Tertre, 18th. Métro: Abbesses. Daily 10am–6pm.
Hôtel de Ville, 11 place de l'Hôtel de Ville, 4th. Métro: Hôtel de Ville. July–Aug 10am–6pm.
Notre Dame, Parvis de Notre Dame, 4th. Métro: Cité. May–Oct daily 10am–7pm.
Bastille, 4 place Bastille, 12th. Métro: Bastille. July–Aug daily 11am–7pm.

U

Useful Addresses

RATP Information, in English, tel: 32 46, www.ratp.fr.
SNCF, tel: 36 35, www.sncf.fr, for train information.
http://parisbytrain.com, a useful website with practical information on how to travel Paris and the surrounding Ile-de-France by train.

V

Visas and Passports

All visitors to France require a valid passport or national ID card issued by one of the EU member states. No visa is required by visitors from European Union (EU) member states, the US, Australia, Canada or Japan. Nationals of other countries may need a visa; if in doubt, check with the French Consulate in your home country. For anyone (including EU nationals) who wants to stay longer than 90 days, it is no longer obligatory to obtain a *carte de séjour*, but it is still advisable to get one, from French Consulates or the Préfecture de Police (www.prefecturedepolice.fr), 9 boulevard du Palais, 4th, tel: 01 58 80 80 80.

W

Weights & Measures

Metric measurements are always used in France. For a quick conversion: 1 metre is about a yard, 100 grams is just under 4oz, 1kg is 2lbs 2oz. Distance is in kilometres: 1km equals five-eighths of a mile, so 80km is 50 miles.

PARIS INFO

www.parisinfo.com has details of all services.
To call the Paris Tourist Office, tel: 08 29 68 30 00; calls cost €0.34 per minute.

LANGUAGE

UNDERSTANDING THE LANGUAGE

GENERAL

French is the native language of more than 90 million people and the acquired language of 190 million. It is a Romance language descended from the Vulgar Latin spoken by the Roman conquerors of Gaul. It still carries the reputation of being the most cultured language in the world and the most beautiful. People often tell stories about the impatience of the French towards foreigners who do not attempt to speak their language. In general, however, if you attempt to communicate with them in French, they will appreciate it and may even overcome their reluctance to respond in English.

Since much of the English vocabulary is related to French, thanks to the Norman Conquest in 1066, travellers will often recognise many helpful cognates: words such as *hôtel, café* and *bagages* hardly need to be translated. You should be aware, however, of some misleading "false friends" *(faux amis)*, words that look like English words but mean something different.
le car coach, also railway carriage
le conducteur bus driver
personne can mean either person or nobody, depending on the context.

The Alphabet

Learning the pronunciation of the French alphabet is a good idea. In particular, learn how to spell out your name.
a = ah, **b** = bay, **c** = say, **d** = day, **e** = uh, **f** = ef, **g** = zhay, **h** = ash, **i** = ee, **j** = zhee, **k** = ka, **l** = el, **m** = em, **n** = en, **o** = oh, **p** = pay, **q** = kew, **r** = ehr, **s** = ess, **t** = tay, **u** = ew, **v** = vay, **w** = dooblah vay, **x** = eex, **y** = ee grek, **z** = zed.

USEFUL WORDS & PHRASES

How much is it? *C'est combien?*
What is your name? *Comment vous appelez-vous?*
My name is... *Je m'appelle...*
Do you speak English? *Parlez-vous anglais?*
I am English/American *Je suis anglais(e)/américain(e)*
I don't understand *Je ne comprends pas*
Please speak more slowly *Parlez plus lentement, s'il vous plaît*
Can you help me? *Pouvez-vous m'aider?*
I'm looking for... *Je cherche...*
Where is...? *Où est...?*
I'm sorry *Excusez-moi/Pardon*
I don't know *Je ne sais pas*
No problem *Pas de problème*
Have a good day! *Bonne journée!*

That's it *C'est ça*
Here it is *Voici*
There it is *Voilà*
Let's go *On y va/Allons-y*
See you tomorrow *A demain*
See you soon *A bientôt*
Show me the word in the book *Montrez-moi le mot dans le livre*
At what time? *A quelle heure?*
When? *Quand?*
What time is it? *Quelle heure est-il?*
yes *oui*
no *non*
please *s'il vous plaît*
thank you *merci*
(very much) *(beaucoup)*
you're welcome *de rien*
excuse me *excusez-moi*
hello *bonjour*
hi/bye *salut*
OK *d'accord*
goodbye *au revoir*
good evening *bonsoir*
here *ici*
there *là*
left *gauche*
right *droite*
straight on *tout droit*
far *loin*
near *près d'ici*
opposite *en face*
beside *à côté de*
over there *là-bas*
today *aujourd'hui*
yesterday *hier*
tomorrow *demain*
now *maintenant*
later *plus tard*

right away *tout de suite*
this morning *ce matin*
this afternoon *cet après-midi*
this evening *ce soir*

On Arrival

I want to get off at... *Je voudrais descendre à...*
Is there a bus to the Louvre? *Est-ce qu'il y a un bus pour le Louvre?*
What street is this? *Sur quelle rue sommes-nous?*
Which line do I take for...? *Quelle ligne dois-je prendre pour...?*
How far is...? *A quelle distance se trouve...?*
Validate your ticket *Compostez votre billet*
airport *l'aéroport*
railway station *la gare*
bus station *la gare routière*
Métro stop *la station de Métro*
bus *l'autobus, le car*
bus stop *l'arrêt*
platform *le quai*
ticket *le billet*
return ticket *aller-retour*
hitch hiking *l'autostop*
toilets *les toilettes*
This is the hotel address *C'est l'adresse de l'hôtel*
I'd like a (single/double) room... *Je voudrais une chambre (pour une/deux personnes)...*
...with shower *avec douche*
...with bath *avec salle de bain*
Is breakfast included? *Le prix comprend-il le petit-déjeuner?*
May I see the room? *Puis-je voir la chambre?*
washbasin *le lavabo*
bed *le lit*
key *la clé*
elevator *l'ascenseur*
air-conditioned *climatisé*

Emergencies

Help! *Au secours!*
Stop! *Arrêtez!*
Call a doctor *Appelez un médecin*
Call an ambulance *Appelez une ambulance*
Call the police *Appelez la police*
Call the fire brigade *Appelez les pompiers*
Where is the nearest telephone? *Où est le téléphone le plus proche?*
Where is the nearest hospital? *Où est l'hôpital le plus proche?*
I am sick *Je suis malade*
I have lost my passport/purse *J'ai perdu mon passeport/porte-monnaie*

Shopping

Where is the nearest bank (post office)? *Où se trouve la banque (Poste) la plus proche?*
I'd like to buy *Je voudrais acheter*
How much is it? *C'est combien?*
Do you take credit cards? *Est-ce que vous acceptez les cartes de crédit?*
I'm just looking *Je regarde seulement*
Have you got? *Avez-vous...?*
I'll take it *Je le prends*
I'll take this one/that one *Je prends celui-ci/celui-là*
What size is it? *C'est quelle taille?*
Anything else? *Avec ceci?*
size (clothes) *la taille*
size (shoes) *la pointure*
cheap *bon marché*
expensive *cher*

enough *assez*
too much *trop*
a piece of *un morceau de*
each *la pièce (eg ananas, €2 la pièce)*
receipt *le reçu*
chemist *la pharmacie*
bakery *la boulangerie*
bookshop *la librairie*
library *la bibliothèque*
department store *le grand-magasin*
delicatessen *la charcuterie/ le traiteur*
fishmonger *la poissonnerie*
grocery *l'alimentation/l'épicerie*
tobacconist *le tabac (also sells stamps and newspapers)*
market *le marché*
supermarket *le supermarché*
junk shop *la brocante*

Sightseeing

town *la ville*
old town *la vieille ville*
street *la rue*
square *la place*
abbey *l'abbaye*
cathedral *la cathédrale*
church *l'église*
keep *le donjon*
mansion *l'hôtel*
hospital *l'hôpital*
town hall *l'hôtel de ville/la mairie*

BASIC RULES

If you speak no French at all, it is worth trying to master a few simple phrases. The fact that you have made an effort is likely to break the ice. More and more French people like practising their English on visitors, especially waiters and the younger generation. Pronunciation is the key; they really will not understand if you get it very wrong. Remember to **emphasise each syllable**, but not to pronounce the last consonant of a word as a rule, unless it is followed by a vowel. Also bear in mind "er", "et" and "ez" endings are pronounced "ay" (this includes the plural "s") and "h"s are silent.

Whether to use "**vous**" or "**tu**" is a vexed question; increasingly the familiar form of "tu" is used, but it is safer to be formal, and use "vous". It is very important to be courteous; always address people as **Mademoiselle**, **Madame** or **Monsieur**, and address them by their surnames until you are confident first names are acceptable. When entering a shop always say, "*Bonjour Monsieur/Madame/Mademoiselle*," and "*Merci, au revoir*," when leaving.

Garçon is the word for waiter but is never used directly; say *Monsieur, Madame* or *Mademoiselle*, to attract a waiter's attention.

nave *la nef*
stained glass *le vitrail*
staircase *l'escalier*
tower *la tour (La Tour Eiffel)*
walk *le tour*
country house/castle *le château*
Gothic *gothique*
Roman *romain*
Romanesque *roman*
museum *le musée*
art gallery *la galerie*
exhibition *l'exposition*
tourist information office *l'office du tourisme/le syndicat d'initiative*
free *gratuit*
open *ouvert*
closed *fermé*
every day *tous les jours*
all year *toute l'année*
all day *toute la journée*
swimming pool *la piscine*
to book *réserver*
town map *le plan*
road map *la carte*

Dining Out

Table d'hôte (the "host's table") is one set menu served at a set price. *Prix fixe* is a fixed-price menu. *A la carte* means differently priced dishes chosen from the menu.
breakfast *le petit-déjeuner*
lunch *le déjeuner*
dinner *le dîner*
meal *le repas*
first course *l'entrée/les hors d'œuvre*
main course *le plat principal*
made to order *sur commande*
drink included *boisson comprise*
wine list *la carte des vins*
the bill *l'addition*
fork *la fourchette*
knife *le couteau*
spoon *la cuillère*
plate *l'assiette*
glass *le verre*
napkin *la serviette*
ashtray *le cendrier*
I am a vegetarian *Je suis végétarien(ne)*
I am on a diet *Je suis au régime*
What do you recommend? *Qu'est-ce que vous recommandez?*

Like anywhere else in the world: the green man means go.

Do you have local specialities? *Avez-vous des spécialités locales?*
I'd like to order *Je voudrais commander*
That is not what I ordered *Ce n'est pas ce que j'ai commandé*
Is service included? *Est-ce que le service est compris?*
May I have more wine? *Encore du vin, s'il vous plaît*
Enjoy your meal *Bon appétit!*

Breakfast and Snacks

baguette **long thin loaf**
pain **bread**
petits pains **rolls**
beurre **butter**
poivre **pepper**
sel **salt**
sucre **sugar**
confiture **jam**
miel **honey**
œufs **eggs**
...à la coque **boiled eggs**
...au bacon **bacon and eggs**
...au jambon **ham and eggs**
...sur le plat **fried eggs**
...brouillés **scrambled eggs**
tartine **bread with butter**
yaourt **yoghurt**
crêpe **pancake**
croque-monsieur **ham and cheese toasted sandwich**
croque-madame **...with a fried egg on top**
galette **type of cake**

pan bagna **bread roll stuffed with salade niçoise**
quiche **tart of eggs and cream with various fillings**
quiche lorraine **quiche with bacon**

First Course

An *amuse-bouche, amuse-gueule* or appetiser is something to "amuse the mouth", before the first course
anchoïade **sauce of olive oil, anchovies and garlic, served with raw vegetables**
assiette anglaise **cold meats**
potage **soup**
rillettes **rich fatty paste of shredded duck, rabbit or pork**
tapenade **spread of olives and anchovies**
pissaladière **Provençal pizza with onions, olives and anchovies**

Main Courses

Viande **Meat**
bleu saignant **rare**
à point **medium**
bien cuit **well done**
grillé **grilled**
agneau **lamb**
andouille/andouillette **tripe sausage**
bifteck **steak**
boudin **sausage**
boudin noir **black pudding**
boudin blanc **white pudding (chicken or veal)**
blanquette **stew of veal, lamb or chicken with creamy egg sauce**
bœuf à la mode **beef in red wine with carrots, onions, mushroom and onions**
à la bordelaise **beef with red wine and shallots**
bourguignon **cooked in red wine, onions and mushrooms**
brochette **kebab**
caille **quail**
canard **duck**
carbonnade **casserole of beef, beer and onions**
carré d'agneau **rack of lamb**
cassoulet **stew of beans, sausages, pork and duck from**

southwest France
cervelle **brains (food)**
châteaubriand **thick steak**
choucroute **Alsace dish of sau-
erkraut, bacon and sausages**
confit **duck or goose preserved
in its own fat**
contre-filet **cut of sirloin steak**
coq au vin **chicken in red wine**
côte d'agneau **lamb chop**
daube **beef stew with red wine,
onions and tomatoes**
dinde **turkey**
entrecôte **beef rib steak**
escargot **snail**
faisan **pheasant**
farci **stuffed**
faux-filet **sirloin**
feuilleté **puff pastry**
foie **liver**
foie de veau **calf's liver**
foie gras **goose or duck liver**
pâté
gardian **rich beef stew with
olives and garlic from the Cam-
argue**
cuisses de grenouille **frogs' legs**
grillade **grilled meat**
hachis **minced meat**
jambon **ham**
langue **tongue**
lapin **rabbit**
lardons **small pieces of bacon,
often added to salads**
magret de canard **breast of duck**
médaillon **round piece of meat**
moelle **beef bone marrow**
mouton navarin **stew of lamb
with onions, carrots and tur-
nips**
oie **goose**
perdrix **partridge**
petit-gris **small snail**
pieds de cochon **pig's trotters**
pintade **guinea fowl**
Pipérade **Basque dish of eggs,
ham, peppers and onion**
porc **pork**
pot-au-feu **casserole of beef
and vegetables**
poulet **chicken**
poussin **young chicken**
rognons **kidneys**
rôti **roast**
sanglier **wild boar**
saucisse **fresh sausage**
saucisson **salami**
veau **veal**
Poissons Fish

à l'américaine **made with white
wine, tomatoes, butter and
cognac**
anchois **anchovies**
anguille **eel**
bar/loup **sea bass**
barbue **brill**
belon **Brittany oyster**
bigorneau **sea snail**
Bercy **sauce of fish stock, butter, white wine and shallots**
bouillabaisse **fish soup, served
with grated cheese, garlic
croutons and spicy rouille
sauce**
brandade **salt cod purée**
cabillaud **cod**
calamars **squid**
colin **hake**
coquillage **shellfish**
coquilles Saint-Jacques **scallops**
crevette **shrimp**
daurade **sea bream**
flétan **halibut**
fruits de mer **seafood**
hareng **herring**
homard **lobster**
huître **oyster**
langoustine **large prawn**
limande **lemon sole**
lotte **monkfish**
morue **salt cod**
moule **mussel**
moules marinières **mussels in
white wine and onions**
oursin **sea urchin**
raie **skate**
saumon **salmon**
thon **tuna**
truite **trout**
Légumes Vegetables
ail **garlic**
artichaut **artichoke**
asperge **asparagus**
aubergine **eggplant, aubergine**
avocat **avocado**
bolets **boletus mushrooms**
céleri rémoulade **grated celery
with mayonnaise**
cèpes **boletus mushrooms**
champignon **mushroom**
chanterelle **wild mushroom**
chips **potato crisps**
chou **cabbage**
chou-fleur **cauliflower**
concombre **cucumber**
cornichon **gherkin**
courgette **zucchini, courgette**
cru **raw**

crudités **raw vegetables**
épinards **spinach**
frites **chips, French fries**
gratin dauphinois **sliced potatoes baked with cream**
haricot **dried bean**
haricots verts **green beans**
lentilles **lentils**
maïs **corn**
mange-tout **snow pea**
mesclun **mixed-leaf salad**
navet **turnip**
noisette **hazelnut**
noix **nut, walnut**
oignon **onion**
panais **parsnip**
persil **parsley**
pignon **pine nut**
poireau **leek**
pois **pea**
poivron **bell pepper**
pomme de terre **potato**
pommes frites **chips, French
fries**
primeurs **early fruit and vegetables**
radis **radis**
roquette **arugula, rocket**
ratatouille **Provençal vegetable
stew of aubergines, cour-
gettes, tomatoes, peppers and
olive oil**
riz **rice**
salade niçoise **egg, tuna, olives,
onions and tomato salad**
salade verte **green salad**
truffe **truffle**
Fruit Fruit
ananas **pineapple**
cerise **cherry**
citron **lemon**
citron vert **lime**
figue **fig**
fraise **strawberry**
framboise **raspberry**
groseille **redcurrant**
mangue **mango**
mirabelle **yellow plum**
pamplemousse **grapefruit**
pêche **peach**
poire **pear**
pomme **apple**
raisin **grape**
prune **plum**
pruneau **prune**
reine claude **greengage**
Sauces Sauces
aïoli **garlic mayonnaise**
béarnaise **sauce of egg, butter,**

wine and herbs
forestière with mushrooms and bacon
hollandaise egg and butter
lyonnaise with onions
meunière fried fish with butter, lemon and parsley sauce
meurette red wine sauce
Mornay sauce of cream, egg and cheese
Parmentier served with potatoes
paysan rustic-style, ingredients depend on the region
pistou Provençal sauce of basil, garlic and olive oil; vegetable soup with the sauce
provençale sauce of tomatoes, garlic and olive oil
papillotte cooked in paper
Dessert Pudding, dessert
chèvre goat's cheese
clafoutis baked pudding of batter and cherries
coulis purée of fruit or vegetables
crème anglaise custard
crème caramel caramelised egg custard
crème Chantilly whipped cream
fromage cheese
gâteau cake
île flottante whisked egg whites floating in custard sauce
pêche melba peaches with ice cream and raspberry sauce
poire Belle-Hélène pear with ice cream and chocolate sauce
tarte tatin upside-down tart of caramelised apples

In the Café

les boissons drinks
café coffee
...au lait or *crème* ...with milk or cream
...déca/décaféiné ...decaffeinated
...espresso/noir ...black espresso
...filtre ...filtered coffee
thé tea
tisane herb infusion
verveine verbena tea
chocolat chaud hot chocolate
lait milk
eau minérale mineral water
gazeux fizzy

non-gazeux non-fizzy
limonade fizzy lemonade
citron pressé fresh lemon juice served with sugar
orange pressée fresh squeezed orange juice
entier full (eg full cream milk)
frais, fraîche fresh or cold
bière beer
...en bouteille ...bottled
...à la pression ...on tap
apéritif pre-dinner drink
kir white wine with cassis, blackcurrant liqueur
kir royale kir with champagne
avec des glaçons with ice
sec neat
rouge red
blanc white
rosé rosé
brut dry
doux sweet
crémant sparkling wine
vin de maison house wine
vin de pays local wine
carafe/pichet pitcher
...d'eau/de vin ...of water/wine
demi-carafe half-litre
quart quarter-litre
panaché shandy
digestif after-dinner drink
armagnac brandy from the Armagnac region of France
calvados Normandy apple brandy
Where is this wine from? *De quelle région vient ce vin?*
cheers! *santé!*
hangover *gueule de bois*

Days of the Week

Days of the week, seasons and months are not capitalised in French.
Monday *lundi*
Tuesday *mardi*
Wednesday *mercredi*
Thursday *jeudi*
Friday *vendredi*
Saturday *samedi*
Sunday *dimanche*

Seasons

spring *le printemps*
summer *l'été*
autumn *l'automne*
winter *l'hiver*

Months

January *janvier*
February *février*
March *mars*
April *avril*
May *mai*
June *juin*
July *juillet*
August *août*
September *septembre*
October *octobre*
November *novembre*
December *décembre*
Saying the date
20 October 2016 *le vingt octobre, deux mille seize*

Numbers

0 *zéro*
1 *un, une*
2 *deux*
3 *trois*
4 *quatre*
5 *cinq*
6 *six*
7 *sept*
8 *huit*
9 *neuf*
10 *dix*
11 *onze*
12 *douze*
13 *treize*
14 *quatorze*
15 *quinze*
16 *seize*
17 *dix-sept*
18 *dix-huit*
19 *dix-neuf*
20 *vingt*
21 *vingt-et-un*
30 *trente*
40 *quarante*
50 *cinquante*
60 *soixante*
70 *soixante-dix*
80 *quatre-vingts*
90 *quatre-vingt-dix*
100 *cent*
200 *deux cents*
500 *cinq cents*
1000 *mille*
1,000,000 *un million*

Note that the number 1 is often written like an upside down V, and the number 7 is always crossed.

TRANSPORT

A – Z

LANGUAGE

FURTHER READING

HISTORY

A Concise History of France, by Roger Price. Excellent historical overview.
Paris: The Secret History, by Andrew Hussey. An entertaining history of Paris.
The Eiffel Tower: And Other Mythologies, by Roland Barthes. A collection of essays by this influential French critic.
The Rival Queens: Catherine de' Medici, Her Daughter Marguerite de Valois, and the Betrayal that Ignited a Kingdom, by Nancy Goldstone. An intricate spider web of spying and political upheaval in 16th-century France.
Marie Antoinette, by Antonia Fraser. An interesting biography of France's most famous queen.
Parisians: An Adventure History of Paris, by Graham Robb. A fascinating look at the individuals who shaped the city.
Sylvia Beach and the Lost Generation: A History of Literary Paris in the Twenties and Thirties, by Noel Riley Fitch. The origins of Shakespeare & Company bookshop and the writers who went there.
Napoleon: A Life, by Andrew Roberts. A compelling biography of the great French leader.

ART & ARCHITECTURE

A Propos de Paris, by Henri Cartier-Bresson. Some 130 stunning black-and-white photographs of the capital, spanning 50 years.
Brassaï: Paris, by Jean-Claude Gautrand. A great collection of the photographer's gritty images along with a biographical essay.

The Cathedral Builders, by Jean Gimpel. The story of the hands and minds behind the great cathedrals of France.
Paris: An Architectural History, by Anthony Sutcliffe. A great book on the architecture of the capital across the ages.
Paris: Art and Architecture by Martina Padberg. A comprehensive guide to the city's art and architecture up to the 21st century.
Robert Doisneau: Paris. A compact book featuring over 600 of the photographer's images of Paris.

EXPAT MEMOIRS

A Moveable Feast, by Ernest Hemingway. Life with the literati in 1920s Paris.
A Year in the Merde, by Stephen Clarke. The best-selling humorous tale of an expat in Paris.
Almost French: A New Life in Paris, by Sarah Turnbull. An engaging story of a woman who moves to Paris for a man but falls in love with the city.
Me Talk Pretty One day, by David Sedaris. Rich in humour, an entertaining tale of miscommunications and cultural differences.
Inside a Pearl: My Years in Paris, by Edmond White. Gossipy and moving account of the author's 15 years in Paris in the 1980s–90s.

FICTION

Murder in the Palais Royal, by Cara Black. One of a series of entertaining crime novels set in and around Paris.
Irene, by Pierre Lemaitre. This taut thriller, set in Paris, follows Commandant Camille Verhoevan

as he struggles to save the enigmatic Alex.
The Elegance of the Hedgehog, by Muriel Barbery. A moving tale of a friendship between a young girl and the concierge of her apartment building.
The Sun King Rises, by Yves Jégo and Denis Lépée. Intrigue and mystery in the court of Louis XIV.
Pure, by Andrew Miller. Atmospheric tale of an engineer sent to clear Paris' largest and oldest cemetery, the Holy Innocents' Cemetery in 1785.
The Red Notebook, by Antoine Laurain. Follows an adorable bookseller on his search through Paris for the owner of a lost handbag.
Delicacy, by David Foenkinos. This very Gallic romance was adapted into a 2011 film starring Audrey Tautou.

FOOD

Paris Bistro Cooking, by Linda Dannenberg. Tasty dishes from a wealth of Paris brasseries.
The Little Paris Kitchen, by Rachel Khoo. Easy-to-make versions of French classics.
The Paris Café Cookbook, by Daniel Young. Recipes and excerpts on recommended cafés.
The Sweet Life in Paris, by David Lebovitz. The Paris-based American chef's observations on Paris and cooking, including 50 recipes.
Mastering the Art of French Cooking by Julia Child. A classic book with 524 recipes for both seasoned cooks and beginners who love good food.
The Paris Gourmet, by Trish Deseine. A guide to Paris foodie heaven by an Irish food writer who has lived in Paris for thirty years.

PARIS STREET ATLAS

The key map shows the area of Paris covered by the atlas section. An index of street names and places of interest shown on the maps can be found on the following pages. For each entry there is a page number and grid reference

Map Legend

Autoroute with Junction	✈ ✈ Airport	Autoroute	Ⓜ Metro
Autoroute (under construction)	✝ ✝ Church (ruins)	Major Roads	ⓇⒺⓇ RER Station
Dual Carriageway	✝ Monastery		🚌 Bus Station
Main Road	Castle (ruins)	} Main Roads	ⓘ Tourist Information
Secondary Road	∴ Archaeological Site		✉ Post Office
Minor Road	Cave	} Minor Roads	Cathedral/Church
Track	★ Place of Interest	Footpath	☾ Mosque
International Boundary	⌂ Mansion/Stately Home	Railway	✡ Synagogue
Province/State Boundary	❊ Viewpoint	Pedestrian Area	Statue/Monument
National Park/Reserve	Beach	Important Building	Tower
Ferry Route		Park	Lighthouse

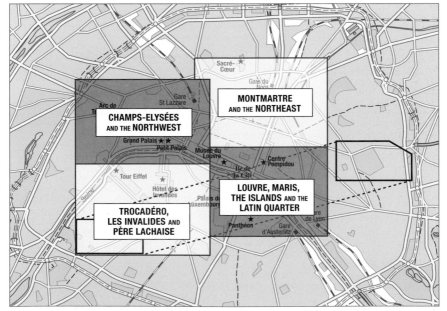

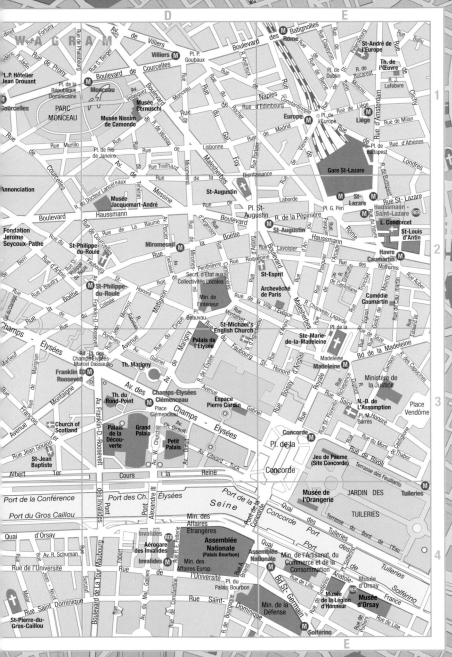

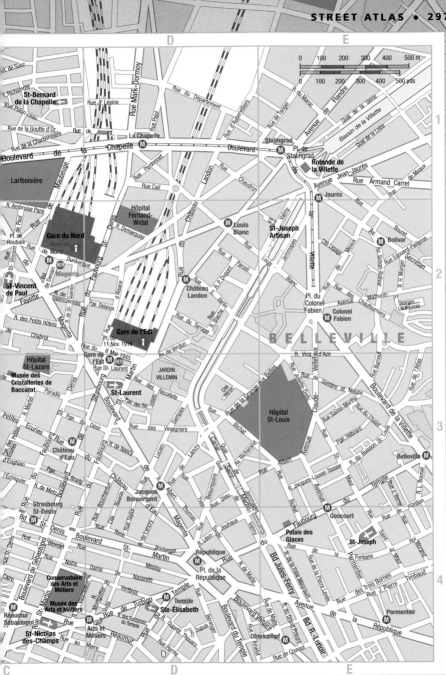

R. de Suez

St-Bernard
de la Chapelle ✚

Rue JF Lépine

R. Richomme

Rue Polon ceau

Rue de la Goutte d'Or

Rue de Jessaint

La Chapelle

Rue de la Charbonnière

Boulevard   de   la   Chapelle Ⓜ

Rue du Département

Rue de Tanger

Rue du Maroc

Avenue de Flandre

Quai de la Seine

Bassin de la Villette

Quai de la Loire

Boulevard

Stalingrad

Pl. de
Stalingrad

Rotonde de
la Villette

Avenue Jean-Jaurès

Rue de Meaux

Lariboisière

Rue   Maubeuge

Rue Pardonner

Rue Cail

Chaudron

Avenue Jean-Jaurès

Rue Armand Carrel

R. Ambroise Paré

Rue de Paris

Hôpital
Fernand-
Widal

R. Demarquay

Rue du Château

Rue Louis Blanc

St-Joseph
Artisan

Av. Bouret

Av.   Secrétan

Bolivar

Pl. de
Roubaix

Gare du Nord
Gare du
de Nord   ℹ

REP Ⓜ
Magenta

Rue du Faubourg

Rue d'Alsace

Rue A. Parodi

Rue J.-P. Dupont

Rue Louis

Rue Blanc

Rue de la Villette

Cité Lepage

Av. Simon-Bolivar

Av. Edouard-Pailleron

R. H. Murger

St-Vincent
de Paul

Rue de Denain

Dunkerque

Château
Landon

Rue A. Varlin

Rue L. Blanche

Pl. du
Colonel
Fabien

Rue des Chaufourniers

Georges
Lardennois

Mathurin

R. de Valenciennes

Rue Magenta

Pge. Delanos

Rue du Terrage

Colonel
Fabien Ⓜ

R. des Petits Hôtels

Gare de l'Est ℹ

Pl. du
11. Nov. 1918

B E L L E V I L L E

Rue Buzelin

Rue du Château d'Atlas

Hôpital
St-Lazare

Gare de
l'Est

Rue du
8 Mai 1945 REP Ⓜ

Rue St-Laurent

Av. de Verdun

R. Vicq d'Azir

Rue de Sambre et Meuse

Boulevard de la Villette

Musée des
Cristalleries de
Baccarat

Rue Strasbourg

✚ St-Laurent

JARDIN
VILLEMIN

Rue des Récollets

Cité
Héron

Rue de la Grange aux Belles

Rue Juliette-Dodu

Rue Sainte-Marthe

Rue du Chalet

Paradis

Rue Denis

Boulevard du Désir

Pge. des Ré...

Rue des Vinaigriers

Rue Bichat

Hôpital
St-Louis

Claude

Pge. Hébrard

Petites   Ecuries

Rue du Faubourg

R. de Nancy

Rue Lucien

Quai de Jemmapes

Av. Richerand

Avenue

R. du Buisson St.-L...

Belleville Ⓜ

R. L. Bonnet

d'Enghien

Rue Château d'Eau Ⓜ

Château
d'Eau

Rue des Marais

Rue Dieu

Rue Bichat

Albert

Rue Jacques-Louvel-Tessier

Rue Sainte-Marthe

Temple

l'Echiquier

R. de Metz

Rue

Rue de Lancry

Quai de Valmy

Yves Toudic

Rue des Récollets

Rue Thomas

Rue Jacquard

Maur

Rue de Vienne

R. d'Orillon

Rue

Strasbourg
St-Denis Ⓜ

St-Denis Ⓜ

Boulevard

Château

Rue René

Jacques
Bonsergent Ⓜ

Rue Léon-Jouhaux

Goncourt Ⓜ

Temple

Rue de la

St-Denis

Rue Taylor

Rue de Lancry

Rue Magenta

Faubourg

du

Bd

St-Joseph

Bd de Sébastopol Ⓜ

Boulevard

St-

Martin

Boulanger

Palais des
Glaces

Rue

Rue de la Fontaine au Roi

Rue

Parmentier

Caire

Blondel

Rue

Maatay

République Ⓜ

Rue de Malte

Bd Jules-Ferry

de

Rue des Trois Bornes

Notre

Dame   de

Nazareth

Pl. de la
République

Rue de la Pierre Levée

Rue J.-Pierre Timbaud

Conservatoire
des Arts et
Métiers

Vertbois

Rue du Grand Prieuré

Réaumur- Ⓜ
Sébastopol

Musée des
Arts et Métiers Ⓜ

Rue Montgolfier

Rue de Turbigo Ⓜ

Temple Ⓜ

Ste-Élisabeth ✚

Béranger

Boulevard Voltaire

Boulevard du Temple

Avenue

de

la

Parmentier Ⓜ

République

St-Nicolas
des-Champs

Arts et
Métiers

Rue au Maire

Rue des fontaines
du Temple

Rue Dupetit Thouars

Rue Perrée

Oberkampf Ⓜ

Bd R.-Lenoir

Rue de Crussol

Amelot

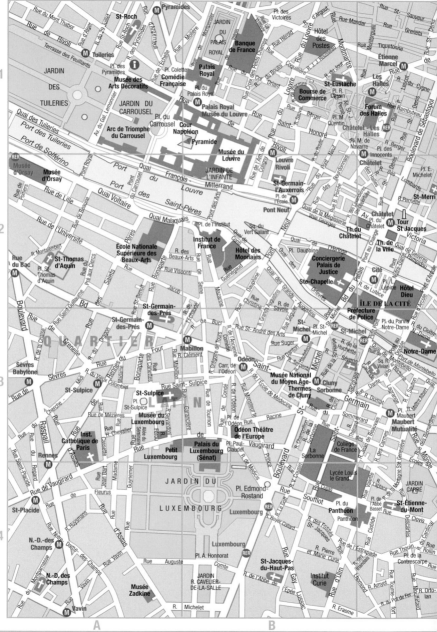

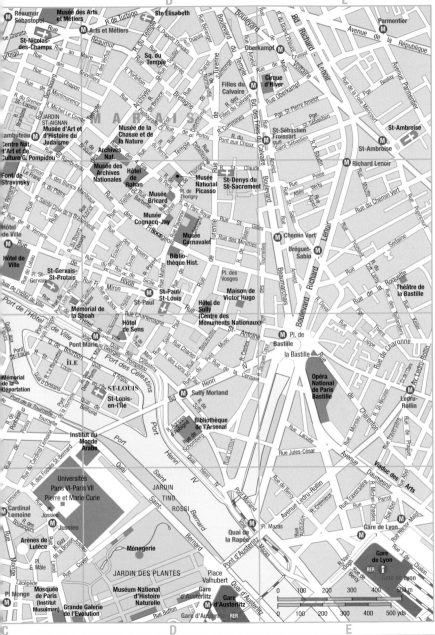

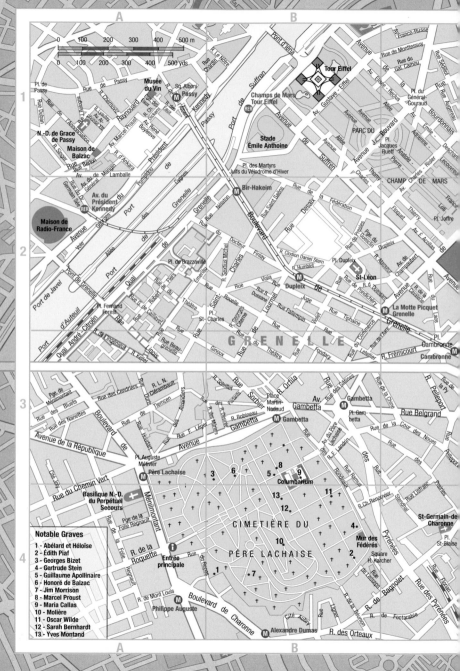

Notable Graves

1 - Abélard et Héloïse
2 - Édith Piaf
3 - Georges Bizet
4 - Gertrude Stein
5 - Guillaume Apollinaire
6 - Honoré de Balzac
7 - Jim Morrison
8 - Marcel Proust
9 - Maria Callas
10 - Molière
11 - Oscar Wilde
12 - Sarah Bernhardt
13 - Yves Montand

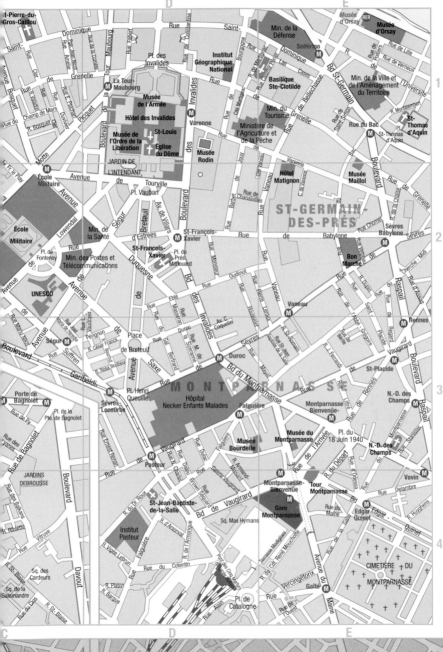

t-Pierre-du-
Gros-Caillou

Dominique

Saint-

Avenue Bosquet

Champ de Mars

Rue du

Rue

Rue de la Comète

Rue Fabert

Pl. des
Invalides

Rue de Constantine

Saint-

Saint-

Bourgogne

Min. de la
Défense

Solférino

Musée
d'Orsay

Musée
d'Orsay

R. de Lille

Rue de Lille

Rue de Verneuil

Dominique

Bd St-Germain

Institut
Géographique
National

Las
Cases

Basilique
Ste-Clotilde

Min. de la Ville et
de l'Aménagement
du Territoire

de

l'Université

La Tour-
Maubourg

Musée
de l'Armée

Hôtel des Invalides

Picpus

Rue de Bellechasse

Min. du
Tourisme

Rue de Grenelle

St-
Thomas
d'Aquin

Varenne

Ministere de
l'Agriculture et
de la Pêche

St-Thomas
d'Aquin

Rue du Bac

Musée de
l'Ordre de la
Libération

St-Louis

Église
du Dôme

Musée
Rodin

Varenne

Boulevard

Rue de la Chaise

Rue de Grenelle

JARDIN DE
L'INTENDANT

Hôtel
Matignon

Musée
Maillol

École
Militaire

Avenue

Tourville

Pl. Vauban

Rue de Chanaleilles

ST-GERMAIN-
DES-PRÉS

Sèvres
Babylone

École
Militaire

Lowendal

Min. de
la Santé

d'Estrées

St-François-
Xavier

Bon
Marché

Sèvres

Babylone

Pl. de
Fontenoy

Min. des Postes et
Télécommunications

St-François-
Xavier

Pl. du
Prés.
Mithouard

Oudinot

Rue

Cherche - Midi

Rue

UNESCO

Avenue

de

des Invalides

Vaneau

Vaneau

Raspail

Rennes

Ségur

Place
de Breteuil

Av. C.
Coqueilin

Sèvres

Vaugirard

Boulevard

de Saxe

Duroc

St-Placide

Boulevard

Garibaldi

Duroc

MONTPARNASSE

Bd du Montparnasse

N.-D. des
Champs

Raspail

Porte de
Bagnolet

Pl. de la
Pté. de Bagnolet

Sèvres-
Lecourbe

Pl. Henri
Queuille

Hôpital
Necker Enfants Malades

Falguière

Montparnasse-
Bienvenüe

JARDINS
DEBROUSSE

Boulevard

Pasteur

Vaugirard

Musée
Bourdelle

Musée du
Montparnasse

Pl. du
18 Juin 1940

N.-B. des
Champs

Vavin

St-Jean-Baptiste-
de-la-Salle

Montparnasse-
Bienvenüe

Tour
Montparnasse

Edgar
Quinet

Institut
Pasteur

Gare
Montparnasse

Rue du
Maine

Edgar
Quinet

Sq. des
Cardeurs

Davout

Bd de Vaugirard

Gaité

Vercingétorix

Avenue du Maine

CIMETIÈRE ♦ DU
MONTPARNASSE

Sq. de la
Salamandre

Pl. de
Catalogne

STREET INDEX

ART AND PHOTO CREDITS

akg-images/Gilles Mermet 30T
akg-images/CDA/Guillemot 30B
Alamy 32R, 32L, 36, 36/37, 64BL,
64/65M, 85BR, 116/117, 158B,
202/203
AWL Images 50
Bigstock 84/85B, 260T
Corbis 34/35, 38/39T, 166ML
Disneyland Paris 12T, 248B, 248T,
248/249B, 247, 249T, 250, 251
Dreamstime 93B, 188B,
200/201B, 201TR, 246, 258B,
260/261B, 262B, 266BL, 266MR,
266/267B
Flickr 178
Fotolia 149BR, 234, 235, 238B,
242/243B, 243T, 260B,
262/263B, 264/265B
Getty Images 28, 29, 34, 37R, 38,
39B, 94/95, 108/109T, 154B,
166/167T, 167BR, 181
Ilpo Musto/Apa Publications 81T,
81B, 90B, 90/91T, 108B,
140/141B, 142B, 147B,
176/177T, 178/179B, 190/191B,
192T, 192B, 227BR, 230B, 238T,
240B, 240T, 245BR, 258T, 259B,
258/259T, 264/265M, 265BR,
267MC, 266/267T, 267BR, 274T
iStock 9MR, 9BR, 31B, 40,
152/153, 200/201T, 227ML, 263T,
264T, 292
Jezza Dennis/Apa Publications
264B
Kevin Cummins/Apa Publications
8MR, 8MR, 9TR, 8/9M, 10/11,
14/15, 18, 22, 42/43, 52L, 55R,
59TC, 60MR, 60/61T, 62BL, 69T,
85TC, 86, 93T, 100B, 102B, 105B,
114, 114/115B, 118/119B,
118/119T, 121B, 120/121T,
126/127T, 130, 131, 132, 133, 136,
138B, 138T, 138/139T, 140/141T,
146/147T, 150, 154T, 164/165B,

164/165T, 168, 170B, 170T, 174B,
174T, 174/175T, 175B, 176T, 176B,
184T, 184B, 184/185T, 185B, 186,
194B, 194/195T, 195B, 196,
198/199, 200T, 200B, 200/201M,
202, 214T, 214/215, 216B, 216T,
216/217T, 229T, 229B, 230TL,
231BR, 238/239, 241B, 240/241T,
242B, 242T, 254, 255, 256T,
264/265T, 273, 274B, 275T, 280,
284
Leading Hotels of the World 140
Leonardo 124B
Mbzt/wiki 136/137
Ming Tang-Evans/Apa Publications
1, 6/7, 8BL, 8ML, 8/9T, 8/9M, 10,
11R, 12B, 12/13B, 13T, 16, 17T,
16/17B, 19, 20T, 20B, 20/21, 23B,
22/23T, 25, 27, 30/31T, 44, 45,
46B, 46T, 46/47, 48B, 48T, 49, 51,
52R, 52/53, 54L, 54R, 54/55, 56L,
56R, 56/57, 58BR, 58MR, 58ML,
58/59M, 59BR, 60MR, 60BL,
60/61M, 61BR, 61TC, 66/67, 68,
68/69B, 72, 73, 75T, 74/75B, 76,
77B, 76/77T, 78B, 78T, 78/79T,
79B, 80B, 80T, 82T, 82/83T, 83B,
84, 84/85M, 87, 88B, 88T, 88/89,
90T, 91B, 92T, 92B, 94T, 94B, 96, 97,
98, 99, 100T, 101B, 101T, 102T,
103, 104B, 104T, 104/105T, 106T,
106B, 107B, 106/107T, 108T,
108/109M, 109BR, 109TC, 109ML,
112, 113, 114/115T, 116T, 116B,
118T, 118B, 120T, 120B, 122T,
122B, 122/123B, 122/123T, 124T,
125T, 124/125B, 126B, 126T, 128T,
128B, 129, 134, 135, 138/139B,
142T, 143B, 143T, 144B, 144T,
144/145T, 148B, 148T, 148/149T,
149TC, 151, 152, 154/155, 156B,
156T, 157T, 156/157B, 158T, 159T,
158/159B, 160BR, 160TR, 160TL,
160/161B, 160/161T, 162B, 162T,

162/163B, 163T, 164, 166MC, 169,
172T, 172B, 172/173B, 172/173T,
180, 186/187B, 186/187T, 188T,
188/189, 190, 191T, 192/193,
194T, 197B, 197T, 198B, 198T,
204B, 204T, 204/205T, 204/205B,
206B, 206T, 206/207, 208/209B,
209T, 210, 211, 212/213B, 213T,
214B, 216/217B, 218TL, 218BR,
218TR, 218/219B, 218/219T, 220T,
220B, 220/221T, 221B, 222T, 222B,
222/223, 224, 224/225, 226B,
226/227B, 226/227T, 227TC, 228,
230/231T, 231TC, 232/233, 236,
244T, 244B, 244/245M, 244/245T,
268, 270, 270/271T, 270/271B,
272B, 274/275B, 276B, 276T, 278,
281, 282/283, 286, 286/287, 289
MK2 64MR
Moonik 256B
Paris Tourist Office/Amélie Dupont
62MR, 62/63M, 63BR, 62/63T,
63TC
Paris Tourist Office/Marc Bertrand
62MR, 146
Photoshot 252/253
Public domain 24T, 24B,
148/149M, 179T, 265TC
Richard Cooke 272T
Robert Harding 84/85T
Roger Viollet 226T
Ronald Grant Archive 64/65T,
65TR
Sipa Press/Rex Features 41
SuperStock 58/59T, 230/231M,
260/261T
The Art Archive 32/33, 145B
The Kobal Collection 64BR,
64/65B, 245TC
TopFoto 208
Wiki 25B, 25TR, 26, 82B,
126/127B, 166BR, 166/167B,
167TC, 176/177B, 230ML, 262T,
266TL

Cover Credits

Front cover: Metro entrance *Getty Images*
Back cover: (top) Eiffel Tower view *Ming Tang-Evans/Apa Publications*

Front flap: (from top) Metro entrance *Kevin Cummins/Apa Publications*; shoppers *Ming Tang-Evans/Apa Publications*; pipes *Ming*

Tang-Evans/Apa Publications; park girl *Kevin Cummins/Apa Publications*
Back flap: Eiffel view *Ming Tang-Evans/Apa Publications*

INDEX

INSIGHT ⊙ GUIDES

PARIS

Editor: Carine Tracanelli
Author: Victoria Trott
Head of Production: Rebeka Davies
Update Production: AM Services
Pictures: Tom Smyth
Cartography: original cartography
Berndtson & Berndtson, updated by
Carte

Distribution

UK
Dorling Kindersley Ltd
A Penguin Group company
80 Strand, London, WC2R 0RL
sales@uk.dk.com

United States
Ingram Publisher Services
1 Ingram Boulevard, PO Box 3006,
La Vergne, TN 37086-1986
ips@ingramcontent.com

Australia and New Zealand
Woodslane
10 Apollo St
Warriewood NSW 2102
Australia
info@woodslane.com.au

Worldwide
Apa Publications (Singapore) Pte
7030 Ang Mo Kio Avenue 5
08-65 Northstar @ AMK
Singapore 569880
apasin@singnet.com.sg

Printing

CTPS-China

All Rights Reserved
© 2016 Apa Digital (CH) AG and
Apa Publications (UK) Ltd

First Edition 1988
Fourteenth Edition 2016

ABOUT THIS BOOK

This edition of City Guide: Paris was commissioned by **Carine Tracanelli** and updated by **Victoria Trott**, a passionate Francophile who has written and updated many Insight Guides to French destinations as well as contributed articles to magazines *Living France*, *France Magazine* and *French Entrée*.

This edition of the book builds on previous editions produced by Fabienne Gondrand, Nick Rider, Andrew Eames, Caroline Radula-Scott, Natasha Edwards and Cathy Muscat. Past contributors whose work is still evident here include Simon Cropper (Chic Shopping and Paris After Dark chapters, and the essay on Parisian suburbs, The Outsiders), Marton Radkai (history chapter), Susan Bell (one-page features on Café Life, The Métro and Paris Schooling), Philippe Artru (architecture), Brent Gregston (Parisiens, Parisiennes), and Paris-based food writer Laura Calder (Paris on a Plate).

Exciting new photography for this edition comes courtesy of Insight regular **Ming Tang-Evans**. Other photographers whose pictures feature in this edition are Ilpo Musto and Kevin Cummings.

SEND US YOUR THOUGHTS

We do our best to ensure the information in our books is as accurate and up-to-date as possible. The books are updated on a regular basis using local contacts, who painstakingly add, amend, and correct as required. However, some details (such as telephone numbers and opening times) are liable to change, and we are ultimately reliant on our readers to put us in the picture.

We welcome your feedback, especially your experience of using the book "on the road". Maybe we recommended a hotel that you liked (or another that you didn't), or you came across a great bar or new attraction that we missed.

We will acknowledge all contributions, and we'll offer an Insight Guide to the best letters received.

Please write to us at:
Insight Guides
PO Box 7910, London SE1 1WE
Or email us at:
hello@insightguides.com